T0311831

CRITICAL REALISM IN ECONOMICS

Critical Realism, with its focus on the causal structures underlying observable phenomena, is one of the most significant developments of recent years in the philosophy of social science. This volume extends its insights into the fields of economic methodology and economic theory in such a way as to open up new forms of investigation in economics and transform the nature of economic reasoning.

It is argued that the specific value of this approach is that it directs attention to the structures, mechanisms, powers and capacities that explain the observed phenomena of economic life and thus provides a more profound understanding of the subject matter of economics. In this way, complacent forms of theoretical practice in economics based on the deductivist method and on statistical explanation are overturned and new avenues of empirical research opened up.

Critical Realism in Economics is more than just an eloquent advocacy of a new way of seeing in economic methodology: it also includes papers from authors critical of this approach, as well as from those who are concerned to elucidate its full implications for contemporary economics. What emerges then from this combination of exposition and critical exchange is a volume of reflection and learning from the pens of some of the leading authorities in the field of economic philosophy. *Critical Realism in Economics* will make fascinating reading for both students and exponents of economic methodology, economic theory and social theory.

Steve Fleetwood is Senior Lecturer in Economics and Sociology in the Department of Economics, School of Social Science at De Montfort University. He is the author of *Hayek's Political Economy: The Socio-Economics of Order* (Routledge 1995).

ECONOMICS AS SOCIAL THEORY
Series edited by Tony Lawson
University of Cambridge

Social theory is experiencing something of a revival within economics. Critical analyses of the particular nature of the subject matter of social studies and of the types of method, categories and modes of explanation that can legitimately be endorsed for the scientific study of social objects, are re-emerging. Economists are again addressing such issues as the relationship between agency and structure, between the economy and the rest of society, and between enquirer and the object of enquiry. There is renewed interest in elaborating basic categories such as causation, competition, culture, discrimination, evolution, money, need, order, organisation, power, probability, process, rationality, technology, time, truth, uncertainty and value, etc.

The objective for this series is to facilitate this revival further. In contemporary economics the label 'theory' has been appropriated by a group that confines itself to largely a-social, a-historical, mathematical 'modelling'. *Economics as Social Theory* thus reclaims the 'theory' label, offering a platform for alternative, rigorous, but broader and more critical conceptions of theorising.

CRITICAL REALISM IN ECONOMICS

Development and debate

Edited by Steve Fleetwood

London and New York

First published 1999
by Routledge
11 New Fetter Lane, London EC4P 4EE

Simultaneously published in the USA and Canada
by Routledge
29 West 35th Street, New York, NY 10001

British Library Cataloguing in Publication Data
A catalogue record for this book is available from the British Library

Library of Congress Cataloging in Publication Data
Critical realism in economics: development and debate /
[editor] Steve Fleetwood.
(Economics as social theory)
A selection of articles previously published in the Review of
social economy (1996) and in Ekonomia (1997), with an
introduction by the editor.
1. Economics – Methodology. 2. Economics –
Philosophy. I. Fleetwood, Steve, 1955–. II. Series.
HB131.C75 1999   98-23387
330–dc21   CIP

ISBN 0–415–19567–5 (hbk)
ISBN 0–415–19568–3 (pbk)

CONTENTS

CONTENTS

CONTRIBUTORS

Thomas A. Boylan is Associate Professor of Economics at the National University of Ireland, Galway, and a former Dean of the Faculty of Arts. He has published widely in the areas of econometrics, growth and development, economic methodology, and the history of political economy. He is the author of *Political Economy and Colonial Ireland* (Routledge 1992) (with T. P. Foley) and *Beyond Rhetoric and Realism* (Routledge 1995) (with P. F. O'Gorman). He is currently a guest editor, with P. F. O'Gorman, for a special issue of *Revue Internationale de Philosophie* on the philosophy of economics.

Steve Fleetwood is a senior lecturer in Economics and Sociology at De Montfort University, Milton Keynes. He is the author of *Hayek's Political Economy: The Socio-Economics of Order* (Routledge 1995) and has published articles on labour economics, methodology of economics, Marxist economics and Austrian economics.

D. Wade Hands is Professor of Economics at the University of Puget Sound in Tacoma, Washington. He has published widely in the history of economic thought and economic methodology. He is the author of *Testing, Rationality and Progress: Essays on the Popperian Tradition in EC Methodology* (Rowan & Littlefield 1993) and the editor (along with John Davis and Uskali Mäki) of *The Handbook of Economic Methodology* (Edward Elgar 1998).

Geoffrey Ingham is a Fellow and Director of Studies in Social and Political Sciences, Christ's College, University of Cambridge, and was a Lecturer in the Faculty of Economics, University of Cambridge, 1971–1994. His main publications include *Strikes and Industrial Conflict: Britain and Scandinavia* (1974) and *Capitalism Divided? The City and Industry in British Social Development* (1984). He is currently writing a book on the development of money, provisionally entitled *The Social Construction of Money*.

Rajani Kanth is currently a Visiting Fellow with the Economics

Department at Harvard University. He has taught at the State University of New York, Purchase; the University of Aarhus, Denmark; the University of Utah, Salt Lake City; the University of New South Wales, Sydney; the Nehru University, New Delhi; and has been a Visiting Fellow at Oxford University. His latest books are *Breaking with the Enlightenment: The Twilight of History and the Rediscovery of Utopia* (Humanities Press 1997) and *Against Economics* (Ashgate 1997).

Clive Lawson is currently a Fellow of Girton College, Cambridge and Research Fellow of the ESRC Centre for Business Research, Department of Applied Economics, University of Cambridge. His current research is into economic methodology and regional innovation and learning in high-technology firms.

Tony Lawson is Lecturer in Economics at the Cambridge Faculty of Economics and Politics. He has published numerous articles on philosophical issues in economics, and is the author of *Economics and Reality* (Routledge 1997). He sits on numerous editorial boards of journals and is editor of the Routledge list 'Economics as Social Theory'. He is also the organiser of the weekly Cambridge Workshop on Realism and Economics.

Paul Lewis is a Fellow of Emmanuel College, Cambridge.

Paschal F. O'Gorman is Associate Professor of Philosophy at the National University of Ireland, Galway, and Secretary of the Royal Irish Academy's National Committee for the History and Philosophy of Science. He has published in a variety of journals, including *Studies in History and Philosophy of Science*, *International Studies in the Philosophy of Science* and the *Cambridge Journal of Economics*. He is the author of *Rationality and Relativity* (Avebury 1989) and co-author with T. A. Boylan of *Beyond Rhetoric and Realism* (Routledge 1995).

Stephen D. Parsons is Principal Lecturer in Economics at De Montfort University, Milton Keynes. He is currently writing a book on the problem of time in the social sciences.

Stephen Pratten is Research Fellow at the ESRC Centre for Business Research, Department of Applied Economics, University of Cambridge. His principal research is in the area of economic methodology and he is currently working on an empirical study examining the implications for competitiveness of developments in corporate restructuring within the UK media industry. He is a member of the editorial board of the *Cambridge Journal of Economics*.

Jochen Runde is Fellow and Director of Studies in economics at Girton College, Cambridge, and Lecturer in Economics at New Hall, Cambridge. His main research area is the methodology of economics, focusing particularly on the areas of probability, uncertainty and decision theory, idealisation and abstraction, causality and causal explanation, and rational choice theory. He is currently working on a comparative study of the Information Theoretic and Austrian approaches to economic analysis, and an empirical study of credit risk assessment procedures in the British retail banking sector.

PREFACE

If being subject to continued development and enthusiastic criticism are signs of a project in a good state then the venture systematised as *critical realism in economics* is in a healthy condition indeed. So much is this so that special issues of economics journals are appearing devoted wholly to this project's development or to debating its limitations. Two such special issues are collected together here. The first set of chapters, constituting Part I of the book, and originally published in the *Review of Social Economy*, are primarily concerned with both critical and constructive developments in the critical realist project in economics. The second set of chapters, constituting Part II, and recently published in *Ekonomia*, mainly consists of criticisms of the project as formulated by economic methodologists adopting alternative perspectives. Part II also includes a response by Tony Lawson.

My reason for reproducing this collection of papers is a suspicion that they have a potential audience significantly wider than that group of economists with easy access to specific journals, coupled with the conviction that they deserve to be widely read. My motivation in combining the two sets of contributions, one largely concerned with developing the project, the other with identifying its limitations, is an expectation that a sufficient understanding of the project can more readily be achieved when the aims, achievements and interpretations of those enamoured with the project are laid alongside the criticisms or reservations of those who hold a more sceptical, and perhaps even a hostile, stance.

This book follows in the wake of another, of course. The basic project of critical realism in economics has recently received its most systematic and comprehensive elaboration in Tony Lawson's *Economics and Reality*. Indeed it is mostly towards arguments found in the latter that the following chapters are developmentally or critically oriented. Because of this emphasis upon extension and debate, some of the contributions which follow inevitably take certain of the basic categories, terminology and indeed results of the critical realist project in economics as given. However, both parts of the current volume contain introductory or preliminary chapters which set the context and terms of the ensuing discussion. As a result, I believe that *Critical Realism in Economics*, though obviously a supplement to Lawson's book, is sufficiently self-contained to be readily accessible, even to any interested newcomer to the discussion.

It remains for me to thank the authors of the chapters for allowing me to include their papers, and the publishers of *Ekonomia* and *Review of Social Economy* for permission to reproduce here material that originally appeared in their pages.

Stephen Fleetwood
De Montfort University
July 1997

Part I

DEVELOPMENT

1

DEVELOPMENTS IN *ECONOMICS AS REALIST SOCIAL THEORY*

Tony Lawson

Social theory explicitly committed to elaborating the nature of social being and/or how we access social reality is experiencing something of a revival in economics.[1] The five chapters which follow can all be counted as contributing to this trend. In fact they all in some way connect with a specific social theory project of the sort in question, one that has been systematised within economics as *critical realism*.[2] Under this head, numerous results, arguments, conjectures and critiques have been produced in recent years,[3] and the chapters included here aim to take some of these specific developments further.[4] My own object in this introductory chapter is merely to facilitate the contributions which follow: to outline something of their context and to sketch certain basic ideas and results that are treated in the following chapters as 'given', that are taken as sufficiently well grounded (if of course always corrigible) premises.

Underlabouring

Within economics critical realism has very much played the role of underlabourer for a more fruitful approach to scientific explanation (Lawson, C., Peacock and Pratten 1996). In this it has been both *critically explanatory* (of the existing situation in economics) and in varying degrees *developmentally constructive* (in elaborating an alternative perspective). In the following paragraphs, as in the ordering of the chapters included here, the move is from the (more) critical to the (more) constructive moment.

One primary object of critical realism in economics has been to identify the basic nature or character of mainstream economics. Most critics of the mainstream project have, in attempting to characterise it, isolated particular substantive claims, such as theories of rationality, or of equilibrium. It has been the contention of critical realism, in contrast, that it is at the level of method that its essence lies. In fact the insight that it is not substantive theory that defines the project is clear enough once we recognise that, despite the mainstream project being widely regarded as persisting, specific substantive theories come and go, often with some rapidity. Even the cherished conceptions of rationality and of equilibrium have been dispensed with in recent contributions regarded as central to the mainstream (see Lawson 1997, Chapter 8). Yet through all its transformations and apparent metamorphoses the essential method of mainstream economics has been found to remain reasonably constant. It is this, then, that must be taken as the most central and defining feature of the mainstream project.[5]

Deductivism

The method of the mainstream project which, according to critical realist analysis, is its characteristic feature is, briefly put, closed system modelling. This is also its essential error. A reliance upon closed systems modelling is an error in that the social world appears to be quintessentially open and hardly susceptible to scientifically interesting local closures. By a closed system here I simply mean situations in which regularities of the form 'whenever event (or state of affairs) x then event (or state of affairs) y' occur. Methods of analysis, including modes of explanation, which are formulated on the presupposition that elaborating regularities *of this form or structure* are at least necessary in science[6] can be labelled *deductivist*. It is deductivism so interpreted that, it has been shown elsewhere (Lawson 1997), characterises mainstream economics and which, in an open social system, is the essential error of modern economics.

Now it does not follow that because deductivism is a mistake, science and explanation are thereby impossible. Rather, the latter need to be more adequately conceptualised. An important observation here is that event regularities of the sort presupposed in deductivism actually occur only under rather specific conditions. In fact, outside astronomy, event regularities of interest in science usually occur only in conditions of experimental control. Once this is recognised, it is easily seen that any conception which ties science to activities involving the elaboration of event regularities serves systematically to fence off science from most of the goings on in the world. Moreover, any such conception is inevitably unable to make sense of the further observation that science *is* after all successfully applied even in situations where event regularities are not in evidence.

These two observations – that event regularities are restricted to rather specific situations and that science is successful even where event regularities are not in evidence – clearly warrant explanation. We *can* make sense of them. But in order to do so we need first of all to augment the ontology of events and experiences that is so basic to mainstream economics, to include underlying structures of things, their powers, mechanisms and tendencies that, if triggered, act even if their effects are not directly manifest. Certain things, by virtue of their intrinsic structures, have various powers (including liabilities): bicycles to facilitate rides, aspirins to relieve head-aches, language systems to facilitate speech-acts, shops to facilitate trade, or autumn leaves to fall to the ground under the influence of gravitational attraction. And it is clear enough that such powers may exist without being triggered (e.g. the aspirin may remain in the bottle; the shop closed on Sundays), or if triggered, may set forth mechanisms and tendencies that are not directly manifest or *actualised* because of countervailing factors. The fall of an autumn leaf, for example, does not conform to an empirical regularity, precisely because it is governed in complex ways by the actions of different juxtaposed and counteracting mechanisms. Not only is the path of the leaf governed by gravitational pull, but also by aerodynamic, thermal, inertial and other mechanisms. Similarly, the headache sufferer may take the aspirin in an environment which is, say, sufficiently noisy that the pain experienced actually worsens despite the aspirin's pain-reducing *effect*.

According to this conception, experimental activity can now be understood as an attempt to intervene in order to insulate a particular mechanism of interest by holding off all other potentially counteracting influences. The aim is to engineer a system in which the actions of any mechanism being investigated are more readily identifiable. Thus, experimental activity is rendered intelligible *not* as the production of a rare situation in which an empirical law is put into effect, but as an intervention designed to bring about those special circumstances under which a non-empirical mechanism can be insulated and its tendencies empirically identified. This explains the restriction of so many event regularities to situations of experimental control: where triggering conditions and effects of mechanisms are found to be correlated. But a mechanism itself, if triggered, can be operative whatever else is going on. This is what is expressed by the notion of *transfactuality* in critical realism. A transfactual statement is not a counter-factual, i.e. it does not express what *would* happen if conditions were different. Rather it refers to something that *is* going on, that is having an effect, even if the actual (possibly observable) outcome is jointly co-determined by (possibly numerous) other influences. On this understanding, for example, a leaf is subject to the gravitational tendency even as I hold it in the palm of my hand or as it 'flies' over roof tops and chimneys. Through this sort of reasoning we can render intelligible the application of scientific knowledge outside experimental situations. If triggered, a mechanism may have its effects irrespective of the context in which it is operative.

It follows that science and explanation are not so much concerned to elaborate patterns at the level of actual events as to identify and understand the causal mechanisms responsible for them. This is as feasible in the social realm as in the natural domain (Lawson 1997). Only under special conditions does this activity involve the generation of strict event regularities, and in the social realm, where the opportunities for meaningful experimental control are limited, such conditions may not materialise at all. The basic error of deductivism, then, is to generalise what must now be recognised as a special case – where a single set of mechanisms is insulated and thereby empirically identified. The error of deductivism in its guise of mainstream economics is to abduct this special case to a context where it may have almost no scientific bearing at all.

Of the chapters included here, it is Stephen Pratten's contribution that builds most directly on this characterisation of mainstream economics as deductivist. Pratten, though, is wanting to move beyond the characterising of mainstream economics. Indeed, his general concern is with the degree to which coherence can be found in the non-mainstream economic traditions. His particular concern is whether the set of contributions systematised as neo-Ricardianism can comfortably fit under the umbrella of a coherent Post-Keynesianism. There is no doubt that the reputed relation of neo-Ricardianism to Post-Keynesianism (or description of the former as Post-Keynesian) involves many tensions and has often been questioned previously. Usually the question of whether the two projects are the same or at least complementary has been taken to turn on substantive issues of some sort. From the perspective elaborated in critical realism, however, this strategy can now be questioned. Specifically, if the essence of the mainstream project is its deductivist methodology, then any truly alternative approach will be non-deductivist in nature and presumably not wholly distinct from the project and perspective elaborated as, or within, critical realism. Elsewhere, indeed, I have suggested that coherence in such traditions as Austrianism and Institutionalism as well as Post-Keynesianism, should also be sought on this basis (Lawson 1994). Pratten's question then can be framed as follows: if mainstream economics is deductivist and the essence of a coherent Post-Keynesianism is akin to critical realism, does neo-

Ricardianism have affinities (mainly) with the latter or the former? His answer is formulated as follows:

> neo-Ricardian economics, to the extent that it takes closure for granted as a natural and useful starting point for analysis, retains an underlying commitment to deductivism and so is difficult to reconcile with Post-Keynesianism. In other words, if Post-Keynesianism is to be a consistent project, its link with neo-Ricardianism appears untenable. Alternatively, if, perhaps for institutional reasons, it is felt that in outlining the nominal characteristics of Post-Keynesianism some reference has to be made to neo-Ricardianism, then the project of seeking coherence may have to be abandoned.

The chapter by Clive Lawson has parallels with Pratten's. Lawson's concern is with the 'new institutionalist' economics, or, more directly, with certain methodological results that certain strands of that school attribute to Menger. If deductivism is the structure of mainstream reasoning it encourages a material form of *social atomism*. That is, to guarantee results of the 'whenever this then that' form the entities of analysis are required to be crypto atomistic (basically pre-programmed). In economics this has inevitably meant that explanations are couched in terms of human (typically 'optimising') individuals. Of course, once the manner in which deductivism drives the project is recognised, it is easy enough to see that notions like economic rationality, at least as formulated in mainstream economics, are little more than a gloss on the proceedings. But the mainstream project needs to present things differently. Specifically, the insistence upon explaining things in terms of individual (typically rational) decisions or some other attribute, i.e. the doctrine of methodological individualism, is recognised as something that warrants an independent justification. One apparent attraction of Menger's work to the mainstream project, then, one explicitly referred to by its 'new institutionalist' strand or offspring, is precisely that it is perceived to have provided an argument to justify the individualist approach.

In fact, the question of whether Menger has actually been successful in this is of particular interest here because Menger also adopts an Aristotelian orientation which, in some significant aspects at least, is not dissimilar to the perspective developed in critical realism. Is, then, methodological individualism, and perhaps by implication the deductivist structure on which it rests, justified after all? Lawson's findings are as follows:

Menger's particular essentialist–realist position, once transposed to the social realm, becomes the position now familiar
as methodological individualism. But it is most noticeable that
the method which is so transposed is hardly justified. That
theory must start with the simplest elements is simply
asserted by Menger. However, this assertion is of crucial
importance as it appears to be the only link provided by
Menger between the notion of theory, which he spends so
much time defending against the Historical School, and the
individualism for which he is so well known. Moreover, . . .
criticisms made of Menger's work, which are understood to
be criticisms of his Aristotelianism, in fact hinge on just this
assertion that exact types are the simplest elements in everything real.

If the usual material form of deductivism (i.e. methodological individualism) is (erroneously) assumed by some economists to be justified in
Menger's contributions, others suppose that a generalised reliance
upon deductivist modes of reasoning is directly grounded in the writings of Popper. Indeed, it is not uncommon to find econometrics
textbooks and articles averting to 'Popperian falsificationism' as
authoritative support for deductivist methods thereafter elaborated.
Jochen Runde's chapter provides a challenge to the claim that Popper
provides deductivism with such a general grounding. Critical realism,
it has been noted, argues that it is only in relatively special conditions
(outside astronomy mostly in well-controlled experimental situations)
that event regularities can be rationally anticipated, so that it is only in
such conditions that predictive accuracy, the central falsificationist
concern, can be accepted as a relevant criterion of theory assessment.
Runde's chapter suggests not only that Popper does not justify deductivism as a general approach, but also that, in his writings on
propensities, something like its limitations as emphasised in critical
realism are recognised by Popper all along. It is true that in his contributions on falsificationism Popper's *emphasis* has served to encourage
a widespread acceptance of the deductivist approach. Nevertheless, it
can be argued that, in his discussions on propensities especially,
Popper always situated the relevance of this method. However that
may be, recent developments in Popper's thinking are such that, with
the publication of his final book *A World of Propensities* (Popper 1990),
a conception sharing many similarities with central features of critical
realism is, according to Runde, quite evident. Thus Runde makes the
following observations:

Whereas in his earlier writings he [Popper] had focused almost exclusively on propensities identified in experimental situations, the shift reported in his 1990 book is his fully taking on board that non-experimental situations have propensities too, that, as he puts it, we live in a world of propensities.

Two important consequences follow directly from this shift, both of them emphasised in CR [critical realism]. First Popper now acknowledges explicitly that only a small proportion of the now expanded ontology of propensities will be amenable to statistical measurement . . .

The second key consequence is that Popper now feels bound to emphasise that, with the exception of the 'unique natural laboratory experiment' of the planetary system, regular associations of events or states of affairs – what he calls 'natural laws of a deterministic character' and 'natural laws of a probabilistic character' – are rarely found to occur outside of situations of experimental control. The reason is simply that in non-laboratory situations there will typically be 'disturbing propensities', the exclusion of which is the very purpose of laboratory experiments.

Given the usual interpretation of Popperianism in economics (as elsewhere) as (naive) falsificationism it is tempting to conclude (although I must emphasise that Runde does not put things in quite this way) that Popper is perhaps more critical realist than Popperian.

Retroduction

I move now to consider the context of contributions more directly concerned with the developmental moment of the realist project. Given the structured ontology elaborated in critical realism, i.e. an ontology which includes structures and mechanisms as well as events and experiences, various obvious questions immediately arise. One that is frequently voiced is what significant and specifically *social* structures are there that economists might attempt more fully to identify and understand? This issue receives some attention below. But before turning to it, a prior question to consider is by what method might a knowledge of underlying structures, etc., be obtained? Specifically, if important features of reality, including of the social world, are *intransitive* (irreducible, for the most part, to our knowledge of them) as well as *structured* (irreducible to phenomena we can directly experience) by what process do we come to know them?

The answer argued for in critical realism is that the essential method involved is neither induction nor deduction but *retroduction*. Induction, of course, involves the move from the particular to the general. It is to reason, for example, that because observed ravens are black then all ravens are black, or because various pieces of copper conduct electricity well then all copper does. Deduction characteristically moves in the opposite direction, from general to particular. It is thus to reason that if all ravens are black, the next one to be seen will be, or if all copper conducts electricity well, a particular piece to hand will do so. Retroduction, in contrast to both induction and deduction, is to move from the level of the phenomenon identified to a different 'deeper' level in order to explain the phenomenon, to identify a causal mechanism responsible. It is, for example, to move from the observation that ravens are black to a theory of a mechanism intrinsic (and also possibly extrinsic) to ravens which disposes them to be black, or it is to move from the recognition that observed pieces of copper conduct electricity well to an account of copper's intrinsic, ionic, structure by virtue of which the power so to conduct electricity is possessed.

But can anything more be said about this process of retroduction? Those working on critical realism, including myself, have generally rested content with making the observation that it 'relies upon a logic of analogy and metaphor amongst other things'. Of course, such a claim requires unpacking and, amongst other things, presupposes a particular conception of metaphor and of how metaphorical reasoning is able to aid this process of scientific illumination. It is a concern with unpacking the account of metaphor in critical realist thinking, and with indicating that, and how, metaphor can fulfil the role ascribed to it, that motivates Paul Lewis' contribution. In arguing for a conception of *generative* metaphor in the context of the *interanimation* theory Lewis finds:

> Scientific metaphors are not merely linguistic ornaments that can be discarded in favour of literal description. On the contrary, metaphors are essential to the conception, development and maintenance of scientific theories in a variety of ways: they provide the linguistic context in which the models that constitute the basis for scientific explanation are suggested and described; they supply new terms for the theoretical vocabulary, especially where there is a gap in the lexicon; and they direct scientists towards new avenues of inquiry, in particular by suggesting new hypothetical entities and mechanisms. Through metaphor scientists draw upon

antecedently existing cognitive resources to provide both the model and the vocabulary in terms of which the unknown mechanisms, etc., governing observable behaviour can be conceived and so investigated. Metaphor thereby performs an indispensable role in scientific theorising.

Social relations

I turn, at this point, to more concrete issues, and specifically to the matter of elaborating and furthering our understanding of a particular social structure. This is the focus of the chapter by Geoffrey Ingham. The criterion accepted in critical realism for a thing or aspect to be designated *social* is a dependency on intentional human action. Clearly rules of language or the highway code are like this: they not only facilitate human acts such as, respectively, speech acts and safe motoring, they are reproduced by the very acts (in total) which they facilitate. If the human race were to disappear tomorrow, human language and the highway code, as emergent *but dependent* properties of human interaction, would disappear as well. Social structure, then, must be viewed as a duality: as both condition and consequence of intentional human agency.

If items such as rules of language can be designated social, their *reality* can be ascribed by virtue of their ability to make a difference. In this sense social structures are just like such natural ones as gravitational and magnetic fields: they cannot be perceived directly, only known to exist – through their revealed abilities to effect other phenomena that can be observed.

Is there more to social structure than rules (or procedures) of action? In critical realism the emphasis is also very much upon social positions and, in particular, *social relations*. Two types of relation must be distinguished: external and internal. Two objects or aspects are said to be externally related if neither is constituted by the relationship in which it stands to the other. Bread and butter, coffee and milk, barking dog and post-person, two passing strangers, provide examples. In contrast, two objects are said to be internally related if they are what they are, and do what they do, by virtue of the relationship in which they stand to one other. Landlord and tenant, employer and employee, teacher and student, magnet and its field are examples that spring easily to mind. In each case it is not possible to have the one without the other; each, in part, is what it is, and does what it does, by virtue of the relation in which it stands to the other.

Internal relations are especially important in the social realm in relating social positions. I, as a university lecturer, have all sorts of obligations, prerogatives, rights and privileges, most of which, for example, are not shared by students. Yet if I were to leave town tomorrow someone else would take over my post and inherit the same set of obligations and rights. In other words, the obligations in question are attached not to individuals *per se* but to the positions which individuals occupy. Now all social positions are oriented towards others: lecturers to students or to governing bodies of universities, landlords to tenants, employers to employees, etc. Indeed, it is not difficult to see that such orientations consist in networks of internal relations. Thus, for example, the set of rights and obligations on offer to landlords *qua* landlords is underpinned by the relationship in which they stand to tenants.

If social relations, external as well as internal ones, are then an integral aspect of the social ontology sustained in critical realism, is it possible to point to relations of significance other than the examples of employer / employee, landlord / tenant, teacher / student, etc., relationships that are usually referred to in the highly abstract discussions of contemporary social theory? Now with this turn to more concrete questions and issues, things start to become more contentious for those inclined to the critical realist project (a matter I briefly return to below). In my own view an especially important social relation being increasingly investigated by those interested in productive systems, evolutionary economics and industrial networking is that of *trust*. But one perhaps even more obviously of significance and interest to economists is the social relation that constitutes the focus of Ingham's chapter: money. Money, Ingham argues, is a social relation. Of course, for many economists money comes in measurable quantities, and mainly acts as a means of exchange. But the inadequacy of such a conception is apparent if we question why this piece of metal, paper or card serves as an acceptable means of payment and / or store of value and not that one. The answer is that the one is backed up by, or rather is part of, a whole system of relations, controls and guarantees. From this perspective, it can be seen that it is this latter system itself, facilitating positions of debtors, creditors, and so forth, that is the basis of money, while backed-up pieces of paper are merely tokens or surface (phenomenal) manifestations of this system of social relations. In short, money is essentially a (rather fundamental) set or system of social relations which exists as an emergent property of human interaction.

It is a version of this view that is endorsed and elaborated upon by Geoffrey Ingham. Ingham in fact picks up the difficulty that economists experience of finding an indispensable role for money in their models, a difficulty often put aside explicitly as a puzzle (e.g. Hahn 1987: 42). Given that, excepting in rhetorical gloss, deductivist modelling inevitably focuses only upon (measurable) surface phenomena (actualities such as events and states of affairs), once money is recognised as a social relation, the inability of mainstream economics to accommodate it remains a puzzle no longer. Ingham finds:

> mainstream economics rarely concerns itself with, and indeed cannot easily accommodate any role for, underlying social structures including, on one level, social relations. In this approach, 'social relations' or 'social structure' can be said to be conceptualised, at best, as the recognition that economic agents take each others' maximising strategies into account, as in game theory. At the same time, mainstream economists widely observe, and continually puzzle over, the difficulty of establishing an indispensable role for money in their theorising. My objective has been to demonstrate that money is itself a social relation in the sense that it cannot be adequately conceptualised other than as the emergent property of a configuration (or 'structure') of social relations. Thus the inability of contemporary mainstream economics to accommodate money is a specific, and rather fundamental, manifestation of the sorts of failings that critical realist and some sociological arguments have established more generally.

Context

I should say something about how the chapters in Part I have been put together. All the authors currently work in Cambridge, and indeed all the chapters in Part I were first presented at the Cambridge *Workshop on realism and economics*. Others working outside Cambridge (and indeed the UK) were invited to contribute. Unfortunately the tight deadline imposed by the *Review of Social Economy* (where the following five chapters originally appeared) really meant that I had to look for work that was already in progress. For obvious reasons I was more familiar with the research of people in Cambridge. I hope that this bias in the selection process will not detract from the worth of the chapters included here. In one way it is a source of strength. For, by way of being first presented at the 'realist workshop' the contributions have received significant criticism from many familiar with the subject matter. In any case, as post-modernists and sociologists of scientific knowledge repeatedly emphasise, all contributions have a specific cultural and social-relational context of some kind; there is no getting away from this fact. The significant point here is that all the papers have been heavily refereed by (in some cases numerous) anonymous assessors who were requested to be critical and, where appropriate, to reject. The outcome is a collection of papers all of which are of a high quality and, without exception, make an important contribution.[7]

Substantive theory

As a final matter I want to say something about the omission, from the chapters which follow, of any contribution concerned to elaborate a specific substantive (highly concrete) theory. Probably the 'request' I come across most frequently in the context of discussing critical realism is for examples of 'critical realist substantive theory' meaning *the* critical realist accounts of some highly concrete phenomena. In my view there can be no such thing. Critical realism in economics is a project oriented to underlabouring for a more fruitful science of economics. It can provide a perspective on the nature of science and society, but it cannot do the work of science. In this sense it is on a par with deductivism. The mainstream modelling project, I have argued, is not, and cannot be, tied to any particular substantive theory. For example, there is not *the* deductivist, or even, say, *the* econometric theory of price or output determination in any context. Nor can there be the critical realist one (and I wonder by the same token whether theories of price-determination, etc., are usefully labelled Post-Keynesian, Austrian or Institutionalist either). Of course, the aim accepted in critical realism is to encourage economists to accept in their researches the broad perspective elaborated under the critical realist head. Specifically, those connected with the project all accept, and seek to promote the insight, that the world is open, structured, dynamic and at least in part holistic, with the aim of science being to illuminate mechanisms, etc., responsible for phenomena identified as of interest. But there can be no expectation that scientists acting on the basis of this perspective will always reach the same conclusions. Given the openness of social reality in particular, researchers may even entertain a range of explanatory theories. If there is wide agreement concerning such highly abstract features as those just noted (that reality is open, structured, dynamic, etc.), things begin to get more contentious once the focus moves to more concrete issues, perhaps even at the (still relatively abstract) level of 'money is a social relation', as I noted above. In any case it is likely that any specific explanatory conception accepted at a given stage will undergo significant development over time.

Of course, for those acting upon critical realism, the aim at each stage *will* be to bring empirical and other evidence to bear with the *intention* of identifying which of the competing accounts is the most adequate. But still there can be no guarantee that agreement will always be reached, or that, if and when agreement is reached, new evidence and thinking will not lead to revised accounts sooner or later. Indeed, if there is to be continuing progress in understanding the latter is only to be expected and actively facilitated.

It would be wrong then, in my view, to cast any substantive theory as *the* critical realist one. But this of course does not mean that the project has nothing to achieve in the economics domain. In fact, given that deductivism probably accounts for more than 90 per cent of modern economics, merely to convince economists of its errors would be a result of no little consequence. And of course, to establish a more viable approach to economics, to *facilitate* successful substantive theories, would equally be of substantial value. The chapters which follow underlabour in a significant way for both these ends.

Acknowledgements

For helpful comments on an earlier draft I am grateful to Steve Fleetwood, Geoff Harcourt, Geoffrey Ingham, Clive Lawson, Mark Peacock, Stephen Pratten, and Jochen Runde.

Notes

1 See, for example, Mäki, Gustafsson and Knudsen (1993); Backhouse (1994); Boylan and O'Gorman (1995); and Nelson (1996).
2 In recent years there have been a number of projects within the social sciences adopting an explicitly *realist* stance. Not all have accepted the perspective of critical realism, of course, including, in economics, the important contributions of Mäki (1988, 1990a, 1990b, 1992a, 1992b, 1993a, 1993b, 1994).
3 Within economics, see, for example, Arestis (1990, 1992, 1996); Davis (1998); Dow (1997a, 1997b, 1997c); Ekström (1992); Fleetwood (1995, 1996a, 1996b); Foss (1994); Hodgson (1993a); Jennings and Waller (1994, 1995); Kanth (1991); C. Lawson (1994); C. Lawson *et al.* (1996); Peacock (1993); Philip (1995); Pratten (1993, 1994, 1995); Rotheim (1993); Runde (1993, 1995a, 1995b, 1995c, 1996, 1997, 1998); Sofianou (1995). Outside economics important contributions include Archer (1995); Collier (1994); Lloyd (1993); Pratt (1995); Sayer (1984, 1985); and of course the numerous contributions of Bhaskar (e.g. 1978, 1993, 1994).
4 Of course many of the results and arguments generated within critical realism overlap with those produced in parallel projects, including, in recent years, those systematised under the heads of *evolutionary economics*, e.g. Hodgson (1992, 1993a, 1993b); Foss (1994); and Vromen (1995), *feminist economics*, e.g. Folbre (1991, 1993, 1994); Harding (1995); Hartmann (1981); Nelson (1993a, 1993b, 1996); Strassmann (1993a, 1993b, 1994); Strober (1994) and *path dependence*, e.g. David (1985, 1986, 1992, 1994) amongst others.

Basically I see all such projects as attempting to deal with the same sorts of problems and issues albeit coming from different angles as it were, adopting different starting points and drawing upon different insights and experiences.

5 Of course there are others who have reached effectively the same conclusion; some, like Marx and Veblen, long ago. But for many it is an insight that has been lost along the way. One set of contributions that has lately emphasised this feature is *feminist economics*. In fact, I was very much hoping to include a paper on *feminist economics and realism* in this issue co-authored by Jane Humphries. Due to the tight deadline I had to impose, however, the paper never emerged on time. I thus content myself here with recording Humphries' summing-up on the centrality of methodology in a recent book review. She writes:

> In other disciplines gender biases have long been acknowledged and solutions sought. In economics feminist revisionism has been laggard. Why?
>
> The answer lies in the uncompromising attachment of economists to their methodology. Economists can live with affirmative action where gender bias is identified with the under-representation of women. They might even tolerate a feminist empiricism according to which the biases of the discipline can be corrected by even stricter adherence to the alleged methodological norms of scientific inquiry. More dispassion, less involvement, a more *scientific* approach will purge androcentrism. What economists cannot permit is a deeper methodological critique.
>
> (1994: 483)

6 That is, irrespective of whether the 'events' in question ever occur, or are even expected to. The emphasis in deductivism is on generalities at the level of surface phenomena rather than at the level of 'deeper' mechanisms which are responsible for whatever event configurations emerge – see below.

7 I should add a remark about the chapter by Clive Lawson. As he and I are related, the initial acceptance of this contribution for publication in the *Review of Social Economy* may appear questionable. In fact, this is the only paper whose processing I have had nothing to do with: it was assessed (by referees unknown to me) and accepted for publication by the *Review of Social Economy* even before I was invited to put this special issue together. On targeting five papers for this issue, and soliciting seven papers (not including Clive's) in anticipation that at least two of the seven would not make it, I requested that Clive's be held back for possible inclusion in case only four of those solicited came through. This latter conjectured possibility proved to be the actual outcome.

Bibliography

Archer, M. S. (1995) *Realist Social Theory: The Morphogenic Approach*, Cambridge: Cambridge University Press.

Arestis, P. (1990) 'Post-Keynesianism: A New Approach to Economics', *Review of Social Economy* 48(3): 222–246.

—— (1992) *The Post-Keynesianism Approach to Economics: An Alternative Analysis of Economic Theory and Policy*, Aldershot: Edward Elgar.

—— (1996) 'Post-Keynesian Economics: Towards Coherence', *Cambridge Journal of Economics*, 20(1): 111–136.

Backhouse, R. (1994) *New Directions in Economic Methodology*, London: Routledge.

Bhaskar, R. (1978) *A Realist Theory of Science*, Hemel Hempstead: Harvester Press (1st edn, Leeds 1975).

—— (1993) *Dialectic: The Pulse of Freedom*, London: Verso.

—— (1994) *Plato Etc.: The Problems of Philosophy and their Resolution*, London: Verso.

Boylan, T. A. and O'Gorman, P. F. (1995) *Beyond Rhetoric and Realism in Economics: Towards a Reformulation of Economic Methodology*, London: Routledge.

Collier, A. (1994) *Critical Realism: An Introduction to Roy Bhaskar's Philosophy*, London: Verso.

David, P. A. (1985) 'Clio and the Economics of QWERTY', *American Economic Review (Papers and Proceedings)* 75(2): 332–337.

—— (1986) 'Understanding the Economics of QWERTY: The Necessity of History', in W. N. Parker (ed.) *Economic History and the Modern Economist*, Oxford: Blackwell: 30–49.

—— (1992) 'Path-Dependency in Economic Processes: Implications for Policy Analysis in Dynamical System Contexts', *Centre for Economic Policy Research*, Stanford University, mimeo.

—— (1994) 'Why are Institutions the "Carriers Of History"?: Path Dependence and the Evolution of Conventions, Organisations and Institutions', *Structural Change and Economic Dynamics* 5(2): 205–220.

Davis, J. B. (1998) 'Davidson, Non-ergodicity and Individuals', in P. Arestis (ed.) *Festrift for Paul Davidson*, Aldershot: Edward Elgar.

Dow, S. C. (1997a) *The Methodology of Macroeconomic Thought*, Aldershot: Edward Elgar.

—— (1997b) 'Methodological Pluralism and Pluralism of Method', in A. Salanti (ed.) *Pluralism in Economics: Theory, History and Methodology*, Aldershot: Edward Elgar.

—— (1997c) 'Whither Mainstream Economics? A Survey of Economic Methodology', *Cambridge Journal of Economics* 21(1): 73–93.

Ekström, M. (1992) 'Causal Explanation of Social Action: The Contribution of Max Weber and of Critical Realism to a Generative View of Causal Explanation in Social Science', *Acta Sociologica*, 35: 107–122.

Fleetwood, S. (1995) *Hayek's Political Economy: The Socio-Economics of Order*, London: Routledge.

—— (1996a) 'Order Without Equilibrium: A Critical Realist Interpretation of Hayek's Notion of Spontaneous Order', *Cambridge Journal of Economics* 20(6): 729–747.

—— (1996b) 'Hayek III: The Necessity of Social Rules of Conduct', in S. Frowen (ed.) *Hayek the Economist and Social Philosopher*, Basingstoke and London: Macmillan.

Folbre, N. (1991) 'The Unproductive Housewife: Her Evolution in Nineteenth Century Economic Thought', *Signs* 16(3): 463–484.

—— (1993) 'How Does She Know? Feminist Theories of Gender Bias in Economics', *History of Political Economy* 25(1): 167–184.

—— (1994) *Who Pays for the Kids? Gender and the Structures of Constraint*, London: Routledge.

Foss, N. J. (1994) 'Realism and Evolutionary Economics', *Journal of Social and Evolutionary Systems* 17(1): 21–40.

Hahn, F. H. (1987) 'The Foundations of Monetary Theory', in M. de Cecco and J. Fitoussi (eds) *Monetary Theory and Economic Institutions*, London: Macmillan: 21–43.

Harding, S. (1995) 'Can Feminist Thought Make Economics More Objective?', *Feminist Economics* 1(1): 7–32.

Hartmann, H. (1981) 'The Family as the Locus of Gender, Class, and Political Struggle: The Example of Housework', *Signs* 6(3): 366–394.

Hodgson, G. (1992) 'Thorstein Veblen and Post-Darwinian Economics', *Cambridge Journal of Economics* 16(3): 285–302.

—— (1993a) *Economics and Evolution: Bringing Life Back into Economics*, Cambridge: Polity Press.

—— (1993b) 'Theories of Economic Evolution: A Preliminary Taxonomy', *Manchester School of Economic and Social Studies* LXI (2): 125–143.

Humphries, J. (1994) Review of Ferber M. and Nelson J. (eds.): *Beyond Economic Man: Feminist Theory and Economics*, *Journal of Economic History*, 54: 483, 484.

Jennings, A. and Waller, W. (1994) 'Evolutionary Economics and Cultural Hermeneutics: Veblen, Cultural Relativism and Blind Drift', *Journal of Economic Issues* XXVIII(4): 997–1030.

—— (1995) 'Cultural: Core Concept Reaffirmed', *Journal of Economic Issues* XXIX(2): 407–418.

Kanth, R. K. (1991) 'Economic Theory and Realism: Outlines of a Reconstruction', *Methodus* 3(2): 37–45.

Lawson, C. (1994) 'The Transformation Model of Social Activity and Economic Activity: A Reinterpretation of the Work of J. R. Commons', *Review of Political Economy* 6(2): 445–464.

Lawson, C., Peacock, M. and Pratten, S. (1996) 'Realism, Underlabouring and Institutions', *Cambridge Journal of Economics* 20(1): 137–151.

Lawson, T. (1994) 'The Nature of Post Keynesianism and its Links to other Traditions', *Journal of Post Keynesian Economics*, 16: 503–538. Reprinted in D. L. Prychitko (ed.) (1998) *Why Economists Disagree: An Introduction to the Contemporary Schools of Thought*, New York: State University of New York Press.

—— (1997) *Economics and Reality*, London: Routledge.

Lloyd, C. (1993) *The Structures of History*, Oxford: Blackwell Publishers.

Mäki, U. (1988) 'How to Combine Rhetoric and Realism in the Methodology of Economics', *Economics and Philosophy* 4(1): 89–109.

—— (1990a) 'Scientific Realism and Austrian Explanation', *Review of Political Economy* 2(3): 310, 344.

—— (1990b) 'Methodology of Economics: Complaints and Guidelines', *Finnish Economic Papers* 3(1): 77–84.

—— (1992a) 'On the Method of Isolation in Economics', *Poznan Studies in the Philosophy of the Sciences and the Humanities* 26: 317–351.

——(1992b) 'Friedman and Realism', *Research in the History of Economic Thought and Methodology* 10: 171–195.

—— (1993a) 'Economics with Institutions: Agenda for Methodological Enquiry', in U. Mäki, B. Gustafsson and C. Knudson (eds) *Rationality, Institutions and Economic Methodology*, London and New York: Routledge

—— (1993b) 'Social Theories of Science and the Fate of Institutionalism in Economics', in U. Mäki, B. Gustafsson and C. Knudsen (eds) *Rationality, Institutions and Economic Methodology*, London and New York: Routledge.

—— (1994) 'Isolation, Idealization and Truth in Economics', *Poznan Studies in the Philosophy of the Sciences and the Humanities* 38: 147–168.

Mäki, U., Gustafsson, B. and Knudsen, C. (eds) (1993) *Rationality, Institutions and Economic Methodology*, London: Routledge.

Nelson, J. (1993a) 'Value-Free or Valueless? Notes on the Pursuit of Detachment in Economics', *History of Political Economy* 25(1): 121–145.

—— (1993b) 'The Study of Choice or the Study of Provisioning? Gender and the Definition of Economics', in M. A. Ferber and J. Nelson (eds) *Beyond Economic Man*, Chicago: Chicago University Press, 23–36.

—— (1996) *Feminism, Objectivity and Economics*, London and New York: Routledge.

Peacock, M. (1993) 'Hayek, Realism and Spontaneous Order', *Journal for the Theory of Social Behaviour* 23(3): 249, 264.

Philip, P. (1995) 'Transcendental Realism – A Foundation for Evolutionary Economics?', *International Journal for Social Economics* 22(12): 19–35.

Popper, K. R. (1990) *A World of Propensities*, Bristol: Thoemmes Antiquarian Books Ltd.

Pratt, A. C. (1995) 'Putting Critical Realism to Work: The Practical Implications for Geographical Research', *Progress in Human Geography* 19(1): 61–74.

Pratten, S. (1993) 'Structure, Agency and Marx's Analysis of the Labour Process', *Review of Political Economy* 5(4): 403–426.

—— (1994) 'Marshall on Tendencies, Equilibrium and the Statical Method', Chap 2. of PhD thesis: *Forms of Realism, Conceptions of Science and Approaches to Industrial Organisations*, Cambridge.

—— (1995) 'Operationalizing Transaction Cost Economics: Implications and Alternatives', De Montford University: mimeo.

Rotheim, R. J. (1993) 'On the Indeterminacy of Keynes's Monetary Theory of Value', *Review of Political Economy* 5(2): 197, 216.

Runde, J. (1993) 'Paul Davidson and the Austrians', *Critical Review* 7(2–3): 381–397.

19

—— (1995a) 'Risk, Uncertainty and Bayesian Decision Theory: A Keynesian View', in S. Dow and J. Hillard (eds) *Keynes, Knowledge and Uncertainty*, Aldershot: Edward Elgar: 197–210.

—— (1995b) 'Review of Young Bak Choi's *Paradigms and Conventions'*, *Economics and Philosophy* 11(2): 379–385.

—— (1995c) 'Chances and Choices: Some Notes on Probability and Belief in Economic Theory', *The Monist* July, 78: 330, 351

—— (1996) 'Keynesian Methodology', in G. C. Harcourt and P. Riach (eds) *Keynes General Theory*, second edition, London: Routledge.

—— (1998) 'Assessing Causal Explanation', *Oxford Economic Papers*, 50: 151–172.

Runde, J. (1997) 'Abstraction, Idealisation and Economic Theory', in P. Arestis, G. Palma and M. Sawyer (eds) *Markets, Unemployment and Economic Policy: Essays in honour of Geoff Harcourt, volume II*, London: Routledge.

Sayer, A. (1984) *Method in Social Science: A Realist Approach*, London: Hutchison.

—— (1985) 'Realism and Geography', in R. J. Johnston (ed.) *The Future of Geography*, London: Methuen, 159–173.

Sofianou, E. (1995) 'Post-Modernism and the Notion of Rationality in Economics', *Cambridge Journal of Economics* 19(3): 373–390.

Strassmann, D. L. (1993a) 'Not a Free Market; The Rhetoric of Disciplinary Authority in Economics', in M. A. Ferber and J. Nelson (eds) *Beyond Economic Man: Feminist Theory and Economics*, Chicago: Chicago University Press, 54–68.

—— (1993b) 'The Stories of Economics and the Power of the Storyteller', *History of Political Economy* 25(1): 147–165.

—— (1994) 'Feminist Thought and Economics; Or, What do the Visigoths Know?', *American Economic Review, Papers and Proceedings* 84(2): 153–158.

Strober, M. H. (1994) 'Rethinking Economics through Feminist Lens', *American Economic Review, Papers and Proceedings* 84(2): 143–147.

Vromen, J. (1995) *Economic Evolution: An Enquiry into the Foundation of New Institutional Economics*, London: Routledge.

2

THE 'CLOSURE' ASSUMPTION AS A FIRST STEP

Neo-Ricardian economics and Post-Keynesianism

Stephen Pratten[1]

Introduction

The position of neo-Ricardian economics[2] remains controversial. Specifically, there is significant debate regarding the extent to which neo-Ricardianism can be incorporated within a coherent Post-Keynesian perspective. Related to this, though as a prior concern, is the question of whether coherence in Post-Keynesian economics is achievable on any conception. While some authors express misgivings regarding the search for coherence,[3] others claim that an adequate account of Post-Keynesian economics can be identified at a substantive level.[4] But the argument that appears to have gained most ground is that coherence must rather be located at a methodological or philosophical level and specifically rooted in a common adherence to critical realism. T. Lawson (1994), in particular, suggests that if anything can render intelligible the most important nominal features of Post-Keynesian economics, including its opposition to orthodoxy, relative openness towards methodological reflection, emphasis upon institutions and historical processes, and sensitivity to agents' own conceptions and their expectations, then it must be something like a shared commitment to a broadly critical realist perspective.[5] Much of the time neo-Ricardian authors appear to share a similar set of concerns. They repeatedly emphasise the importance of history, the role of social institutions and express a deep-rooted distrust of orthodox economics.[6] But, despite such apparent correspondences, one discerns within Post-Keynesianism a continuing sense of disquiet regarding neo-Ricardian economics. That is to say the Post-Keynesian–

neo-Ricardian relationship appears to represent a long-standing puzzle within this literature.[7] It is significant to note that Lawson, when elaborating the key characteristics of Post-Keynesianism, consciously sets to one side neo-Ricardian economics. This strategy is defended precisely on the basis that the relationship between neo-Ricardianism and Post-Keynesianism constitutes a highly contested issue. Lawson writes:

> If coherence within Post-Keynesianism cannot be found amongst those features that appear to be widely agreed upon by Post-Keynesians, then the inclusion of controversial features is unlikely to change matters. Alternatively, if coherence can be brought to, or found within, the agreed features, it should then be that much easier to assess whether, conditional upon coherence being required, those features not considered here do, or could, or should not, etc., belong.
>
> (1994: 506)

In this chapter I indicate how anchoring Post-Keynesianism within critical realism does serve to clarify its relationship with neo-Ricardian economics. Specifically in adopting this strategy, I not only outline a suitable criterion for assessing whether neo-Ricardian economics belongs within a coherent Post-Keynesianism but also provide an account which renders intelligible the noted continuing uncertainty expressed by Post-Keynesians on whether to embrace neo-Ricardianism. The chapter is structured as follows. In the next section I briefly review the arguments, central to Lawson's thesis, that

1   orthodoxy must be characterised by its method (rather than any substantive claim), and in particular by its (unquestioning) acceptance of deductivism, and
2   that Post-Keynesian coherence lies in its adopting a non-deductivist perspective along the lines of critical realism.

In the following section I argue that neo-Ricardianism remains tied to deductivism, indicating that it underpins the main theoretical contributions of its proponents, and is fairly explicit in their general methodological reflections. My conclusion, set out in the final section, is that neo-Ricardianism cannot sustain the, albeit often hesitant, moves towards critical realism typical of Post-Keynesianism but rather must, ultimately, be seen as constrained in the manner of orthodox approaches.

Critical realism, deductivism and closure

In considering whether neo-Ricardianism belongs within a coherent Post-Keynesian economics, and in attempting to make sense of the continuing puzzle surrounding the relationship between neo-Ricardianism and Post-Keynesianism, my contention is that it is useful to turn to the recent methodological literature and in particular to a set of contributions systematised as critical realism.[8] An important contribution of critical realism has been to elaborate the nature of the mainstream project and thereby explain its numerous failings.[9] In the present context, critical realists, by tracing the inadequacies of contemporary orthodox economics back to entrenched methodological misconceptions, bring into focus precisely what Post-Keynesians are opposing. Specifically it has been demonstrated that the essence of orthodox economics lies not at the level of substantive theory but at that of method. The numerous nominal characteristics and recent developments in contemporary orthodox economics can, in fact, be readily accounted for once we recognise that project's commitment to an essentially positivist account of the structure of scientific results and associated, profoundly limiting, deductivist mode of explanation. In particular, the conception of science as necessitating the search for regularities of the form 'whenever event (type) x then event (type) y' can be seen to underpin most substantive orthodox positions. In critical realist contributions such regularities are referred to as *closures*. The failings of the mainstream project have been revealed to be due to the continued attempts to investigate an intrinsically open social system by way of methods that presuppose that the social system is everywhere closed.

The inadequacy of this conception is exposed once some reflection is given to the nature of those situations within which such event regularities hold. Critical realists recognise that *closed systems* are rarely spontaneously occurring. Two observations are especially pertinent here. First, outside astronomy most of the strict event regularities uncovered in science have been produced in situations of experimental control. Second, experimental results are frequently applied outside the experimental situation where event regularities are no longer found. In order to render intelligible these observations critical realists argue that it is necessary to interpret the world as *structured* and *open* thereby breaking away from the essentially flat ontology, exhausted by events and experiences, associated with the positivist position. That is, the confinement of most event regularities, but not of the application of scientific knowledge to situations of experimental control, can be explained if it is acknowledged that the world is structured in that actual events and states of affairs are produced by equally real underlying structures, mechanisms, powers and open in that actual phenomena are typically conjointly determined by numerous often countervailing mechanisms. On this conception the noted observations can be explained by seeing the achievement of the well-controlled experiment as the insulation of some fixed or relatively stable causal mechanism from the action of countervailing factors so that the mechanism of interest can be empirically identified. The event regularity so uncovered, in other words, relates the 'triggering' conditions of some mechanism and the way it acts. But the mechanism itself, when triggered, acts inside and outside the experimental conditions, thereby explaining how it is that experimentally determined results can be applied in non-experimental contexts. Laws on this conception refer not to event regularities produced in experimental situations but to the causal mechanisms they reveal. In short, event regularities are not the scientific object but a human contrivance which allows underlying causal mechanisms to be revealed.[10]

T. Lawson (1994, 1995) demonstrates that, rather than any substantive claims, it is the retention of methods that hinge upon the discovery, or elaboration, of putative 'event regularities' which characterises orthodox economics. In short, the argument is simply that while substantive theories come and go, the modelling strategies that presuppose deductivism to be relevant are continually sustained. Once it is recognised that the essence of orthodoxy is its method then the Post-Keynesian opposition to it can be seen as an, albeit often tacit, call for a move beyond deductivism. If this response can be interpreted as involving the adoption of something approximating critical realism then it opens up the possibility of incorporating more compelling treatments of complex human agency and structured social processes.[11] That is, it is only by abandoning the entire deductivist framework and embracing something like critical realism that progress beyond the orthodox project can be made.

Accepting this set of arguments the question of whether neo-Ricardianism is part of Post-Keynesianism amounts to questioning whether it is deductivist in structure. Already we can see why the question of the relation between the two has previously been handled inadequately. For previous attempts have supposed that what is at issue in characterising both orthodoxy and Post-Keynesianism is substantive theory rather than methodology. If the basis of coherence within Post-Keynesianism turns on its move beyond deductivism then the issue of whether neo-Ricardianism belongs within a coherent Post-Keynesianism must be considered at a methodological level. It is a failure previously to appreciate this that helps explain the continuing puzzle surrounding the relationship between neo-Ricardianism and Post-Keynesianism.

The neo-Ricardian retention of deductivism

While neo-Ricardian authors, at least at the level of presentation, emphasise their openness to the analysis of social processes, institutional structures, history, and the like, I shall argue that their theoretical contributions together with their meta-theoretical claims to be scientific, in fact, turn on the deductivist method. More specifically, I show that inspection of the key methodological themes and distinctions which neo-Ricardians accept as central to their project reveals a reliance upon a deductivist mode of explanation.

The core of classical political economy

Many neo-Ricardian authors follow Garegnani in arguing that implicit in Sraffa's analysis, and buried within the contributions of the classical authors, is a crucial distinction between two different kinds of relations which in turn promotes a separation of analysis into successive logical steps.[12] Garegnani asserts the existence of

> a field where general quantitative relations of sufficiently definite form can be postulated, and another field where relations in the economy are so complex and variable according to circumstances as to allow not for general quantitative relations of sufficiently definite form, but rather for a more inductive kind of analysis, continuously supported by what Marshall used to call 'specific experience'.
>
> (1990a: 123–124)

More substantively Garegnani writes:

> The surplus theories have so to speak, a *core* which is isolated from the rest of the analysis, because the wage, the social product and the technical conditions of production appear there as already determined. It is in this 'core' that we find the determination of the shares other than wages as a residual: a determination which . . . will also entail the determination of the relative prices of commodities. Further as a natural extension of this, we shall find in the 'core' an analysis of the relations between, on the one hand, the real wage, the social product and the technical conditions of production (the

independent variables) and, on the other hand, the shares other than wages constituting the surplus, and the relative prices (the dependent variables).

(1984: 236)

While Garegnani emphasises that this distinction relates to some aspect of the nature of the relationships studied,[13] it is taken for granted that quantitative relations exist both within the core and outside and that it is these which constitute the basis for scientific generalisations. The analysis undertaken within the core seems to be regarded as distinctive mainly because it can be formulated at a relatively high level of generality.[14] It is important to note here that these general claims appear to be interpreted as, or as depending upon, event regularities of our real social world. Garegnani argues, for example, that within the core 'the price equations can be held to provide a rigorous representation of reality' (1990b: 155).[15] Meanwhile, outside the core it is assumed that quantitative relations of a functional form obtain, but it is acknowledged that they are likely to be less general, more time-space specific or hold only approximately. Thus, one way or another, formulations of these non-core regularities seem, on empirical grounds, to be considered more questionable than core relations, with any deductions derived when deploying them regarded as less secure. Thus Garegnani writes that outside the core:

> the possibility of formal relations in fields of analysis like the determination of outputs, accumulation and distribution appears to exist only under special assumptions, and in that sense either as approximate (though of course highly useful) descriptions of reality or, alternatively, as intellectual experiments intended to analyze the logical implications of particular hypotheses.
>
> (1990b: 155)

Elsewhere he notes:

> Beyond these relations engendered by the necessary connection between the price of a commodity and resource remunerations there lay the second field of analysis where no similarly definite quantitative relations could be postulated about reality. (This did not exclude the possibility or usefulness of obtaining relations on the basis of *special hypotheses*.) Because they were special hypotheses, however, these relations could not be applied to reality with the generality

associated, for instance, with the equality between prices and costs in the price equations.

(1990a: 124)

Although not always explicitly stated, then, it seems to be taken for granted that deductivism is appropriate for the set of core relations and seems to be accepted as extendable in principle (if with certain qualifications) to other parts of the economy. Garegnani writes:

> In the classical theories we find a 'core' where the real wage, the outputs and the techniques are taken as given or as independent variables. This is so because the view taken of the forces determining those variables makes it convenient to determine them *separately* from prices and the dependent distributive variables . . . That separate 'determination' has, however, the usual explanatory or . . . 'predictive' meaning.
>
> (1991: 112)

Neo-Ricardians, as we have seen, recognise that the analysis of the core involves the isolation of these relations from all kinds of other determinations and reciprocal influences that are important but reserved for analysis in the second field of analysis. Garegnani writes:

> the study of the *reciprocal influences* between real wages, levels of output and technical conditions of production . . . treated as independent variables in the core, were seen to pertain to this second field of analysis. And into this second field there would also fall the study . . . of the reverse influence of the shares other than wages, or of relative prices, on those same independent variables. In this second field all those dependencies could be studied together with all the social and political factors, independent monetary factors, or independent technical changes. The multiplicity of these dependencies, and their variability according to circumstance, made it necessary to study them *separately* from the relations of the core and not *simultaneously* with them.
>
> (1990a: 125)

This procedure is justified on the promise that it represents an essential first step. Bharadwaj notes:

> This 'separation' as a first step, may appear unduly restrictive. On the contrary, it opens up the possibility of introducing a

wider range of determinants and the real dynamics of the process of change – precisely because, the more complex, historically specific, institutional and social forces that govern changes . . . can thereby be introduced.

(1990: 73–74)

Garegnani, similarly, notes 'the relationships studied in the core are simply a step, though generally a necessary step, in the analysis of those central questions dealt with outside the core' (1990b: 151–152). According to Eatwell and Green, the analysis of the core is not complete until it has been filled out by supplementary analysis, they write that:

theoretically general constructs . . . rely on concrete histori-cally specific factors for their completion and solution . . . the classical analysis of prices must be 'closed' by the addition of concrete information on the historical and institutional factors affecting, say, the determination of wages.

(1984: 201)

The point, though, is that no matter how this process of *filling in* is to be done, and whatever the methods, the core is postulated as a set of insulated relationships, with only the values of the independent vari-ables open to outside determination.

It is true that the distinctive nature of the relations of the core are strongly asserted when neo-Ricardian authors differentiate their approach from that of orthodox theory. In particular, the theory of value, which is seen as corresponding to the analysis of the core,[16] is said to perform a strictly limited role within the neo-Ricardian perspective. Garegnani suggests that this

limitation of the theory of value in the classical authors appears to have been the result of an instinctive methodolog-ical adaptation to the requirements of economics, where, because of the impossibility of experiment and of the complexity and variability of the material, 'the function of analysis and deduction . . . is not to forge long chains of reasoning, but to forge rightly many short chains'; the limited scope of the theory of value and the analysis by separate stages, are a way of keeping the 'chains of reasoning' short as Marshall realised to be necessary.

(1987: 563)

It is claimed that this stands in stark contrast to orthodoxy:

> The attempt of marginalist authors to widen the scope of general quantitative relations inevitably tended to shape the method of economics *as a whole* along those relationships. All those phenomena that, though recognised to influence the economy, were obviously refractory to a treatment in terms of quantitative relations, which should be both sufficiently general and sufficiently well defined in their properties were excluded from economics and left to other sciences.
>
> (1990a: 126)[17]

However, if, as I have accepted, mainstream economics is characterised by its deductivist methodology, then this contrast drawn between neo-Ricardianism and orthodoxy seems somewhat overstated.[18] In both orthodoxy and neo-Ricardianism the relevance of deductivism is taken for granted.[19]

It might plausibly be argued that neo-Ricardianism in contrast to orthodoxy does not regard deductivism as holding universally in that it is allowed that, outside the core, relations of a non-quantitative nature may hold which call for a quite different kind of approach. This seems to be supported when neo-Ricardians emphasise that the separation of analysis promotes an openness towards historical and institutional factors:

> By limiting the scope of the quantitative relations of known general properties to those of the core, the classical economists recognized the multiplicity of the factors affecting both distribution and accumulation, and allowed the study of these social and historical factors to be an integral part of economics. For example, the separate determination of the wage outside the core of the theory allowed for a role for historical factors both with respect to the notion of subsistence that we find in the given economy, and more generally, with respect to all the other events that influence the relative bargaining position of the classes involved. These historical factors are often embodied, so to speak, in the conventions and institutions within the limits of which and through which competition must operate.
>
> (Garegnani 1990a: 126)

Elsewhere he notes:

the flexibility resulting from the classical reasoning 'by stages' and the recognition it implies of the multiplicity and vari- ability of the relations examined outside the 'core', appear to be a more or less conscious recognition of the role which broader social, institutional and political factors, in a word historical factors, play in economic phenomena, particularly in the spheres of distribution, accumulation and technical change.

(1987: 563)

But even if comments such as these suggest (an occasional) recogni- tion that the deductivist structure is not appropriate for a certain set of relations outside the core there remains the need to justify the presupposition that, for a sub-set of social phenomena, the elabora- tion of constant relationships is appropriate. It would appear that all the criticisms which apply to orthodox economics for unreflectively deploying deductivism in the analysis of all aspects of economic phenomena also apply to neo-Ricardianism for applying it to a signifi- cant part. In an open social system neo-Ricardians can provide more adequate accounts of historical processes, institutional forms, etc., only by abandoning their commitment to deductivism.

Normal positions and gravitational forces

A further set of distinctions, accepted as vital by neo-Ricardian authors, is between positions and/or values of variables interpreted as normal and the positions and values of variables that actually occur. And this set of distinctions highlights once more how firmly embedded deductivism is within this project. Eatwell writes:

satisfactory analysis of value and distribution in a capitalist economy should endeavour to explain and determine the normal or long period position of the system whereby long- period is meant not that which occurs in a long period of time, but rather that which is determined by the dominant forces of the system within a period in which those forces are constant or changing but slowly.

(1987: 599)

Bharadwaj characterises this method as 'trying to identify relations that appear to be fairly persistent, so that they may by viewed as dominant tendencies at work in the economy' (1990: 65). Garegnani similarly, drawing on Marx, claims that the adoption of this procedure represents the condition for finding 'the actual tendencies of [the] movements [of the phenomena]' (1979: 77). Milgate notes 'in isolating the systematic, regular and persistent forces the traditional method deferred to the equalising effects of competition and focused upon natural or long-period conditions as the basis for providing statements of general validity (i.e., statements of "tendency")' (1982: 34).

This reference to persistent forces and tendencies might appear to suggest the acknowledgement of a structured ontology of the sort elaborated in critical realism. Indeed, it seems to have been this kind of presentation that has led some commentators to insist that neo-Ricardianism is consistent with 'realism', where the latter appears to be a short-hand for the critical realism accepted by some Post-Keynesians. Lavoie, for example, notes: 'some may doubt that there is any link between realism and neo-Ricardianism. This is not so.' He goes on to quote Milgate's characterisation of the neo-Ricardian method as involving the 'abstract characterisation of the actual economy' aimed at capturing 'the systematic, regular and persistent forces at work in the system' (Lavoie 1992: 9).

Now the notion of distinguishing dominant tendencies or forces is clearly legitimate. Indeed, it is precisely because certain mechanisms come to dominate others over restricted regions of time and space and thereby give rise to partial event regularities which require explanation, that science is able to go to work in an open social world. However, neo-Ricardians do not simply identify dominant tendencies, they suggest that the system can in fact be represented as a formal system within which functional relations, characterising these dominant tendencies, obtain. Eatwell, for example, argues:

Theory proceeds by the extraction from reality of those forces which are believed to be dominant and persistent, and the formation of these elements into a formal system, the solution of which is to determine the state or magnitude of the variables under consideration. It is obvious that the solution will not, except by a fluke, correspond to the actual magnitudes of the variables ruling at any one time, for these will be the outcome not simply of the elements grouped under the heading 'dominant and persistent', but also of the multitude of other forces excluded from the analysis as transitory, peculiar or specific (lacking general significance) which may in any given situation, exert a more or less powerful effect. None the less, the practice of analysis necessarily embodies the assumption that forces comprising the theory are dominant, and that the determined magnitudes will on average, tend to be established. In any satisfactory analytical scheme these magnitudes must be centres of gravitation, capturing the essential character of the phenomena under consideration.

(1982a: 211)

Elsewhere and more explicitly he notes:

In defining the object of analysis and identifying the forces which determine it, the assumption is made, implicitly, that the forces of which the theory is constituted are the more dominant, systematic and persistent. Transitory and arbitrary phenomena are abstracted from intentionally: as are those forces which are related to specific circumstances as opposed to the general case. The *dominant forces are expressed in algebraic form, as functions and constants, and constitute the data of the theory. The model may then (if it has been specified correctly) be solved to determine the magnitude of the object.* It is known that, except by a fluke, the magnitude determined as a solution will not be exactly that observed in reality. It cannot be, since a variety of transitory forces, known and unknown, have been excluded. None the less, since the theory is constructed on the basis of dominant and persistent forces, the magnitude determined by the analysis is the *centre of gravity* of the actual magnitude of the object.

(Italics added, 1979: 94–95)

Thus, despite the noted references to forces, tendencies and so on the emphasis is upon normal positions. And it is the focus upon these which is reckoned to facilitate the identification of certain constant relationships between variables that would obtain if temporary or accidental causes did not interfere. There is an acknowledgement of open systems here – it is recognised that there are likely to exist all sorts of disturbing, accidental or temporary influences preventing event regularities from obtaining. Garegnani explicitly recognises that economics is a field 'where experiment is impossible and . . . the material of the science is so highly complex and variable as generally to limit considerably the weight one can attribute to any observed, purely empirical regularity' (1990d: 72). However, while recognising the reality of open systems, neo-Ricardianism, in its method, remains tied to closed systems; its results are formulated in terms of outcomes, events, states of affairs, and their correlations or 'functional relations', and remains clearly deductivist in structure. Rather than event regularities holding at an immediate level, relationships between theoretical variables are seen as holding counterfactually, once isolated from the transient influences which invariably disturb them. It is taken for granted that it is legitimate, even necessary, to seal off phenomena of interest from interfering forces so as to facilitate concentration upon definite functional relations.

Now, it is true that, on a critical realist reading, any statement about a tendency that is transfactually in play may, in some situations, facilitate essentially hypothetical considerations regarding what would happen if the system could be closed. However, rather than this procedure of imagining closed systems being seen as an essential prerequisite for science, it is recognised as highly partial. To focus on event regularities even as counterfactuals is to concentrate on situations that are rare even in the natural realm – mainly those of experimental control – and more or less without counterpart in the social sphere. Tendency statements, in critical realism, relate to the operation of non-actual but real mechanisms which if triggered act unconditionally. Laws designate the activity of generative mechanisms independently of any particular sequences of events. A tendency here is understood not as a second-best kind of empirical generalisation but as a mechanism having effects even when they are not directly manifest. A tendency statement can be true even if the tendency referred to is never actualised at the level of events because of offsetting tendencies. It does not merely (and possibly does not at all) stipulate what would have happened had the situation been different. Thus the operation of the tendency does not depend upon the closure or otherwise of the system in which the mechanism operates: the mode of application of lawlike statements is the same in open and closed systems. It is the inferences that can be drawn from our knowledge of such tendencies which differ in the two cases.

Clearly in any attempt to legitimise the focus upon closed systems for a perspective which recognises the social realm to be quintessentially open, some kind of link between normal positions and actual positions has to be elaborated. Garegnani notes:

> if what is asserted in the theory about the variables is to be valid, there must ultimately exist some forces that bring the actual magnitudes towards the levels determined in the theory, with which the former magnitudes can in fact never coincide exactly.
>
> (1990c: 347)

Eatwell emphasises that:

Competition ... not only established the object of analysis, natural prices and the general rate of profit, but made meaningful analysis possible, since it allowed the operations of the capitalist economy to be characterised in a manner which permitted theoretical statements of general validity to be made about them.

(1982a: 210–211)

He goes on to argue:

Simple labelling of forces as dominant is not enough. These forces must operate through a process which establishes their dominance and through which the 'law-governed' nature of the system is manifest. That process is competition, which both enforces and expresses the attempts of individual capitals to maximise profits. Thus an important aspect of the behaviour of a capitalist market economy may be characterised at a sufficient level of generality, as the general rate of profit with associated normal prices, to permit the formulation of general causal statements, i.e., to permit analysis. Without this step ... it would not be possible to develop any form of general economic theory.

(ibid.: 211)

Of course, what is required here is not only some account of why actual variables should fluctuate around theoretical values[20] but also why the system under scrutiny should be characterised by the purported regularities. But the last element is missing. It remains unclear how competition or gravitational forces could guarantee that strict functional relations should characterise the system. Rather, it is merely assumed that if a system is to be amenable to scientific analysis then event regularities must exist at some level.

Concluding remarks

A degree of consensus on the most important nominal features of Post-Keynesianism is a prerequisite for any attempted assessment of the coherence of that project. If such agreement is forthcoming this opens up the possibility of competing accounts of coherence. In this chapter I have accepted that (just as mainstream economics can be characterised by its insistence upon a deductivist method), the least contentious, most widely accepted nominal features of Post-Keynesianism can be accounted for by that project's anti-deductivist stance. Specifically, these nominal aspects of Post-Keynesianism can be explained by reference to a tacit commitment to something like critical realism. In this chapter I have suggested that neo-Ricardian economics, to the extent that it takes closure for granted as a natural and useful starting point for analysis, retains an underlying commitment to deductivism and so is difficult to reconcile with Post-Keynesianism. In other words, if Post-Keynesianism is to be a consistent project, its link with neo-Ricardianism appears untenable. Alternatively, if, perhaps for institutional reasons, it is felt that in outlining the nominal characteristics of Post-Keynesianism some reference has to be made to neo-Ricardianism, then the project of seeking coherence may have to be abandoned. In providing a criterion for assessing whether neo-Ricardianism belongs within a coherent Post-Keynesianism it has become clear why the nature of this relationship has remained unresolved. It is not until it is recognised that the degree of coherence within Post-Keynesianism turns upon methodological issues, and essentially involves the abandonment of the deductivist framework, that progress in understanding its relationship with neo-Ricardianism could be made.

I have drawn lines particularly starkly in this chapter. No doubt there are all sorts of tensions to be unpacked within neo-Ricardian economics between the constraints that the deductivist view of explanation impose and the tentative acknowledgement of a structured social reality. This, of course, is no less true of those theorists who have more traditionally been viewed as orthodox. Moreover, since the rootedness of Post-Keynesianism in something like critical realism is rarely made explicit, there are likely to be tensions here also. Post-Keynesians do not consciously ground their work within critical realism or any related philosophical perspective and, given the dominance of the deductivist method in contemporary economics, this can lead to inconsistencies. It may therefore be the case that Post-Keynesianism remains uneasily anchored within critical realism. Meanwhile neo-Ricardian economics faces a clear dilemma. It can either retain its commitment to deductivism, and continue to run parallel to, if not actually constitute a sub-strand of, orthodoxy, or abandon this commitment and in the process lose what are perhaps its most distinctive characteristics.

Notes

1 An earlier version of this chapter was presented at the Cambridge Workshop on Realism and Economics. I am indebted to Sergio Cesaratto, Steve Fleetwood, Fred Lee, Clive Lawson, Tony Lawson, Pat Northover,

Fabio Petri, and Jochen Runde for valuable discussions on various aspects of this chapter. I am also grateful to five referees of the [ROSE] journal who provided constructive criticism of the paper. The usual disclaimers apply.

2 The label neo-Ricardian economics is applied to a range of positions (see Roncaglia 1991). Moreover, the term is not universally accepted – many authors who consciously develop Sraffa's approach view the reference to neo-Ricardianism as profoundly misleading. This is especially the case for the authors I primarily focus upon within this chapter who perceive Sraffa as rehabilitating a *classical approach* encompassing Marx's political economy. Garegnani, for example, writes that the relationship between Marx and the classical economists, particularly Ricardo 'should be seen in terms of a strict continuity at the level of economic analysis' (1989b: 372). Sraffa is then seen as returning to this approach:

> A resumption of the classical approach had naturally to start from the highest points of analytical development which that approach had achieved in the past – and in many respects these points are those at which we find that approach in Marx's work.
>
> (1989b: 372)

To the extent that reference to neo-Ricardianism indicates an implicit denial of any continuity with Marx, this label is seen as objectionable (see Eatwell 1974 and Milgate 1987). Even so, I persist in deploying the term neo-Ricardian economics primarily because this has become a widely adopted convention within the literature and appears to be sufficiently well established as to avoid confusion.

3 For example, Harcourt and Hamouda write:

> the real difficulty arises when attempts are made to synthesize the strands [of post-Keynesian economics] in order to see whether a coherent whole emerges. Our own view is that to attempt to do so is vainly to search for what Joan Robinson called 'only another box of tricks' to replace the 'complete theory' of mainstream economics which all strands reject.
>
> (1988: 230–231)

4 Kregel (1991: 81) suggests that 'the only way to make progress is by attempting to use the monetary theory that we find in the General Theory ... to form a foundation for a Post Keynesian theory of price ... and to attempt to link this to the theory of prices and production we find in the Sraffa model'.

5 While Lawson, in his account of the nature of Post-Keynesian economics, draws upon critical realism most systematically, there are numerous others, including Arestis (1990); Arestis *et al.* (1994); Dow (1990, 1995), who point to the relevance of critical realism when considering the coherence of Post-Keynesianism. See also Runde (1993).

6 See, for example, Eatwell (1994).

7 For one expression of this Post-Keynesian unease regarding neo-Ricardian economics see Joan Robinson's (1979) reaction to Garegnani.

8 Critical realism has been stimulated to a large extent by the writings

of R. Bhaskar (1978, 1986). Critical realism has in the last ten years been increasingly adopted in social and psychological research and more recently has begun to gain some ground within economics, see Fleetwood (1995), C. Lawson (1994), T. Lawson (1994, 1995), Pratten (1993), Runde (1993) and Sofianou (1995).

9 For detailed elaboration see T. Lawson (1995).

10 Bhaskar sums up the nature of the experiment as

> an attempt to trigger or unleash a single kind of mechanism or process in relative isolation, free from the interfering flux of the open world, so as to observe its detailed workings, or record its characteristic mode of effect and/or to test some hypothesis about them.
>
> (1986: 35)

For further discussion, see Bhaskar (1978).

11 Indeed, the typical emphasis of Post-Keynesians upon historical processes, social institutions, and agents' conceptions and expectations can be interpreted as calling for the adoption of a structured, transformational, and relational social ontology of the kind advanced and elaborated by critical realism, see T. Lawson (1994).

12 Thus Garegnani argues:

> the classical economists distinguished between [a] field of analysis ... where necessary quantitative relations could be found between rates of remuneration, and between these rates and relative prices, and other fields where no such necessary relations could be established, and where actual relations had to be studied in their multiplicity and diversity according to circumstances.
>
> (1983: 163–164)

Sraffa is seen as returning to this approach, providing 'a consistent version of what we may call the "core" of the surplus theories of Ricardo or Marx: the determination, that is, of the relationships linking the real wage, the rate of profits and prices' (1989a: 365–366).

13 Thus he writes:

> To avoid misunderstandings, it should be noted that the distinction between the part of the theory to be found in that core and the part outside it, has to do with a difference only in the *nature of the relationships* studied. It has therefore little to do with the comparative interest or importance which one wished to attach to those two kinds of relationships, as should be evident from the fact that questions as central as distribution, aggregate demand, accumulation or technical change fell largely outside the core.
>
> (1987: 562)

14 When considering the interpretation of the core it is interesting to note both Hahn's reaction to, and Garegnani's defence of, Sraffa's claim that outputs are taken as given in his analysis and that as a consequence, 'no

question arises as to the variation or constancy of returns' (Sraffa 1960: v). Hahn writes that this claim reduces Sraffa's analysis to 'just a fancy way of presenting accounts ex-post' (1982: 359). Garegnani insists that Hahn would be correct only

> if the modern *simultaneous* determination of prices and outputs by 'demand and supply' were the only conceivable way to determine outputs. Only then would taking outputs as data when determining prices be equivalent to 'presenting accounts ex-post'. However, ... a separate determination of outputs is possible and was in fact associated with the different classical theory of distribution ... and this is precisely what underlies Sraffa's assumption of given outputs and the independence of his analysis from constant returns to scale.
>
> (1990a: 129)

15 In elaborating upon the way in which the theory of value focuses upon real relations Garegnani draws upon Marx:

> There are, on the one hand, the 'apparent relations' or 'connections,' which are those perceived by the unsystematic observer and which are represented in Adam Smith's 'adding up' theory of prices ... in such an inconsistent representation of the economic system 'the contradictory character of capital is totally concealed and effaced ... no contradiction to labour is evident'. There are on the other hand, the real relations constituting the intrinsic or inner connections of the bourgeois system. These are the relations brought to light by systematic scientific analysis. They centre on the constraint that binds changes in wages to changes in profits and rents and reveal the economic antagonism between classes.
>
> (1984: 243)

Critical realists would, of course, wish to sustain the distinction between apparent relations and underlying real relations if it were being deployed as a way of referring to a structured ontology encompassing not only events and states of affairs but also underlying structures, mechanisms, etc.

16 'The "core" might in fact be described as constituting the "theory of value" as we find it in the surplus theories' (Garegnani 1984: 260).

17 Later he notes:

> once marginal theory is abandoned, it no longer seems possible to determine individual incomes, and therefore the quantities demanded, by means of functional relations having properties that are sufficiently definite and at the same time sufficiently general as to render the procedure meaningful at the level of general theory, as distinct from special 'models'.
>
> (1990a: 131)

18 Indeed, if the core/non-core division relates to the level of generality over which quantitative relations are taken to hold, it becomes clear that such a

distinction cannot differentiate neo-Ricardianism from orthodoxy since parallel distinctions are emphasised by prominent orthodox theorists. See, for example, T. Lawson's (1995: 8–10) interpretation of Hahn's distinction between axioms and assumptions.

19 Once it is recognised that neo-Ricardian economics retains a deductivist conception of explanation it comes as no surprise that the question of whether neo-Ricardian economics can be incorporated within an appropriately defined orthodoxy has been raised. Hahn (1975, 1982) has questioned the traditionally accepted view that neo-Ricardian economics stands opposed to orthodoxy, suggesting that Sraffa's *Production of Commodities* is in fact concerned with a special case of neoclassical theory. Garegnani (1990a) has countered by situating Sraffa's contributions within a revival of the classical approach. While the focus of the deductive project may be somewhat different, the conception of explanation and science appears to be the same. If it is the case that orthodoxy can best be understood by relating it to the adoption of a particularly inappropriate deductivist method, then it would seem that neo-Ricardian economics should be identified as a branch of orthodox economics.

20 Some authors have addressed the issue of why capitalist economies might possess the gravitational properties attributed to them. However, even here the focus appears to be primarily upon mathematical tractability rather than empirical adequacy – for example, examining the conditions for the stability of the system, see, for example, the various approaches adopted and criticised in M. Caminati and F. Petri (1990).

Bibliography

Arestis, P. (1990) 'Post Keynesianism: A New Approach to Economics', *Review of Social Economy* 48(3): 222–246.

Arestis, P., Mariscal, I. and Howells, P. (1994) 'Realism in Post-Keynesian Quantitative Analysis', in M. Glick (ed.) *Competition, Technology and Money*, Aldershot: Edward Elgar.

Bharadwaj, K. (1978) 'Maurice Dobb's Critique of Theories of Value and Distribution', as reprinted in K. Bharadwaj (1989), *Themes in Value and Distribution*, London: Unwin Hyman.

—— (1990) 'Sraffa's Return to Classical Theory,' in K. Bharadwaj and B. Schefold (eds) *Essays on Piero Sraffa: Critical Perspectives on the Revival of Classical Theory*, London: Routledge.

Bhaskar, R. (1978) *A Realist Theory of Science*, London: Harvester Wheatsheaf.

—— (1986) *Scientific Realism and Human Emancipation*, London: Verso.

Boggio, L. (1987) 'Centre of Gravitation', in J. Eatwell, M. Milgate and P. Newman (eds) *The New Palgrave: A Dictionary of Economics*, London: Macmillan.

Caminati, M. and Petri, F. (eds) (1990) 'Convergence to Long Period Positions', *Studies in the Surplus Approach to Political Economy*, Special Issue, 6, 1–2.

Chick, V. (1995) 'Is There a Case for Post Keynesian Economics?', *Scottish Journal of Political Economy* 42(1): 20–36.

Dow, S. C. (1990) 'Post-Keynesianism as Political Economy: A Methodological Discussion', *Review of Political Economy* 2(3): 345–358.

—— (1995) 'Interview', in J. E. King, *Conversations with Post Keynesians*, London: Macmillan.

Eatwell, J. (1974) 'Controversies in the Theory of Surplus Value: Old and New', *Science and Society* Autumn, 281–303.

—— (1979) 'Theories of Value, Output and Employment,' as reprinted in J. Eatwell and M. Milgate (eds) (1983) *Keynes's Economics and the Theory of Value and Distribution*, London: Duckworth.

—— (1982a) 'Competition', in I. Bradley and M. Howard (eds) *Classical and Marxian Political Economy*, London: Macmillan.

—— (1982b) 'Preface' to M. Milgate (1982) *Capital and Employment*, London: Academic Press.

—— (1987) 'Natural and Normal Conditions', in J. Eatwell, M. Milgate and P. Newman (eds) *The New Palgrave: A Dictionary of Economics*, London: Macmillan.

—— (1994) 'Institutions, Efficiency, and the Theory of Economic Policy', *Social Research* 61(1): 35–53.

Eatwell, J. and Green, R. (1984) 'Economic Theory and Political Power', in B. Pimlott (ed.) *Fabian Essays in Socialist Thought*, London: Heinemann.

Fleetwood, S. (1995) *Hayek's Political Economy: The Socio-Economics of Order*, London: Routledge.

Garegnani, P. (1976) 'On a Change in the Notion of Equilibrium in Recent Work on Value and Distribution', as reprinted in J. Eatwell and M. Milgate (eds) (1983) *Keynes's Economics and the Theory of Value and Distribution*, London: Duckworth.

—— (1979) 'A Reply to Joan Robinson', as reprinted in J. Eatwell and M. Milgate (eds) (1983) *Keynes's Economics and the Theory of Value and Distribution*, London: Duckworth.

—— (1983) 'The Classical Theory of Wages and the Role of Demand Schedules in the Determination of Relative Prices', *American Economic Review*, Papers and proceedings, 73(2). As reprinted in J. C. Wood (ed.) (1995) *Piero Sraffa: Critical Assessments*, Vol. II, London: Routledge.

—— (1984) 'Value and Distribution in the Classical Economists and Marx', *Oxford Economic Papers* 36(2). As reprinted in J. C. Wood (ed.) (1994), *Piero Sraffa: Critical Assessments*, Vol. II, London: Routledge.

—— (1987) 'Surplus Approach to Value and Distribution', in J. Eatwell, M. Milgate and P. Newman (eds) *The New Palgrave: A Dictionary of Economics*, London: Macmillan.

—— (1989a) 'Some Notes on Capital, Expectation and the Analysis of Change', in G. R. Fiewell, *Joan Robinson and Modern Economics*, London: Macmillan.

—— (1989b) 'On Sraffa's Contribution to Economic Theory', in G. R. Fiewell, *Joan Robinson and Modern Economics*, London: Macmillan.

—— (1990a) 'Sraffa: Classical versus Marginalist Analysis', in K. Bharadwaj and B. Schefold (eds) *Essays on Piero Sraffa: Critical Perspectives on the Revival of Classical Theory*, London: Routledge.

—— (1990b) 'Reply', in K. Bharadwaj and B. Schefold (eds) *Essays on Piero Sraffa: Critical Perspectives on the Revival of Classical Theory*, London: Routledge.

—— (1990c) 'Comment on Keynes and Sraffa', in K. Bharadwaj and B. Schefold (eds) *Essays on Piero Sraffa: Critical Perspectives on the Revival of Classical Theory*, London: Routledge.

—— (1990d) 'Quantity of Capital', in J. Eatwell, M. Milgate and P. Newman (eds) *The New Palgrave: Capital Theory*, London: Macmillan.

—— (1991) 'The Labour Theory of Value: "Detour" or Technical Advance?', in G. A. Caravale (ed.) *Marx and Modern Economic Analysis, Volume I: Values, Prices and Exploitation*, Aldershot: Edward Elgar.

Hahn, F. H. (1975) 'Review of Political Economy: The Wrong Issues and the Wrong Argument', *Economic Record* 51, September: 360–364.

—— (1982) 'The Neo-Ricardians', *Cambridge Journal of Economics* 6(4): 353–374.

Harcourt, G. C. and Hamouda, O. F. (1988) 'Post Keynesianism: From Criticism to Coherence', as reprinted in C. Sardoni (ed.) (1992) *On Political Economists and Modern Political Economy: Selected Essays of G. C. Harcourt*, London: Routledge.

Kregel, J. A. (1991) 'The Organising Principle in Post-Keynesian Economics', in W. Adriaansen and J. van der Linden (eds) *Post-Keynesian Thought in Perspective*, Wolters-Noordhof: Groningen.

Lavoie, M. (1992) *Foundations of Post-Keynesian Economic Analysis*, Aldershot: Edward Elgar.

Lawson, C. (1994) 'The Transformational Model of Social Activity and Economic Analysis: A Reconsideration of the Work of J. R. Commons', *Review of Political Economy* 6(2): 186–204.

Lawson, T. (1994) 'The Nature of Post-Keynesianism and its Links to Other Traditions: A Realist Perspective', *Journal of Post-Keynesian Economics* 16(4): 503–538.

—— (1995) 'A Realist Perspective on Contemporary "Economic Theory"', *Journal of Economic Issues* 29(1): 1–32.

Milgate, M. (1982) *Capital and Employment*, London: Academic Press.

—— (1987) 'Neo Ricardianism', in J. Eatwell, M. Milgate and P. Newman (eds) *The New Palgrave: A Dictionary of Economics*, London: Macmillan.

Pratten, S. (1993) 'Structure, Agency and Marx's Analysis of the Labour Process', *Review of Political Economy* 5(4): 403–426.

Robinson, J. (1979) 'Garegnani on Effective Demand', as reprinted in J. Eatwell and M. Milgate (eds) (1983) *Keynes's Economics and the Theory of Value and Distribution*, London: Duckworth.

Roncaglia, A. (1991) 'The Sraffian Schools', *Review of Political Economy* 3(2): 187–219.

Runde, J. (1993) 'Paul Davidson and the Austrians', *Critical Review* 7(2–3): 381–397.

Sofianou, E. (1995) 'Post-Modernism and the Notion of Rationality in Economics', *Cambridge Journal of Economics* 19(3): 373–389.

Sraffa, P. (1960) *Production of Commodities by Means of Commodities*, Cambridge: Cambridge University Press.

3

REALISM, THEORY AND INDIVIDUALISM IN THE WORK OF CARL MENGER

Clive Lawson[1]

Introduction

Recent years have witnessed a revival of interest in the study of institutions in economics. Accompanying this, there has come an increased awareness of the writings of earlier economists in which a focus on institutions is central. The work of Carl Menger occupies a significant position in this regard. Menger's work is especially attractive to those who seek to distance themselves from the heterodox 'old institutionalist' school associated with the work of Thorstein Veblen, John. R. Commons, etc., and to produce instead a 'new institutionalism' more in line with the contemporary mainstream approach to 'theorising'. Thus Langlois observes that:

> It is perhaps fair to say that this modern institutionalism reflects less the ideas of the early institutionalists than it does those of their *opponents* . . . Menger has perhaps more claim to be the patron saint of the new institutional economics than has any of the original institutionalists.
>
> (Langlois 1986: 2)

This modern or 'new' institutionalism[2] sees itself as distinct from the older institutionalism by virtue of its desire to provide a 'theory' of institutions:

> The problem with . . . the early institutionalists is that they wanted an economics with institutions but without theory; the problem with many neoclassicals is that they want economic

43

theory without institutions; what we should really want is both institutions and theory – not only pure economic theory informed by the experience of specific institutions, but also an economic theory *of* institutions.

(ibid.: 5)

The reason that Menger is so important to the 'new institutionalists' is that he (like they, and like orthodox economists in general) associates theory with individualism at the level of method.[3] Indeed, Menger is often supposed to have provided the main defence of individualistic theorising in economics. Why then is Menger not embraced by mainstream economists in a more whole-hearted fashion? At least part of the explanation is that Menger also appears to accept a form of Aristotelian essentialism. This is seen to give rise to untenable claims about 'ultimate' entities and to problems of determining how knowledge of them is obtained. However, in some quarters at least, these problems have been down-played in the optimism resulting from Menger's apparent contribution to (the individualist notion of) theorising in the context of institutions.

In this chapter, building upon the insights recently sustained under the heading of critical realism (and in particular that aspect of critical realism referred to as transcendental realism), I want to argue that this optimism is misplaced. Indeed, it is found, on close examination, that not only does Menger after all fail to provide any justification of the methodological individualist approach to theorising, but also that the problems previously associated with this Aristotelianism arguably stem from, and only from, those ideas which underlie his individualism. I briefly indicate that a resolution of these problems, and the provision of a coherent approach to theorising, in fact follow lines akin to the Aristotelian element in Menger's thought. However, this lends weight to institutionalism of the 'old' sort rather than the 'new'.

Menger: realism and theory

It is widely accepted that Menger's work not only typifies but also adequately defends a particular form of individualism. However, until recently an Aristotelian strand in Menger's thought has received relatively little attention (exceptions include Kauder 1958, 1965 and Hutchison 1973). Recent accounts, in contrast, have tended to argue that some form of Aristotelianism or essentialist–realism is as fundamental to Menger's work as his individualism (see Smith 1986, 1990a, 1990b; Mäki 1986, 1990; Fabian and Simons 1986). One limitation to these recent accounts, however, has been a failure to distinguish, and to investigate the link between, Menger's Aristotelianism and his individualism. In the following, the nature of the relationship between Menger's Aristotelianism and his individualism, and the implications that follow for the conception of 'theory' which those such as the new institutionalists find so attractive, are central.

The main focus is Menger's *Untersuchungen über die Methode der Socialwissenschaften, und der Politischen Ökonomie Insbesondere*,[4] his major contribution to the *Methodenstreit* with the German Historical School and especially Gustav Schmoller. Now it is worth bearing in mind, as Smith notes, that 'it is a highly refined and purified – and indeed simplified – version of Aristotle's general philosophy that is at issue when we are dealing with nineteenth and twentieth century Austrian thought' (Smith 1990a). Thus little time will be spent here elaborating an Aristotelian position in any depth. However, it is necessary to summarise briefly the distinction between Platonic and Aristotelian essences.

For Plato, abstract entities (forms) exist independently of physical objects (which are simply imperfect copies of such forms). It is our given knowledge of these forms which allows us to recognise and distinguish such physical objects. However, if, according to Aristotle, different objects can be recognised as being the same kind of thing, this is because of qualities intrinsic to those objects. Thus, it is because of qualities that all dogs possess, a nature or essence, that enables us to recognise any one of them as a dog. The problem is then to identify what it is that allows us to recognise individuals as examples of some general category, i.e., what is constant. In the case of dogs, any individual will change all of its constituent parts during its lifetime, and perhaps even lose a limb, and yet we still recognise it as a dog, even though no two dogs are the same. The 'something' which remains constant throughout the change of an individual (dog), Aristotle argues, is the internal, or intrinsic, structuring of that thing. It is the thing's internal structure that allows it to act in the ways that it does and establishes it as a certain *kind* of thing. But a nature does not exist independently of objects of a kind – it just *is* the internal (intrinsic) structuring of those objects. Aristotle is a realist in that he views certain entities or things as existing independently of the inquirer. Aristotle is an essentialist realist in that he views essences as existing independently of (external to) the inquirer but, contra Plato, not as existing independently of the object (they structure).

Two aspects of this essentialist–realist position characterise Menger's ideas about theory. The first is that 'theory' must involve knowledge which extends, in time, beyond present or immediate knowledge. For this to be so, theory must involve knowledge *of* really existing and *enduring* objects – objects which endure beyond imme-diate experience. In Menger's words: '[t]he purpose of the theoretical sciences is understanding of the real world, knowledge of it extending beyond immediate experience' (Menger 1985: 55). The second aspect of Menger's position is that it involves some form of abstraction (at its most general: 'leaving something out'). Central to Menger's ideas, as discussed more fully below, is the idea that theoretical or general knowledge cannot be evaluated in terms of actual observations: 'testing the exact theory [general knowledge claims] . . . by the full empirical method [by confrontation with concrete reality] is simply a methodological absurdity' (ibid.: 69).

Combining these two aspects, for Menger, *theory is of something which exists and endures but is not directly manifest or observable*. It is this 'something', which provides the object of theory and corresponds to the notion of real essence in Aristotelian thought. Theoretical research concerned with producing such general knowledge is termed 'exact science' by Menger, and it is in elaborating his ideas about exact science that his particular notion of essence, and an understanding of how such essences come to be known, are most clearly identified.

Theory as exact science

In exact science, the role of *real essences* is occupied by exact (or strict) types and exact laws (the relationships between exact types). It is then exact types and relations that constitute the objects of general knowl-edge. To explain precisely what Menger means by 'exact' science here it is useful to contrast it with the method he terms the empirical–realistic approach. Theory on the empirical–realistic approach involves simply spotting patterns in the ongoing flux of reality. In Menger's words, this approach attempts to 'arrange the totality of the real phenomena in definite empirical forms and in an empirical way to determine the regularities in their coexistence and succession' (Menger 1985: 56).

Menger argues that such an approach cannot produce general knowledge, as defined above, because it cannot produce knowledge of what is persistent throughout change. In other words, such knowl-edge is not of exact types and exact laws but of empirical types and empirical laws, i.e., types and laws in the appearance of things, in events. Menger focuses upon and criticises the search for both empir-ical types and empirical laws. In the case of empirical *types*, these cannot produce general knowledge because phenomena are not strictly repeated:

Phenomena in all their empirical reality are, according to experience, repeated in certain empirical forms. But this is never with perfect strictness, for scarcely ever do two concrete phenomena, let alone a larger group of them, exhibit a thorough agreement. There are no strict types in 'empirical reality', i.e., when the phenomena are under consideration in the totality and the whole complexity of their nature. This might be the case if each individual concrete phenomenon were set up as a particular type. By this the purpose and usefulness of theoretical research would be completely invalidated. The desire to determine strict categories of empirical forms comprising 'all empirical realities' (according to their full content) is therefore an unattainable goal of theoretical research.

(ibid.: 57)

The problem, then, is that there is no thorough agreement between the form of a thing in two separate instances. When Menger comes to criticise the search for empirical *laws*, he appeals to a form of the problem of induction. Laws cannot be arrived at by observing regularities:

A 'law' obtained from the above [inductive] point of view can in truth only state that in reality, regularly or without exception, phenomena belonging to the empirical form C have followed the concrete phenomena belonging to the empirical forms A and B, or that they were observed coexistent with them. The conclusion that the phenomenon C follows the phenomena A and B *in general* (that is, in all cases, even those not observed!), or that the phenomena under discussion here are *in general* coexistent, transcends experience, the point of view of strict empiricism. From the standpoint of the above manner of consideration it is *not strictly* warranted. Aristotle recognised this correctly when he denied the strictly scientific character of induction.

(ibid.: 57)

In other words, the problem with the empirical–realistic method is that it tries to ground general knowledge in constant conjunctions of events whereas, Menger maintains, in reality events are not constantly conjoined. However, Menger still believes that we must *think* in terms of regularities; his point being that these do not exist at the level of *actual* events. Thought, and statements of thought, must take the form of 'if X then Y' statements, but these cannot, then, be of actual events. Instead, such statements must be of exact (or strict) types and laws:

> [t]here is one rule of cognition for the investigation of theoret-
> ical truths which as far as possible is verified beyond doubt
> not only by experience, but simply by our laws of thinking . . .
> that strictly typical phenomena of a definite kind must
> always, and, indeed in consideration of our laws of thinking,
> simply of *necessity*, be followed by strictly typical phenomena
> of just as definite and different a type.
>
> (ibid.: 60)

Thus Menger is arguing that our very ways of thinking lead us to form theories of the 'if X then Y' type, but since such regularities do not exist in the ongoing flux of concrete reality these theories must be *of* something else. In short, theoretical investigation must be about the natures or essences of things (exact types) and the relationships between things in their essential form (exact laws) for thinking itself to be possible.

The exact method, individualism and the 'simplest elements in everything real'

Although Menger spends considerable time discussing his claim that science seeks out exact types and laws in addition to empirical types and laws, he spends very little time explaining precisely what is meant by these 'exact' entities. To some extent the task of discovering exact laws is a secondary one, and simply relates to the relations between exact types. The main issue is really how such *types* are to be found? In explaining how we arrive at them Menger simply asserts that to discover strict types, the *simplest elements in everything real must be sought out*. Such elements 'must be thought of as strictly typical just because they are the simplest' (Menger 1985: 60). Now Menger at no stage explains why the simplest elements must be thought of as strictly typical. This is especially significant given Menger's extension of his analysis to the economic realm. Certainly, Menger moves on to apply the exact method to economic science, spelling out what he terms the 'most original factors of human economy', i.e., needs, goods, and the desire for the most complete satisfaction of needs possible:

> the investigation of the most original, the most elementary
> factors of human economy, the . . . investigation of the laws by

which more complicated forms of the phenomena of human economy develop from those simplest elements.

The most original factors of human economy are the needs, the goods offered directly to humans by nature (both the consumption goods and the means of production concerned), and the desire for the most complete satisfaction of needs possible.

(ibid.: 63)

The relevant economic type is the agent with needs and the intention and means to satisfy such needs. From this exact type, Menger argues, economists must then attempt to 'build up', via the rule of cognition, the more 'complicated phenomena of human economy'. This is, of course, the aspect of Menger's account which is most familiar and indeed, in Hayek's words, the central message in Menger's work, namely, that:

in social science we start from our acquaintance with elements and use them to build models of possible configurations of the complex structures into which they can combine and which are not in the same manner accessible to direct observation as are the elements.

(Hayek 1973: 8)

Thus, Menger's particular essentialist–realist position, once transposed to the social realm, becomes the position now familiar as methodological individualism. But it is most noticeable that the method which is so transposed is hardly justified. That theory must start with the simplest elements is simply asserted by Menger. However, this assertion is of crucial importance as it appears to be the only link provided by Menger between the notion of theory which he spends so much time defending against the Historical School, and the individualism for which he is so well known. Moreover, I argue that criticisms made of Menger's work, which are understood to be criticisms of his Aristotelianism, in fact hinge on just this assertion that exact types are the simplest elements in everything real.

Problems with Menger's essentialism?

The two most prominent criticisms of Menger's position are the following. The first is made by Hutchison, a strong defender of Popperian falsificationism, who unsurprisingly finds the main problem in Menger's position to be the fact that exact propositions are 'in principle unfalsifiable' (Hutchison 1973: 178). As such, for Hutchison and Popper, Menger's position is demarcated as *un*scientific. Now, of course Popperian falsificationism has itself received much criticism (Popper himself rejecting many of his early ideas). Moreover, it is interesting to note that much of this criticism is contained in, and so pre-dated by, Menger's own position. If general knowledge is to be possible and is of real things which endure, and if strict regularities do not exist in concrete reality then knowledge must be of entities which are not directly manifest in, and so cannot be evaluated simply by direct reference to, concrete reality. However, Hutchison argues that the root of the problem in Menger's work is his adherence to a particular form of essentialism. Hutchison interprets Menger's position as 'methodological essentialism' and, characteristically, uses the work of Popper to provide a critique.

> Methodological essentialists are inclined to formulate scientific questions in such terms as 'what is matter?' or 'what is justice?' and they believe that a penetrating answer to such questions, revealing the real or essential meaning of these terms and thereby the real or true nature of the essences denoted by them, is at least a necessary prerequisite of scientific research, if not its main task.
>
> (Popper 1961: 29)

Hutchison, like Popper, is trying to convey the idea that essentialism involves a 'digging down' to smaller and smaller (simpler and simpler) elements. Now, as will become clear below, this criticism is not generally of much relevance to Aristotelian–essentialist positions. However, Menger does encourage such a criticism by equating essences with the *simplest elements* of things; elements which must be thought of as strictly typical 'just because they are the simplest'.

A second frequently highlighted problem with Menger's position is that it is not obvious how exact knowledge might be arrived at. Unfortunately, Menger once more says very little on the matter. However, in defending the exact method Menger gives various examples which are illustrative, a familiar one (often used to defend Menger against falsificationist criticisms such as Hutchison's) being the geometry example. Here Menger likens attempts to falsify the results of theoretical research to: 'the mathematician who wants to correct the principles of geometry by measuring real objects' (Menger 1985: 70). Simple elements such as points, straight lines, etc., are built up into complex configurations which, whilst not existing in their pure form in concrete reality, do appear useful to understanding that reality. The rules of geometry itself are not arrived at inductively from observing regularities but, once 'apprehended', do aid architects to design houses, engineers to design bridges, etc. Thus it is generally concluded that, for Menger, knowledge of exact types is arrived at by 'pure or categorical intuition' (Kauder 1958). Now there have been some attempts to defend Menger's notion of intuition, but these turn on the idea of perceiving 'general' categories such as reds and greens, e.g.:

> it is not the work of any separate or special faculty of 'intuition' but is rather involved of necessity in every act of perceiving and thinking – a fact which makes itself felt in the ubiquitous employment of general terms in all natural languages.
>
> (Smith 1990a: 267)

However, the ability to recognise the general features of things is not the same as the ability to recognise the essential qualities which account for such features, which must be what exact types are. As Prendergast notes, this is precisely the point which led later Austrians, in the context of the logical positivist critique of intuition, to look to Weber for a grounding of their approach rather than the Aristotelian strand in Menger's thought (Prendergast 1986). However, the point, to repeat, is that the heart of the problem is not so much Menger's Aristotelianism,[5] as his ungrounded assertion that exact entities are merely the simplest elements. Menger's Aristotelianism involves the idea that general knowledge can only be of something which exists and endures. This idea does not reduce to Menger's conception of the simplest elements. One more illustration is useful here, this time of an account given by Mäki (1990) which is sympathetic towards Menger's Aristotelianism. Mäki's discussion of Menger is couched in terms of 'Universals', Menger being an example of, what Armstrong terms, an immanent realist about Universals (see Armstrong 1978).[6] Mäki points out that to be an 'immanent realist' about Universals means that these 'general' qualities exist in the particulars, by virtue of the natures or internal structures of the particulars. Mäki draws upon the work of Harré and Madden (1975) in particular here, in which the notion of 'power', which is tied to a thing's nature or real essence, is central: ' "X has the power to A" means "X can or will do A, in the appropriate conditions, in virtue of its intrinsic nature" ' (Mäki 1990: 299).

In all this, Mäki is clearly right to argue that the existence of universals depends upon common or related intrinsic natures or structures. However, Mäki simply attributes this idea to Menger; there is no discussion of how it relates to Menger's comments about simplest elements. Consideration of the examples provided by Menger offers little help in this regard. The geometry analogy serves only to deflect attention from this issue of simplicity and structure. Euclidean points and straight lines do not have powers in the sense that Mäki, Harré and Madden intend. Moreover, where Menger does provide examples of exact types directly (and these are the examples upon which Mäki focuses) they are almost always of 'pure states' of things like pure oxygen, alcohol, gold or water. But these examples are no more useful. In concrete reality, of course, entities such as oxygen, etc., exist mostly in their impure states. But any of these *may* exist in a pure state, the question is one of whether impurities exist too in any instance. Pure gold can exist independently of its impurities, but an essence, or internal structure in Aristotle's sense, does not and cannot exist independently of the thing it structures.

To take stock, while Menger describes (and relies upon) an Aristotelian notion of theory in his disputes with the German Historical School, I have argued that his precise ideas about the contents of such theory (as the simplest elements in everything real) not only do not follow, but also appear to be the real root of various criticisms usually attributed to his Aristotelianism. In the next section I draw attention to recent developments in the philosophical literature which are quite consistent with the kind of (Aristotelian) theory Menger advocates, but share none of the disadvantages noted above. However, as will become clear, in this case Menger's individualism appears somewhat arbitrary. The position I wish to draw attention to is that developed especially by Bhaskar (1978, 1986 and 1989) but also in an economic context by, especially, T. Lawson (1989, 1992, 1994a and 1994b) and Pratten (1994).

Transcendental realism

A comprehensive review of transcendental realism[7] is clearly outside the scope of the present chapter.[8] However, the main points of similarity and difference between this position and that of Menger can be brought out relatively easily. To summarise (rather tersely), for transcendental realism, theoretical propositions are *transfactual* or normic statements. Such statements are not arrived at by intuition or indeed by any *a priori* basis but by an *a posteriori* process of *retroduction*.

A transfactual or normic statement is a kind of conditional:

> which specifies the exercise of possibilities which need not be manifest in any particular outcome. Such conditionals are *normic*, rather than subjunctive. They do not say what would happen, but what is happening in a perhaps unmanifest way.

Whereas a powers statement says A would y in appropriate circumstances, a normic statement says that A really is y'ing, whether or not its actual (or perceivable) effects are counteracted. They are not counter-factuals, but *transfactuals*; they take us to a level at which things are really going on irrespective of the actual outcome.

(Bhaskar 1978: 51)

Gravity is acting on the sheet of paper on which I am writing, but so too is the table, my pen and my arm, holding it in place. To leave out reference to these latter factors and talk solely of gravity is still to talk about something real. A transfactual 'takes us to a level where things are actually going on irrespective of the actual outcome' (ibid.: 51). In contrast, a counterfactual is concerned with what would be the case in certain circumstances or if such and such were (or were not) the case.

Now in transcendental realist accounts, to talk about such factors having effects which may not be manifest (to make transfactual statements) presupposes that the world must be stratified. More specifically, transcendental realism postulates, in response to an investigation into the conditions of the possibility of experimental activity in science (Bhaskar, 1978: 33–36), a threefold stratification of reality into the empirical, actual and (metaphorically) 'deep'; all of which are real. An illustrative example is that of the falling leaf. The falling of the leaf itself is a real event (the actual) but may be experienced in many different ways (the empirical). However, the event does not simply happen but is governed/caused by various mechanisms, e.g., gravity, aerodynamic forces, etc. (the 'deep'). Experiment is then concerned to isolate one (set of) mechanism(s) or, alternatively, to actively bring different strata into phase with one another. Now, whereas a distinction is often made between the actual and the empirical, the proposition of a deeper level which is still real, if only knowable empirically via its effects is not so commonly held. (Within transcendental realism, the term 'empirical realism' is used to capture the position in which the actual and 'deep' are not differentiated.) However, it is only through acknowledging this additional level of reality that the intelligibility of experimental activity can be sustained (see also Chalmers 1992). For example, that which is identified as gravity in experimental conditions continues to *act* (endure) outside such conditions, in a multitude of circumstances. Outside of experimentally controlled conditions, confirmation of the idea of gravity does not involve the identification of the movement of material objects towards each other at a certain velocity depending on their masses, but the 'tendency' of such – leaves tend to fall downwards.

Coming to know about, or formulate, a description of some mechanism (such as gravity) involves a mode of inference which has been termed, following Hanson (1965), retroduction. The important point to note here is that retroduction is actually neither induction nor deduction. It is neither a movement from the particular to the general (induction) nor from the general to the particular (deduction); both of which occur at one level. Instead the focus is upon moving from the level of events to the underlying mechanisms governing them. The process of coming to specify a mechanism such as gravity draws upon analogy and metaphor, of bringing to bear already understood mechanisms which, were they to exist, would account for the observed phenomena. Now retroduction involves the stipulation of a mechanism at a 'deep' (non-actual real) level. To be more precise, the object of retroduction is a non-actual, real mechanism which is transfactually operating.

There is nothing mysterious about the concept of a mechanism here, it is nothing other than the way of acting of a thing (although the class of 'things' is not restricted to material objects such as copper and dogs but extends to genetic codes, electronic structures, magnetic fields, etc. (Bhaskar 1978: 98). It should be noted that there are, though, two paradigm cases for the non-actual real, i.e., the powers of a particular kind and the relations between the elements of a system, where the form of the combination of the elements causally governs or codetermines the elements (see Bhaskar 1986: 131–132). What is generic is that they are structures that are transfactually operative and generative, but not necessarily determining, of events. Moreover, there are no reasons for thinking that the process of explanation must stop at any one level. When one mechanism has been identified and described and shown to explain various phenomena, it becomes itself something to be explained. For example, to locate a tendency or statement of some chemical in terms of its atomic structure does not preclude an investigation of this stratum in terms of a theory of electrons which in turn may be explained in terms of theories of sub-atomic structure, etc. (see Bhaskar 1978: 169); this is of course apart from the fact that different questions will require a focus on different essential characteristics of the thing under investigation.[9]

As well as a structured and stratified reality, the intelligibility of experimental activity requires that reality is, at least in part, differentiated, i.e., that some mechanisms can actually be isolated. The importance of experimental activity is that it seeks to isolate one (set of) mechanism(s), i.e., create the conditions in which only one (set of) mechanism(s) is operative, e.g., creating a vacuum and dropping an apple into it in an attempt to isolate the mechanism which gives us the law of gravity. When, and if, such mechanisms can be isolated (i.e. a closed system is produced) then laws can be formulated of the 'if X then Y' type, which are understood (and operate) outside the conditions of experimental control (i.e., in open systems) as tendencies. However, whilst the fact that experimental activity is possible implies that part of reality is differentiated in this way, this does not imply that all reality takes this form. Indeed, if in the social world, human agents have real choice, i.e., the capacity to do otherwise, then such closures are in principle impossible. However, this does not make retroduction impossible, but it does mean that strictly predictive criteria for the evaluation of theories about the social world are inappropriate (T. Lawson 1989).

Transcendental realism and Menger's exact science

In comparing the above account to Menger's exact science, we find significant agreement concerning the nature, and status, of theory. The notion of transfactuality is presumably what Menger has in mind when he is defending the status of theoretical or exact science in the face of criticism, from the German Historical School. Moreover, Menger's general characterisation of the empirical–realistic approach corresponds very closely to the position denoted as empirical realism in transcendental realist accounts, i.e., where the 'actual' and the 'deep' are not distinguished. However, on closer inspection it is clear that these levels or strata are not themselves sufficiently distinguished by Menger. When Menger talks about the simplest elements, of pure states of gold, of a lack of ignorance, error, etc., these are not transfactuals but either empirical claims or counterfactuals. In other words, once the distinction between transfactual and counterfactual is introduced, it is relatively easy to see that when Menger is defending his method he is talking about one thing and when giving examples of it he is talking about another.

The second point is that in transcendental realism (which distinguishes different strata and focuses upon underlying structures, mechanisms and powers, rather than the 'simplest elements') the problems identified with Menger's position are avoided. The idea of natures of things as ultimate entities (the criticism made by, amongst others, Hutchison) is clearly irrelevant; there is no claim that the mechanisms postulated in the transcendental realist account are without need of further explanation. As the example from chemistry given above demonstrates, the idea that there are different levels or strata to be explained is not inconsistent with the idea of explaining something's activity in terms of its nature or internal structure.

Further, real essences are arrived at in the *a posteriori* process of actively doing science. Retroduction involves a movement from some event or state of affairs to mechanisms which could have produced them, which are then in need of verification, further investigation, etc. There is no obvious end to the explanatory endeavour. The point is that retroduction, as an *a posteriori* process, is immune from the logical positivist criticisms of intuition, without abandoning an essentialist–realist position.

If it is the case that transcendental realism, especially in maintaining the idea of a structured reality, avoids the problems noted with Menger's position, it is also the case, as argued elsewhere, that the conception of a structured ontology sits uneasily with *any form* of individualist position.[10] With objects of theoretical investigations conceptualised as transfactually operative mechanisms it is arbitrary when investigating the social world to exclude such objects as rules and relationships from having an explanatory role. Rules and relationships endure and govern or facilitate actions and events, but are not directly perceivable or manifest. However, they can be retroduced, like any other object of theoretical inquiry, allowing general knowledge (in Menger's sense), which extends beyond immediate experience. The atomic structure of copper and the relationship between husband and wife are both structures, while one governs the ways of acting of pieces of copper the other facilitates human activities (although the former is an instance of the first paradigm case of the non-actual real (natural kinds) and the latter is an instance of the second (codetermining relations)). This is not to say that such things as rules or social relations are the same kinds of things as human agents.[11] But if social relations are both real and enduring then they are legitimate objects of research of the kind Menger calls for. However, in this case, the label of methodological individualism appears to be arbitrary, and the idea of 'building up' configurations from simplest elements quite misguided.

Conclusion

The focus of this chapter has been upon Menger's notion of theory, especially in relation to those ideas which underlie the individualism for which he is so well known. This choice of focus has been prompted by the current prominence of new institutionalist contributions which both resurrect the familiar theme of the relation between theory and individualism and identify Menger's work as an exemplar, and even justification of such a theoretical–individualist position. The conclusion here is not only that a necessary link between theory and individualism is absent in Menger's account, but also that various criticisms made of his general position in fact relate to ideas which underlie his individualism. This point is significant for at least two reasons. First, while the criticisms noted above are well known, these are usually attributed to an Aristotelian strand in Menger's position. However, and as the brief outline of transcendental realism above demonstrates, these criticisms are easily avoided within an essentialist–realist position – such problems only arise when exact types are equated not to really enduring structures but to some notion of the simplest elements. Second, these more recent realist accounts, while sharing Menger's conception of (or, better, intention for) theory, emphasise a basic ontology of structures and generative mechanisms which renders arbitrary any adherence to a form of individualism. Moreover, if we maintain Menger's basic notion of theory (as knowledge which extends beyond immediate experience) but insist that the objects of knowledge are transfactually operative structures (and not 'simplest elements'), an important aspect of social 'theory' would involve describing social practices and understanding (retroducing to) the non-manifest rules and relationships which give rise to them. Perhaps paradoxically, this activity is one which is easily identified (if rarely explicit) in the work of much of the old institutionalist economics.[12]

Notes

1 I am very grateful to Lucy Delap, John Foster, Geoff Harcourt, Rolf Johannes and Tony Lawson for helpful comments on an earlier draft. I would also like to thank the Cambridge Political Economic Society Trust for financial support.

2 Although, as various authors point out, there are severe problems involved in treating the new institutionalism as a precisely defined or homogeneous group (e.g., see Coates 1986 and Mäki 1987), the following are generally accepted to be representative examples on: collective action – Olson (1965; 1982) and Sandler (1992); law – especially Posner (1973); property rights – Coase (1937, 1960); Furubotn and Pejovich (1974); economic history – North and Thomas (1973); North (1981); theory of the firm – Alchian and Demsetz (1972); Williamson (1975, 1985); Aoki *et al.* (1990); modern Austrian school – Kirzner (1992) especially as influenced by Hayek (e.g., 1948, 1967); game theoretic approaches – Schotter (1981, 1986) and Sugden (1986); and evolutionary approaches – Nelson and Winter (1982).

3 Although it is common to find theory and individualism associated in economics, the link is rarely explicit – whether it is the individualist or non-individualist position which is being taken. Two especially illustrative (sets of) examples are those provided by the contributions of Koopmans (especially 1947, 1949a, 1949b) and Field (1979, 1981) and the exchanges

that their work initiated (especially see Vining 1949a, 1949b, Bardhan 1987 and Basu *et al.* 1987). For both Koopmans and Field the central issue is that of the nature of institutional analysis, and for both theory is assumed to correspond to individualism. In the case of Koopmans, as Vining later points out, in commenting that theory must be concerned with real entities that persist or are stable, Koopmans simply equates such persistence with the natures of individual agents whose 'modes of action and response . . . are the ultimate determinants of the levels of economic variables' (1947: 164). Field, unlike Koopmans, is a defender of the old institutionalist approach. His argument against the new institutionalism is that some features of an economic system simply cannot be *endogenised* (which appears to mean 'cannot be incorporated into an economic model involving "tastes, technology, endowments and a maximizing behavioural rule"' (1979)). Institutions for Field are simply 'instrumentalities' which are useful in that they persist. Thus although Field is arguing that such instrumentalities cannot be neglected, their nature (as simply persisting and not resulting from the short-run maximising behaviour of individuals) precludes 'theoretical' investigation (endogenisation) and so must be understood on a 'case by case basis in detail' (1979).

4 Translated as 'Investigations into the method of the social sciences with special reference to economics'.

5 Some qualification is necessary here, in that it is not Aristotle's essentialist–realism which is the problem. There is a case to be made that Aristotle also relies upon some form of *nous* or intuition (see Bhaskar 1994: 183).

6 Basically on this view 'Universals [general properties, relations etc. shared by particular objects e.g. colour, marital status etc.] exist in the particulars that instantiate them' (Mäki 1990: 295).

7 Transcendental realism can be understood as a subset of the more general position of critical realism.

8 However, see Collier (1994: 31–134).

9 This is not to encourage a reductionist view of explanation, the point is that we cannot have an explanation until we know what is to be explained (see also Collier 1994: 45–50).

10 On the specific tensions involved in the work of various new institutionalists which follow from an adherence to an individualist position, see C. Lawson *et al.* (1996).

11 Indeed, to use more Aristotelian terms, human agents may be more precisely termed efficient causes and social structure as material causes of social outcomes. However, to hold to such a distinction in no way entails 'building up' in the usual sense.

12 For an elaboration of this notion of theory in relation to the work of one important institutionalist, J. R. Commons, see C. Lawson (1994).

Bibliography

Alchian, A. and Demsetz, H. (1972) 'Production, Information Costs and Economic Organisation', *American Economic Review* 62: 777–795.

Aoki, M., Gustafsson, B. and Williamson, O. E. (eds) (1990) *The Firm as a Nexus of Treaties*, London: Sage.

Armstrong, D. M. (1978) *Universals and Scientific Realism, Vol. 1, Nominalism and Realism*, Cambridge: Cambridge University Press.

Bardhan, P. (1987) 'Alternative Approaches to the Theory of Institutions in Economic Development', working paper, University of California.

Basu, K., Jones, E. and Schlicht, E. (1987) 'The Growth and Decay of Custom', *Explorations in Economic History*, Jan.: 1–21.

Bhaskar, R. (1978) *A Realist Theory of Science*, Brighton: Harvester.

—— (1986) *Scientific Realism and Human Emancipation*, London: Verso.

—— (1989) *The Possibility of Naturalism*, Brighton: Harvester.

—— (1994) *Plato Etc.: The Problems of Philosophy and their Resolution*, London: Verso.

Chalmers, A. (1992) 'Is a Law Reasonable to a Hume?', *Cogito*, Winter: 125–129.

Coase, R. (1937) 'The Nature of the Firm', *Economica* 4(44): 386–405.

—— (1960) 'The Problem of Social Cost', *Journal of Law and Economics* 3: 1–44.

Coates, A. W. (1986) 'Book Review', *Kyklos*, 39: 628–630.

Collier, A. (1994) *Critical Realism: An Introduction to Roy Bhaskar's Philosophy*, London: Verso.

Fabian, R. and Simons, P. M. (1986) 'The Second Austrian School of Value Theory', in W. Grassl and B. Smith (eds) *Austrian Economics: Historical and Philosophical Background*, London: Croom Helm.

Field, A. J. (1979) 'On the Explanation of Rules using Rational Choice Models', *Journal of Economic Issues* 13(1), March: 49–72.

—— (1981) 'The Problem with Neoclassical Institutional Economics: A Critique with Special Reference to the North/Thomas Model of the Pre-1500 Europe', *Explorations in Economic History* 18(2), April: 174–198.

Furubotn, E. and Pejovich, S. (eds) (1974) *The Economics of Property Rights*, Cambridge, MA: Ballinger.

Hanson, N. R. (1965) *Patterns of Discovery*, Cambridge: Cambridge University Press.

Harré, R. and Madden, E. (1975) *Causal Powers*, Oxford: Basil Blackwell.

Hayek, F. A. (1948) *Individualism and Economic Order*, Chicago: University of Chicago Press.

—— (1967) *Studies in Philosophy, Politics and Economics*, Chicago: University of Chicago Press.

—— (1973) 'The Place of Menger's Grundsatz in the History of Economic Thought', in J. R. Hicks and W. Weber (eds) *Carl Menger and the Austrian School of Economics*, Oxford: Clarendon Press.

Hodgson, G. M. (1989) 'Institutional Economic Theory: The Old Versus the New', *Review of Political Economy* 1: 249–269.

Hutchison, T. W. (1973) 'Some Themes from Investigations into Method', in J. R. Hicks and W. Weber (eds) *Carl Menger and the Austrian School of Economics*, Oxford: Clarendon Press.

Kauder, E. (1958) 'The Intellectual and Political Roots of the Older Austrian School', *Zeitschrift für Nationalökonomie* 17: 411–425.

—— (1965) *A History of Marginal Utility*, Princeton, NJ: Princeton University Press.

Kirzner, I. M. (ed) (1992) *Method, Process and Austrian Economics: Essays in Honour of Ludwig von Mises*, Lexington, MA: D. C. Heath.

Koopmans, T. C. (1947) 'Measurement Without Theory', *Review of Economics and Statistics* 29(2): 161–172.

—— (1949a) 'Identification Problems in Economic Model Construction', *Econometrica* 17: 125–144.

—— (1949b) 'Methodological Issues in Quantitative Economics: A Reply', *Review of Economics and Statistics* 31(2): 36–91.

Langlois, R. (ed.) (1986) *Economics as a Process: Essays in the New Institutional Economics*, Cambridge: Cambridge University Press.

Lawson, C. (1994) 'The Transformational Model of Social Activity and Economic Analysis: A Reinterpretation of the Work of J. R. Commons', *Review of Political Economy* 6(2): 259–278.

Lawson, C., Peacock, M. and Pratten, S. (1996) 'Realism, Underlabouring and Institutions', *Cambridge Journal of Economics* 20(1): 137–151.

Lawson, T. (1989) 'Realism and Instrumentalism in the Development of Econometrics', *Oxford Economic Papers*, 41(1): 236–258.

—— (1992) 'Realism, Closed Systems and Friedman', *Research in the History of Economic Thought and Methodology*, 10: 149–169.

—— (1994) 'Critical Realism and the Analysis of Choice, Explanation and Change', *Advances in Austrian Economics* 1(1): 1–24.

—— (1995) 'A Realist Perspective on Contemporary Economic Theory', *Journal of Economic Issues*, Dec.: 1–32.

Mäki, U. (1986) *Carl Menger's Conception of Economics as Exact Science*, Mimeo.

—— (1987) 'Book Review', *Economics and Philosophy* 3: 367–373.

—— (1990) 'Mengerian Economics in Realist Perspective', *History of Political Economy* 22(5): 289–310.

Menger, C. (1985) *Investigations into the Method of the Social Sciences with Special Reference to Economics*, 1883, translated by F. J. Nock, New York: New York University Press.

Nelson, R. and Winter, S. (1982) *An Evolutionary Theory of Economic Change*, Cambridge, MA: Harvard University Press.

North, D. C. (1981) *Structure and Change in Economic History*, New York: Norton.

North, D. C. and Thomas, R. P. (1973) *The Rise of the Western World: A New Economic History*, Cambridge: Cambridge University Press.

Olson, M. (1965) *The Logic of Collective Action*, Cambridge, MA: Harvard University Press.

—— (1982) *The Rise and Decline of Nations*, New Haven, CT: Yale University Press.

Popper, K. R. (1961) *The Poverty of Historicism*, 2nd edition, London: Routledge.

—— (1962 [1945]) *The Open Society and its Enemies*, London: Routledge.

Posner, R. (1973) *Economic Analysis of Law*, Boston: Little Brown.

Pratten, S. (1994) 'Marshall on Tendencies, Equilibrium and Statical Method', in *Forms of Realism, Conceptions of Science and Approaches to Industrial Organisation*, PhD thesis, University of Cambridge.

Prendergast, C. (1986) 'Alfred Schutz and the Austrian School of Economics', *American Journal of Sociology* 92: 1–26.

Rutherford, M. (1989) 'What is Wrong with the New Institutionalist Economics (and What is Still Wrong with the Old)?', *Review of Political Economy* 1(3): 299–319.

Sandler, T. (1992) *Collective Action: Theory and Applications*, Brighton: Harvester Wheatsheaf.

Schotter, A. (1981) *The Economic Theory of Social Institutions*, Cambridge: Cambridge University Press.

—— (1986) 'The Evolution of Rules', in R. Langlois (ed.) *Economics as a Process: Essays in the New Institutional Economics*, Cambridge University Press: Cambridge.

Smith, B. (1986) 'Austrian Economics and Austrian Philosophy', in W. Grassl and B. Smith (ed.) *Austrian Economics: Historical and Philosophical Background*, London: Croom Helm.

—— (1990a) 'Aristotle, Menger, Mises: An Essay in the Metaphysics of Economics', *History of Political Economy* 22(5): 63–288.

—— (1990b) 'On the Austrianness of Austrian Economics', *Critical Review* 4.

Sugden, R. (1986) *The Economics of Rights, Cooperation and Welfare*, Oxford: Basil Blackwell.

Vinning, R. (1949a) 'Methodological Issues in Quantitative Economics: Koopmans on the Choice of Variables to be Studied and of Method of Measurement', *Review of Economics and Statistics* 31(2): 77–86.

—— (1949b) 'Methodological Issues in Quantitative Economics: A Rejoinder', *Review of Economics and Statistics* 31(2): 91–94.

Williamson, O. E. (1975) *Markets and Hierarchies: Analysis and Antitrust Implications*, New York: Free Press.

—— (1985) *The Economic Institutions of Capitalism: Firms, Markets, Relational Contracting*, New York: Free Press.

4

ON POPPER, PROBABILITIES
AND PROPENSITIES

Jochen Runde[1]

A puzzling feature of the many contributions in economics that refer to Karl Popper's writings is how few of them mention his propensity interpretation of probability.[2] This may well be because this interpretation was initially proposed with physics in mind (Popper 1967). Yet by the end of his life it had become clear that his propensity theory had developed into something with much wider implications. As he puts it in his last book, after he had first proposed it in the 1950s the

> theory had further grown so that it was only in the last year that I realized its cosmological significance. I mean that we live *in a world of propensities*, and that this fact makes our world both more interesting and more homely than the world as seen by earlier states of the sciences.
>
> (Popper 1990: 9)

My aim in this chapter is to document this development, to point out its affinities with Critical Realism (CR), and to raise some implications for two prominent Popperian themes in economics.

One of the difficulties in reporting Popper's views on propensities is that there is some slippage over time in the way that he uses the term. In his earlier writings he leans towards the view that propensities are dispositions, generated in particular experimental situations, towards the realisation of certain experimental outcomes. These dispositions are interpreted as holistic properties of experimental situations, but expressed in terms of the possible outcomes or *effects* of the situation concerned (rather than the generating factors – forces, fields, and so on – which, in conjunction with the relevant boundary conditions, combine to cause those effects).[3] In his last book, however, Popper also refers to forces *as* propensities, suggesting that propensities may be regarded as causal factors as well as what is generated by the operation of causal factors. To avoid confusion I shall use the term propensity in the former sense, in the first two sections below. Some ambiguities that arise in Popper's later interpretation are considered at the end of the chapter.

Probabilities as propensities

Popper introduced his propensity theory of probability in two papers published during the 1950s. I shall concentrate on the second of these, his 1959 paper in the *British Journal for the Philosophy of Science*.[4] The purpose of this paper is to provide an interpretation of probability, or more accurately, of statements of the form 'the probability of *a* given *b* is *r*' (where *r* is a real number in the interval [0,1]). In symbols, this statement may be written:

$$p(a, b) = r$$

Popper divides into two broad categories the different ways statements of this kind are interpreted: the subjective interpretation (sometimes called the epistemic interpretation) and the objective interpretation (sometimes called the aleatory interpretation).[5] On the subjective interpretation, probability is regarded as a property of our knowledge of the external world. Here *r* is regarded as the degree of belief that a knowledge of *b* confers on *a*. As Popper consistently rejected the subjective interpretation throughout his career, I shall say no more about it here (other than that he does concede that there may be something like a measure of rational belief *r* in *a* given *b*, but that this measure is unlikely to conform to the standard probability axioms).

On the objective interpretation, probability is regarded as a property of the external world. Here *a* represents the possible outcome of experiment *b* and *r* the relative frequency with which *a* occurs in a sufficiently long series of repetitions of *b*. Before developing his propensity theory, Popper had been a proponent of the 'purely statistical' version of the objective interpretation of probability. On this interpretation, $p(a, b) = r$ is an estimate or hypothesis 'asserting *nothing but* that the relative frequency of the event *a* in a sequence of trials defined by *b* is equal to *r*' (1959: 26). Popper went on to abandon this view due to problems connected with the interpretation of quantum theory and because of its inability to account for single-case probabilities (probabilities that can be ascribed to a single event occurring at a particular spatio-temporal location). While the problems relating to the interpretation of quantum theory precipitated his change of mind, it was his solution to the problem of single-case probabilities that provides his main argument in support of the propensity interpretation. I shall accordingly leave to one side the genesis of his ideas on probabilities as propensities.

Popper places great emphasis on his contention that, according to the purely statistical interpretation, the probability of an event of a certain kind is *nothing but* the relative frequency of this kind of event in a long sequence of events. This means that single-case probabilities can be assigned in a 'formal' sense only, namely, only to the extent that the event concerned is a member of a sequence and, so to speak, 'shares in' the probabilities of that sequence (see Popper 1959a, section 71). Popper believes that this restriction raises a problem which he illustrates in the following way. Suppose that our sequence consists of an infinite number of throws of a loaded die with a probability of very nearly 1/4 of turning six up, into which a finite number (two or three) of throws of a fair die has been interpolated. Clearly the limiting frequency of sixes in the hybrid sequence is 1/4. The problem is that this number does not reflect the probability of getting a six in any given throw of the fair die, even though, according to the frequency view, this should be equal to 1/4.[6]

Popper accordingly seeks to provide a theory on which objective single-case probabilities are defined and are equal to the limiting relative frequency in an infinite sequence. He does so by placing certain conditions on the sequence concerned, conditions that are not met in terms of the purely statistical interpretation. In particular, he insists that an admissible sequence of events must always be a sequence of *repeated* experiments or, more generally, that admissible sequences must be either virtual or actual sequences that are *characterised by a set of generating conditions* whose repeated realisation produces the elements of the sequence (Popper 1959b: 34). The difficulty raised in the above example then dissolves once the hybrid sequence is recognised as mixing two different experimental set-ups. Once attention is restricted to the two admissible sequences, the limiting relative frequency of sixes is 1/4 in the actual sequence throws of the loaded die and 1/6 in the virtual sequence of throws of the unbiased die.

The modification to the purely statistical view that Popper proposes, then, is to insist that, rather than defining probability as a property of some sequence alone, the sequence must itself be defined in terms of the set of generating conditions that produce each of the events being recorded. In this way, Popper argues, probability becomes a measure of unobservable but nevertheless physically real dispositional properties. These dispositional properties, which he regards as analogous to forces that can interact and combine, are aspects of the *physical experimental arrangements* that are assumed to be the same in each experiment. Since these arrangements are objective, according to Popper, so too are the associated probabilities or propensities. It then becomes possible to define a single-case probability $p(a, b)$ because a is an event produced according to the generating conditions b rather than because a is a member of the sequence b. The statement $p(a, b) = r$ reports the propensity r that a singular event a has to occur in situation b.

How is the hypothesis of propensities to be tested and how are they to be measured? According to Popper (1983: 288–289), every scientific theory implies that under certain specified conditions certain other things will happen.[7] The testing of scientific theories thus involves attempting to generate counterexamples to their predictions in controlled experiments, namely, in situations in which these specified conditions are met. Popper argues that this 'fundamentally clear and simple' procedure of experimental testing applies as much to probabilistic hypotheses (hypotheses that predict a spread of outcomes) as it does to non-probabilistic or what he here calls 'causal' hypotheses (hypotheses that predict unique outcomes or, as he puts it, 'hypotheses asserting a propensity equal to 1'). Predictions about probabilistic hypotheses are tested (and propensities measured) by repeating the experiment under the specified conditions and calculating the associated frequency distribution of the outcomes obtained. Predictions about causal hypotheses are also tested by repeated experiment although in this case, of course, corroboration demands the associated relative frequency of outcomes be close to unity.

A necessary condition for testing hypotheses about the probability/propensity of experimental outcomes in this way is that the relevant experiments be independent (the sample proportion of a sequence of independent events should be approximately normal and therefore make it possible to use standard hypothesis testing procedures to decide whether the conjectured probability ought to be regarded as refuted or corroborated by the test).[8] Independence is ensured if the conditions under which tests are made remain unchanged with each repetition of the experiment, that is, that the experiments in question are truly repeated experiments. I shall return to this point below.

A world of propensities

In his last book Popper signals a late and important development in his thinking. After noting that he had first proposed the propensity interpretation in the 1950s 'after 35 years of study', he writes that it

was 'only in the last year' that he realised its cosmological significance: 'that we live in *a world of propensities*' (Popper 1990: 9).[9]
Unfortunately Popper's account of the route that took him to this realisation does not reveal much beyond what I have already summarised
above. It is, however, possible to reconstruct his later position as a
generalisation of his earlier thinking on propensities. I shall attempt to
do so in this section and to argue that the ultimate position that
emerges in Popper's last book shares the central metaphysical tenets
of CR.

As Popper himself makes clear, his final position was less a product
of dramatic revisions of his thinking than an extension of broad
themes that had been evident in his writings at least thirty years
earlier. The first of these is his earlier espousal of something like the
'layered' ontology of CR, distinguishing between, on the one hand, the
level of the actual such as events or states of affairs, and, on the other,
of the underlying and often unobservable powers that contribute to
bringing about such events or states of affairs. In Popper's words,

> part of the usefulness of these concepts [propensities] lies
> precisely in the fact that they suggest that theory is concerned
> with properties of an *unobservable* physical reality and that it is
> only some of the more superficial effects of this reality which we
> can observe, and which thus makes it possible for us to test a
> theory.
>
> (1959b: 31)

In experiments that produce non-deterministic outcomes, moreover, it
is quite possible that the relevant propensities may not be actualised
in any single trial, or for that matter, even a sequence of trials of that
experiment (although such propensities nevertheless remain a real
property of the physical situation concerned). Implicit in Popper's
earlier position, then, is the CR notion of generative mechanisms
acting transfactually, that is, that there need not be a one-to-one relation between the generative mechanisms in play in some situation and
some particular ensuing set of outcomes.[10]

The second broad theme already present in Popper's early writings
is that propensities are not inherent in objects but are properties of
whole physical situations. It is then *not* the case, according to the
propensity theory, that a loaded die has an intrinsic propensity of, say,
1/4 to turn six up in a particular throw. What may be the case is that
the die has a propensity to do so *when thrown in a particular situation*.[11]
For, and as Popper points out, the propensities of a loaded die will be
very different according as to whether it is thrown onto a hard surface,

an elastic surface or an extremely soft surface. Propensities and there-fore probabilities, then, are *situationally dependent*. The way and extent to which dispositional properties inherent in particular situations are actualised, in terms of the language of CR, depend on the context in which those properties are exercised.

So much for Popper's earlier views on propensities. What was it that changed in his thinking towards the end of the 1980s? The rele-vant passages, sparse as they are, are these:

> To sum up: propensities in physics are properties of *the whole physical situation* and sometimes even of the particular way in which a situation changes. And the same holds of the propen-sities in chemistry, in biochemistry, and in biology.
>
> Now, in our real changing world, the situation and, with it, the possibilities, and thus the propensities, change all the time.
>
> (Popper 1990: 17)

Although the step that Popper takes between these two passages appears to be a small one, it has significant implications. The essential insight is that *all* situations, whether physical, psychological or mixed, have propensities. Whereas in his earlier writings he had focused almost exclusively on propensities identified in experimental situa-tions, the shift reported in his 1990 book is his fully taking on board that non-experimental situations have propensities too, that, as he puts it, we live in a world of propensities.

Two important consequences follow directly from this shift, both of them emphasised in CR. First, Popper now acknowledges explicitly that only a small proportion of his now expanded ontology of propen-sities will be amenable to statistical measurement. The problem is that it is often not possible to engineer or gain access to the repeated exper-iments necessary for the statistical measurement of propensities:

> in many kinds of events . . . propensities cannot be measured because the relevant situation changes and cannot be repeated. This would hold, for example, for the different propensities of some of our evolutionary predecessors to give rise to chim-panzees and to ourselves. Propensities of this kind are, of course, not measurable, since the situation cannot be repeated. It is unique.
>
> (Popper 1990: 17)

In short, Popper's generalised version of his theory of propensities leads to the conclusion that the propensities of non-repeatable and transient situations cannot be captured by statistical means. In fact, if the relevant situation occurs only once, all but one unique combination of its associated propensities will never be actualised and may remain forever unknown.[12]

The second key consequence is that Popper now feels bound to emphasise that, with the exception of the 'unique natural laboratory experiment' of the planetary system, regular associations of events or states of affairs – what he calls 'natural laws of a deterministic character' and 'natural laws of a probabilistic character' – are rarely found to occur outside of situations of experimental control. The reason is simply that in non-laboratory situations there will typically be 'disturbing propensities', the exclusion of which is the very purpose of laboratory experiments:

> In most laboratory experiments we have to exclude many disturbing extraneous influences such as changes of temperature of the normal moisture of the air. Or we may have to create an artificial environment of extreme temperatures – say, near to absolute zero. In this we are led entirely by our hypothetical insight into the theoretical structure of our world. And we have to learn from our experimental mistakes that lead to unsatisfactory results: results are satisfactory only if they can be repeated at will; and this happens only if we have learnt how to exclude the interfering propensities.
>
> But what does this all show us? It shows that in the non-laboratory world, with the exception of our planetary system, no such strictly deterministic laws can be found.
>
> (Popper 1990: 23–24)

This conclusion, following CR, is of course not restricted to deterministic laws. It applies equally to the probabilistic laws Popper discusses in his early writings on the propensity interpretation of probability, the stable relative frequencies with which propensities are realised in particular experimental situations. We therefore have three possibilities:

1   Situations of experimental control that yield 'causal' laws of a deterministic character.
2   Situations of experimental control that yield laws of a probabilistic character.
3   Non-laboratory situations in which natural laws, be they of a deterministic or probabilistic character, cannot be found.

Popper concentrates exclusively on the distinction between (1) and (2) in his earlier writings on the propensity interpretation of probability. His omission of (3) was understandable at the time, since he was then concentrating on situations of experimental control (which, to repeat, is a necessary condition for the statistical measurement of propensities). With the introduction of (3) in his writings on propensities, however, the essential contrast is no longer between (1) and (2), but between (1) and (2) on the one hand and (3) on the other. The significant difference, of course, is that whereas both (1) and (2) refer to experimental situations in which 'disturbing propensities' are excluded, (3) does not. [13]

A common counter to the view that deterministic or probabilistic laws are rarely found outside of experimental situations is to attempt to point to examples of such laws. I have already mentioned one that is accepted by Popper, the 'unique natural laboratory experiment' of the planetary system. But are there any others? An example that often comes up in this connection is the stability of mortality rates, 'the expectation of life' which even Keynes (1973a: 113) held 'is only slightly uncertain'. Popper's response to this example is illuminating:

> as a strong argument, one of my critics appealed to the survival tables of the life assurance companies which, admittedly, seem to incorporate this view. . . . Nevertheless, the view that the propensity to survive is a property of health *and not* of the situation can easily be shown to be a serious mistake. As a matter of course, the state of health is very important – an important aspect of the situation. But as anybody may fall ill or become involved in an accident, the progress of medical science – say, the invention of powerful new drugs (like antibiotics) – changes the *prospects* of everybody to survive, whether or not he or she actually gets into the position of having to take such a drug. The *situation* changes the possibilities and thereby the propensities.
>
> (Popper 1990: 14–15)

Of course, even the regular movements of the planets is itself contingent on the planetary system remaining undisturbed (and by most accounts, eventually, the system will be disturbed). But it is a system that, relative to our own life-histories, changes so slowly as to be imperceptible. There are other such systems, but these are typically ones that we have constructed ourselves – such as the complicated ensemble of isolations that ensure that the lights go on (almost) every time we flick the switch.

In summary, then, the intellectual journey Popper began in his writings on probability is one that took him from the purely statistical interpretation to the propensity interpretation, which, in its ultimate generalised form, leads to a picture of an open world in which measurable probabilities drop out and only propensities remain. I have indicated the points at which Popper's final position is at one with CR. Many of these were already evident in the 1950s: the distinction between unobservable generative mechanisms and their observable effects, the notion of generative mechanisms operating transfactually, the situational dependence of experimental outcomes and the role of controlled experiments in the identification and measurement of propensities. The further step that Popper appears to have taken in the late 1980s is to take on board fully the possibility that all physical situations, irrespective of whether or not they are situations of experimental control, may have propensities. Laboratory experiments, from this new perspective, become a means of ensuring that propensities are actualised in a regular lawlike way by excluding countervailing influences. It then follows that there is nothing to ensure the lawlike actualisation of propensities outside of experimental situations, that is, in situations in which countervailing influences may always be in play.

Falsification, situational analysis and propensities as causes

I conclude by raising three interesting questions that arise in the light of the preceding discussion.[14] The first two concern the ideas for which Popper is best known in economics: falsification and situational analysis. The third, which is of a more general nature, concerns Popper's later tendency to treat propensities as causes. I shall comment briefly in each case, hopefully in a way that may stimulate a more thorough investigation of the issues involved.

Propensities and Popperian falsification

Popper is perhaps best known in economics in his guise as the prophet of falsification in science. The broad outline of this doctrine is well known.[15] At its core is the idea that although no amount of evidence can confirm a theory, observations can disconfirm a theory. The recommendation is that scientists should proceed by proposing bold conjectures and putting these conjectures to the severest tests they can devise. Theories are provisionally accepted so long as they have not been falsified.

My first question is this. How do Popper's writings on the propensity theory of probability bear on the debate that occurred during the 1980s over the role of falsification in economics? It is fair to say that the emphasis in this debate was on logical, epistemological and methodological issues, the metaphysical and ontological presuppositions underlying Popper's views on the testing of theories receiving considerably less attention.[16] Certainly the propensity theory itself was seldom, if ever, mentioned.[17] The parts of Popper's writings discussed in the foregoing sections may therefore help to fill something of a gap in the discussion. For it is in these writings that he specifies a key ontological precondition for testability: that in order to test and falsify a theory it must be possible to subject it to repeated experiment (Popper 1983: 288–291). This can only be achieved, as he later puts it, *'by creating, at will, artificial conditions that either exclude, or reduce to zero, all the interfering and disturbing propensities'* (Popper 1990: 23). In situations in which it is not possible to conduct repeated experiments, then, the scope for falsification is considerably reduced if not precluded entirely.

The possibility that falsification encounters obstacles in economics that are avoided in many of the natural sciences has of course been raised before (for example, Caldwell 1982: 124–128, 1984). But the response of authors such as Blaug (1984) and Hausman (1985) that these difficulties are not unique to economics does not disturb the basic point that there is at least one key difference: economics offers considerably less scope for conducting repeated experiments. It then follows, at least from Popper's post-1950s position, that economics is likely to offer correspondingly less scope for falsification than do many natural sciences.[18] Space precludes my pursuing this point more fully here. But it is worth noting that it squares neatly with Hands's (1985) observation that whereas the economic literature on falsificationism draws almost exclusively on Popper's writings on the natural sciences, Popper's own writings on economics display a preference for what he calls situational analysis (see below).[19] Again, the account given in the previous sections provides a plausible basis for the distinction between the two positions that Hands discerns in his writings, that is between subject matter that is amenable to investigation by repeated experiment and subject matter that is not.

Propensities and situational analysis

My second question concerns possible implications of the development of Popper's views on propensities for his writings on situational analysis. Again there are far more issues here than could ever be covered in just a few paragraphs; I mention just two.

Popper describes situational analysis in different ways in different parts of his writings. The basic idea, however, is that the explanation of social behaviour should be sought in terms of the 'situation' in which the relevant agents find themselves (where the situation, at least in Popper's later formulations, is described in terms of how the agent sees it). It is generally assumed that there is a unique action that follows from the 'logic' of each situation.[20] The actions of agents are then explained as 'rational' responses to their situations. Such explanations must be animated by a 'rationality principle' which states that 'the various persons or agents involved act *adequately* or *appropriately*; that is to say, in accordance with the situation' (Popper 1985: 361). All of this will strike a chord with economists, of course, and in places Popper (1976: 117–118) indeed describes situational analysis as a generalisation of the method of economic theory or marginal utility analysis.

Popper is sometimes criticised for being vague about exactly how situational analysis should be pursued. These criticisms have led some to suggest that it be reformulated on the lines of the 'cleaner' deductive–nomological model of explanation, with the rationality principle serving as the necessary covering law (see Caldwell 1991: 13–17). This move would bring situational analysis directly within the fold of the deductivist approach of modern economic theory, effectively reducing it to what Latsis (1976) calls situational determinism. The first point I want to make here is that this move would be incompatible with Popper's later views on propensities. For the 'whenever these conditions then that outcome' formulation that is the hallmark of deductivism runs into severe difficulties with generative mechanisms that operate transfactually, or alternatively, with propensities outside of situations of experimental control (see Lawson 1997; Runde 1998, for details). It is a move, moreover, that would leave Popper in the position of advocating a form of determinism in the explanation of social phenomena, and which would be extremely difficult to square with his stated view that:

> with the introduction of propensities, the ideology of determinism evaporates. Past situations, whether physical or psychological or mixed, do not determine the future situation. Rather, they determine *changing propensities that influence future situations without determining them in a unique way*. And all our experiences – including our wishes and our efforts – may

contribute to the propensities, sometimes more and sometimes less, as the case may be.

(Popper 1990: 17–18)

What all this entails, if correct, is that the covering-law model should be abandoned as a general approach to explanation. Again this is a topic that introduces issues far wider than can be considered here. But I should like to close by noting, and this is my second point, that Popper's writings on propensities suggest a fresh answer to a much debated problem: the status of the rationality principle. It has been suggested that this principle might be interpreted as saying that all agents act appropriately to the situation *as they see it*, for example, as equivalent to a (falsifiable or non-falsifiable) universal law within the social sciences, or as a methodological principle that is retained because it has been useful in the past (see Caldwell 1991: 18–20; Hands 1985: 85–89). The alternative possibility, following CR, is to interpret rationality, not in terms of a universal law or methodological principle, but as a *capacity* people have that may itself be actualised to different degrees depending on the situation concerned (see Lawson 1997). This suggestion may have affinities with the first of the three interpretations listed above: situational analysis would still proceed by invoking the 'logic' of the situation as the actors see it. But rationality, on this alternative interpretation, would now be one of possibly many causal factors in the situation being explained, the extent of its impact depending on the degree to which it is actually manifest in that situation.[21]

Propensities as causes

We have seen that in his early writings on the propensity theory of probability, Popper proposes that probabilities be regarded as a measure of the dispositions, generated in experimental situations, towards the realisation of particular experimental outcomes. Propensities, on this view, are properties of whole physical situations, but as something that is generated in such situations rather than something that is doing the generating.[22] While Popper originally regarded propensities as *analogous* to forces, then, he did not regard them *as* forces (see Popper 1959b: 30–31). In his 1990 book, however, he appears to change his mind on this point, arguing that propensities include forces:

Propensities . . . are not mere possibilities but are physical realities. They are as real as forces, or fields of forces. And vice versa: forces are propensities. They are propensities for setting bodies in motion. Forces are propensities to accelerate, and fields of forces are propensities distributed over some region of space and perhaps changing continuously over this region (like distances from some given origin). Fields of forces are fields of propensities.

(Popper 1990: 12)

My final question, then, is what should we make of this? How are forces to be understood both as part of the generating conditions described by b (members of the set of causes of a) *and* as propensities (the disposition a has to be realised in situation b)?

There are two possibilities. The first is trivial and simply amounts to recognising that forces referred to in the description of situation b may themselves be propensities in the sense of being possible outcomes of some other situation c. The proviso, of course, is that such forces have to be actualised (that is *there*, triggered, in play) in situation b in order to qualify as members of b. Unfortunately this interpretation does not entirely resolve questions that might be raised about Popper's remarks that forces are 'propensities for setting bodies in motion' or 'propensities to accelerate'. Are forces things which even have the capacity to accelerate? If propensities are properties of whole physical situations, is it consistent to describe isolated forces as propensities in the way Popper seems to be doing? And even if forces may count as propensities in the sense I have suggested, isn't it simply courting confusion to call them propensities in their capacity as members of the generating conditions b? Far better, in view of these considerations, would be to stick with Popper's original formulation and to replace the remarks in the passage quoted above with something like 'forces, in certain situations, contribute to generating propensities towards objects moving or accelerating'.[23]

The second possibility is connected with Popper's use of the term 'causation', which he describes as 'just a special case of a propensity equal to 1, a *determining* demand, or force for realization' or, a little further on, where $p(effect, cause) = 1$. Causation, according to Popper, *is* thus the actualisation of a possibility. But this interpretation raises an interesting challenge. For Popper also wants to reject the old deterministic 'push' theory of causation 'that puts before us a mechanism operating with pushes, or with more abstract causes that are all in the past – the past kicking us and driving us with kicks into the future, the past that is *gone*' (Popper 1990: 20–21). How is this anti-determinism to be reconciled with Popper's conception of causation as a force or determining demand?

The argument seems to go something like this. Popper begins with the premiss that determinism is false (an old theme in his writings, the truth of which I shall take for granted here).[24] If determinism is false, then the future must be open in the sense of admitting more than one possibility that could be actualised. It then follows that the deterministic theory of causation, according to which the future is uniquely determined, has to be replaced. Popper proposes to substitute his new 'pull' view of causation, according to which 'it is not the kicks from the back, from the past, that *impel* us but the attraction, the lure of the future and its competing possibilities, that *attract* us, that *entice* us' (Popper 1990: 20–21). On this view a possibility that is ultimately realised (has propensity 1) is selected over its competitors in the run-up to its actualisation (during the course of which the propensities of all competing possibilities drop to 0).[25] A propensity of 1 is also a force, then, in the sense that it is something that can no longer be halted, that it no longer faces any obstacles that might deny its 'demand for realisation'.

The two distinct interpretations of the notion of propensities as causes (or causation) in Popper's last book, then, may be traced to the two distinct ways in which he uses the term 'force'. On the one hand, he uses 'force' in the standard sense of a power with the capacity to move physical objects. To the extent that such powers contribute to producing propensities, they are causes. And to the extent that they are themselves outcomes of other situations, it follows that causes may also be propensities (so long as they are actualised in those other situations). On the other hand, Popper uses 'force' to describe the special case of a propensity equal to 1. But 'force' in this second sense refers not to individual causes, but to causation itself. I have suggested that the first interpretation is relatively straightforward, at least when fully spelled out. The second interpretation and the associated 'pull' view of causation, however, are more problematic. It is not clear, for example, how the idea of causation as a determining demand applies in situations in which the actualisation of a propensity does not involve anything more definite than a spread of outcomes (at the quantum level, for instance). But that is perhaps not the most serious difficulty. More serious is that the 'pull' view of causation reduces the force of Popper's point that propensities are properties of pre-existing physical situations. Instead, the image conjured up borders on one in which propensities that are actualised somehow contribute to drawing out of the past the necessary conditions appropriate to their realisation. This seems a highly implausible view: it would be equivalent, in general, to claiming that the results of laboratory experiments themselves influence the setting up of the experimental situation in which those results occur.

Let me close by saying that although treating propensities as causes does not square too well with his earlier writings on propensities, it may yet be more fruitful to place relatively more emphasis on the causal factors that generate propensities rather than on propensities themselves. The main lessons in the story of the development of Popper's views on propensities lie in its account of why law-like regularities generally presuppose situations of experimental control and why the adoption of the propensity view leads to the 'evaporation of the ideology of determinism'. However, there is little point in restricting scientific analysis to the study of propensities *per se*, at least outside of well-controlled experimental situations, for they are generally too unique, too impermanent and too irregular in their manifestation to provide much in the way of general knowledge about the world. In view of this fact, following CR, the best way forward may be to take as a point of entry in economic analysis propensities that *ex posteriori are* found to be realised in more or less systematic ways in certain kinds of situations – the propensity of productivity to vary with output, the propensity of stock market prices to fluctuate, or the propensity of wages to be downwards rigid, for example – and then to proceed by retroducing the underlying causal factors that give rise to them. After all, and as Popper already remarks in his 1959b paper (p. 31), a good part of the usefulness of the propensity view lies in its suggestion that our theories are concerned with an unobservable reality of causal factors, generative mechanisms and so on, and that it is only through some of its more superficial effects (propensities that have been realised) that this reality can be identified.

Notes

1 I am grateful to Bruce Caldwell, Allin Cottrell, John Davis, Tony Lawson, David Miller, Eckehard Rosenbaum, three anonymous referees and especially Sue James and Joseph Melia for their very helpful comments on earlier versions of this chapter.
2 Gillies and Ieotto-Gillies (1991), O'Donnell (1989: 341), O'Driscoll and Rizzo (1985: 66) and Runde (1993) are the only exceptions I know of, but even they only mention it in passing.
3 Popper (1959a: 37) writes, for example, that the conjecture that probabilities are dispositional properties of experimental conditions 'allows us to interpret the probability of a *singular* event as a property of the singular event itself'.
4 The first (Popper, 1957), was originally presented in Popper's absence by his then student Paul Feyerabend at the Ninth Symposium of the Colston Research Society.

5 Popper's particular formulation of this distinction should not be taken too literally. For it would otherwise exclude both Keynes and de Finetti, both of whom Popper would regard as subjectivists, Keynes because he believes that *r* does not generally correspond to a real number, and de Finetti because he denies that probability is relational (see Keynes 1973a; de Finetti 1985). An excellent recent survey of the different ways in which probability is interpreted, and which is organised on the basis of much the same distinction, can be found in Howson (1995).

6 It is debatable whether many frequency theorists would accept this example, and it is perhaps for this reason that Popper sometimes refers to the 'purely statistical' interpretation rather than the frequency interpretation. According to Howson (1995: 21), for example, the intended model of Mises's (1939) frequency theory was in fact repeatable trials endowed with dispositions to generate certain limiting frequencies. If so, this would preclude Popper's hybrid sequence (as well as robbing his proposals of some of their novelty). By the same token, however, the criticism of the propensity theory Howson (1995: 21–22) offers in rejoinder seems to presuppose – incorrectly – that single case probabilities are relative to a reference class rather than being a property of the world (see Miller 1995: 138). Economists might be interested to note that Popper's example would also be ruled out on the theories of statistical probability proposed by Keynes (1973a) and Knight (1921), both of which presuppose the effective homogeneity of each 'trial' in the relevant reference class or sequence (Runde 1995).

7 Although this book, *Realism and the Aim of Science*, appeared only in 1983, most of it was written in the years 1951–56. Popper was therefore working on it at roughly the time he was working on his 1959 *BJPS* article (indeed, the section on the propensity theory of probability in the book coincides very closely with this article).

8 See Gillies (1995: 109–114).

9 A shorter version of the lecture that comprises the first half of the book ('A World of Propensities: Two New Views of Causality') was first delivered at the 1988 World Congress of Philosophy in Brighton (Popper 1990: vii). Although the phrase 'in the last year' may not be entirely fair to earlier writings in which he hints that there may be propensities outside experimental situations (Miller 1995: 144), it therefore seems safe to say that Popper arrived at the full generalisation of his propensity theory in the second half of the 1980s.

10 A loaded die that has a propensity/probability of 1/4 to turn 6 up when thrown in a particular situation, for example, does so whether or not the 6 is actualised in any particular throw.

11 I assume that the 'situations' or 'experiments' I refer to always contain an irreducible indeterministic element, that is, 'gaps' in the causal determination of outcomes.

12 This will be the case, for example, when a biased die is thrown once in a particular situation and then destroyed. Of course, as Popper (1990: 17) points out, 'there is nothing to prevent us from supposing that such propensities exist, and from estimating them speculatively'.

13 In the rare cases in which (3) is mentioned by mainstream economists, this is typically only so as to exclude it as not being amenable to economic theory (e.g. Lucas 1981: 223–224). In contrast, CR and members of the various heterodox traditions in economics tend to concentrate on (3) and

argue that mainstream methods illegitimately presuppose situations of either (1) or (2).

14 There are of course many more, not least the impact of Popper's later views on the metaphysics and importance he attaches to universal laws in his *Realism and the Aim of Science* (Popper 1983).

15 I here concentrate on falsification in the practical sense of conclusive experimental proof of the falsity of a theory, rather than falsificationism in the 'logical–technical' sense of the demarcation criterion that Popper proposes to distinguish between statements that belong to the empirical sciences and other sciences (see Popper 1983: xxii).

16 Caldwell's (1991) otherwise excellent survey of this debate provides a case in point, explicitly bracketing the metaphysical foundations of Popper's ideas. See also the commentaries by Blaug (1994) and Hausman (1988).

17 This neglect may be due to the fact that many of the authors concerned concentrate on Popper's pre-propensity *The Logic of Scientific Discovery*.

18 It is interesting to note that the relatively small (but growing) amount of experimental work that is being conducted in economics has a distinctly Popperian flavour. The dominant approach in this work is to attempt to recreate the assumptions of neoclassical economic models in a laboratory setting, by specifying an 'environment' (tastes and technology), an 'institution' (the language by which agents communicate, the order in which they move and the rules under which messages become contracts and thus allocations) and 'behaviour' (that agents are utility maximisers, choose as if they are risk averse, and so on). The usual aim is to test hypotheses about rational behaviour, which are regarded as being corroborated (in the context of the environment and institution posited) so long as they are not falsified (see, for example, Smith 1991, 1994).

19 Hands argues convincingly that the positions Popper adopts in these two branches are not easily reconciled (situational analysis relies on a rationality principle that Popper regards as false and unfalsifiable, for example, which conflicts with the falsifiability doctrine). Hands accordingly distinguishes between Popper$_n$ and Popper$_s$, where the n stands for natural sciences and the s stands for the Popper who has written on situational analysis and the rationality principle. It is noteworthy that Hands is careful not to use the s to denote the social sciences, since Popper also believed that situational analysis might be used to explain evolutionary episodes.

20 Of course there may be more than one action for each agent that follows from the 'logic' of his or her situation, particularly in game-theoretic situations in which the pay-offs to any one agent of taking some course of action depend on the actions of other agents. Popper does not have much to say about situations of this kind.

21 Of course this proposal does imply that the scope of situational analysis will depend on the transparency of 'the logic of the situation' and the extent to which rationality can be imputed to the actors concerned. Situational analysis is unlikely to be much help in the explanation of social phenomena characterised by mass hysteria, for example, or high levels of uncertainty.

22 Popper's aim, after all, was to provide an interpretation of probability that would permit the probability of a singular event to be interpreted as a property of the singular event itself: the statement $p(a, b) = r$ gives the probability/propensity of the outcome a rather than of the description of the situation b in which a arises.

23 The commonly cited CR example, 'the leaf is subject to the gravitational tendency even as I hold it in the palm of my hand' (Lawson 1994: 268), on the present argument, should also be restated on something like the following lines: 'Gravity is a force or power that imbues leaves with a tendency to fall to the ground' (a tendency which may not be actualised because I hold the leaf in the palm of my hand).

24 See Popper (1982).

25 In an open world, of course, the situation will typically be changing over time and, with it, the associated propensities.

> What may happen in the future – say, tomorrow at noon – is, to some extent, open. There are many possibilities trying to realize themselves, but few of them have a very high propensity, given the existing conditions. When tomorrow noon approaches, under constantly changing conditions, many of these propensities will have become zero and others very small; and some of the propensities that remain will have increased. At noon, those propensities that realize themselves will be equal to 1 in the presence of the then existing conditions.
>
> (Popper 1990: 22)

Bibliography

Blaug, M. (1984) 'Comment on Hutchison: Our Methodological Crisis', in P. Wiles and G. Routh (eds) *Economics in Disarray*, Oxford: Basil Blackwell: 30–36.

—— (1994) 'Why I Am Not a Constructivist', in R. E. Backhouse (ed.) *New Directions in Economic Methodology*, London: Routledge: 109–136.

Caldwell, B. (1982) *Beyond Positivism: Economic Methodology in the Twentieth Century*, London: George Allen & Unwin.

—— (1984) 'Some Problems with Falsificationism in Economics', *Philosophy of the Social Sciences* 14: 489–495.

—— (1991) 'Clarifying Popper', *Journal of Economic Literature* 29: 1–33.

de Finetti, B. (1985) 'Cambridge Probability Theorists', *The Manchester School* 53: 348–363.

Gillies, D. A. (1995) 'Popper's Contribution to the Philosophy of Probability', in A. O'Hear (ed.) *Karl Popper: Philosophy and Problems*, Cambridge: Cambridge University Press: 103–120.

Gillies, D. A. and Ietto-Gillies, G. (1991) 'Intersubjective Probability and Economics', *Review of Political Economy* 3: 393–417.

Hands, D. W. (1985) 'Karl Popper and Economic Methodology: A New Look', *Economics and Philosophy* 1: 83–99.

Hausman, D. M. (1985) 'Is Falsificationism Unpractised or Unpractisable?', *Philosophy of the Social Sciences* 15: 313–319.

—— (1988) 'An Appraisal of Popperian Methodology', in N. de Marchi (ed.) *The Popperian Legacy in Economics*, Cambridge: Cambridge University Press: 65–85.

Howson, C. (1995) 'Theories of Probability', *British Journal for the Philosophy of Science* 46: 1–32.

Keynes, J. M. (1973a) 'Treatise on Probability', *The Collected Writings of John Maynard Keynes*, vol. VIII, London: Macmillan.

—— (1973b) 'The General Theory and After Part II: Defence and Development', *The Collected Writings of John Maynard Keynes*, vol. XIV, London: Macmillan.

Knight, F. H. (1921) *Risk, Uncertainty and Profit*, Chicago: Chicago University Press.

Latsis, S. (1976) 'A Research Programme in Economics', in S. Latsis (ed.) *Method and Appraisal in Economics*, Cambridge: Cambridge University Press: 1–41.

Lawson, T. (1994) 'A Realist Theory for Economics', in R. E. Backhouse (ed.) *New Directions in Economic Methodology*, London: Routledge: 257–285.

—— (1997) *Economics and Reality*, London: Routledge.

Lucas, R. E. (1981) *Studies in Business-Cycle Theory*, Cambridge, MA: MIT Press.

Miller, D. (1995) 'Propensities and Indeterminism', in A. O'Hear (ed.) *Karl Popper: Philosophy and Problems*, Cambridge: Cambridge University Press: 121–147.

Mises, von, R. (1939) *Probability, Statistics and Truth*, London: George Allen and Unwin.

O'Donnell, R. M. (1989) *Keynes: Philosophy, Economics and Politics*, London: Macmillan.

O'Driscoll, G. P. and Rizzo, M. (1985) *The Economics of Time and Ignorance*, Oxford: Basil Blackwell.

Popper, K. R. (1957) 'Propensities, Probabilities, and the Quantum Theory', in D. Miller (ed.) *Popper Selections*, Princeton, NJ: Princeton University Press: 199–206.

—— (1959a) *The Logic of Scientific Discovery*, London: Hutchinson.

—— (1959b) 'The Propensity Interpretation of Probability', *British Journal for the Philosophy of Science* 10: 25–42.

—— (1967) 'Quantum Mechanics without "The Observer"', in M. Bunge (ed.) *Quantum Theory and Reality*, Heidelberg: Springer Verlag.

—— (1976) *Unended Quest*, LaSalle, Illinois: Open Court.

—— (1982) *The Open Universe: An Argument for Indeterminism*, London: Hutchinson.

—— (1983) *Realism and the Aim of Science*, London: Hutchinson.

—— (1985) 'The Rationality Principle', in D. Miller (ed.) *Popper Selections*, Princeton, NJ: Princeton University Press: 357–365.

—— (1990) *A World of Propensities*, Bristol: Thoemmes.

Runde, J. H. (1993) 'Paul Davidson and the Austrians: Reply to Davidson', *Critical Review* 7: 381–397.

—— (1995) 'Chances and Choices: Some Notes on Probability and Belief in Economic Theory', *The Monist* 78: 330–351.

—— (1996) 'Assessing Causal Explanations', unpublished, Cambridge University.

—— (1998) 'Assessing Causal Economic Explanations', *Oxford Economic Papers* 50: 151–172.

Smith, V. (1991) 'Theory, Experiment and Economics', in V. Smith, *Papers in Experimental Economics*, Cambridge: Cambridge University Press: 783–801. Reprinted from the *Journal of Economic Perspectives* 3, Winter, 1989.

—— (1994) 'Economics in the Laboratory', *Journal of Economic Perspectives* 8: 113–131.

5

METAPHOR AND CRITICAL
REALISM

Paul Lewis[1]

Introduction

Critical realism asserts that the world investigated by science consists of objects that are structured and intransitive: *structured* in the sense that they are irreducible to the events of experience; and *intransitive* in the sense that they exist and act independently of their identification. That is, the world is constituted not only by events given directly in experience, but also by the unobserved and perhaps even unobservable entities, structures, mechanisms, and so on, which, existing and acting independently of scientists' knowledge of them, govern observable events and states of affairs. Critical realism thus stands in stark contrast to positivism and idealism (including postmodernism), which restrict the objects of scientific knowledge to, respectively, directly experienced events (and their putative constant conjunctions), and the linguistic and conceptual resources of the scientific community.

The aim of science, according to a critical realism, is the identification of the mechanisms, structures, powers, and so on, that produce the phenomena of experience. However, given that the critical realist ontology entails that such objects are not simply given in experience, the question arises of how knowledge of them is possible. It is hardly comprehensible that such knowledge could be created out of nothing. Rather, knowledge comes about through the transformation of pre-existing knowledge-like material.

Advocates of critical realism frequently refer to the important role that the 'logic of analogy and metaphor' plays in this knowledge-production process (Bhaskar 1989: 12; Lawson 1997: 212). However, there has been a failure to develop from a critical realist perspective a detailed, systematic account of metaphor's role in scientific theorising. This chapter aims to remedy the omission. The chapter fills the gap in the literature on critical realism, by first outlining a theory of metaphor, the interanimation approach, and then employing the theory to bring out both the fundamental role that metaphor plays in science, construed according to critical realism, and the fact that it is only from something akin to a critical realist perspective that the true importance of metaphor can be demonstrated.

Reference and critical realism

An understanding of the importance of metaphor for the development of scientific explanations requires an account of the way that our theoretical terms, in the transitive domain, allow us to get to grips with the world, existing independently of the scientist in the intransitive domain. This is the issue of reference, a discussion of which is a necessary preliminary to an account of the role of metaphor in reality depiction. The treatment in this paper follows that of Lyons (1977), Harré (1986), and Bhaskar (1991).

'Referring' is a human practice through which, by any means available, one person attempts to draw the attention of another person to something in their common public space. Reference is effected by a speaker making an utterance in a particular context, not something made by individual vocabulary terms (lexemes) *per se*. Individual terms are said to have a 'sense' and a 'denotation'. The 'sense' of a lexeme is its dictionary definition (which, as we shall see, is potentially revisable, rather than some set of necessary properties of that which the lexeme denotes). By 'denotation' is meant the relation between the lexeme and the things (if any) – entities, states of affairs, and so on – which it designates in the world. So the lexeme 'amphibian' denotes the class of amphibians.

'Meaning' will also be regarded as an utterance-dependent concept, so that we may speak properly of the meaning of an utterance but not of an individual lexeme. In summary, then, referring utterances have meaning and make a reference.

Bhaskar (1991) distinguishes between *conversational referring* (*c ref*) and *practical referring* (*p ref*). A referring expression, in the sense of c ref, is a denoting term which a person has used in order to pick out a hypothetical entity, mechanism, etc., for the attention of the relevant linguistic community. Achieving reference in the sense of p ref, and thus fixing, for the moment, the denotation of a term, involves the use of a material practice (experimental manipulation, perception, measurement, for example), guided by a (revisable) description (c ref), in order to establish a physical relationship with some entity, mechanism, or similar.

On a critical realist interpretation, science involves both c ref and p ref. Typically, what happens is that in attempting to explain some phenomenon, scientists come up with a theory that advances existential hypotheses about the entities, mechanisms, and so on, as yet unobserved, that are the putative referents of the theory. The scientists then embark upon an investigation, guided by the relevant theory, to determine whether the putative referents of the theory actually exist. The scientists' attention is drawn to the possible existence of the referents by theory, a set of cognitive practices. This is c ref. The hunt for the putative referents consists in a set of material practices, whereby the scientists attempt to intervene in the world in order to establish (corrigibly, of course, according to the causal criterion for existence)[2] the existence of the theory's putative referents. This is p ref. Concepts are prior to the discovery of existents; c ref is prior to p ref. The appearance of a theoretical term which seems to denote something extra-observational (given current technology) is taken as grounds for a search of the real world for an entity which could serve as the term's referent. Securing reference then requires the material practice of locating a specimen that meets certain requirements prescribed by the relevant theory (Hacking 1983; Harré 1986).

Reference may be achieved even though the description offered (c ref) does not fit the referent. In referring, scientists provide a description (c ref) which enables their audience to pick out some hypothetical entity and which is sufficiently accurate to guide them when they physically intervene in the material world (p ref) in order to establish whether or not – judged according to the standards of the relevant community – the putative referent of the theory actually exists. It need not matter that the theoretical description of the referent turns out to be factually inaccurate. So long as the scientists possess the relevant linguistic competence to point the entity out to their audience, and so long as the description is sufficiently accurate to permit the physical manipulation of the referent required in order to satisfy the standards imposed by the relevant linguistic community for the causal criterion for existence, then the existence of the referent can be (fallibly) established and reference to it obtained.

Critical realism's approach to reference, with its dual emphasis both upon empirical, material practices and upon the intersubjectively agreed standards according to which the scientific community judges existential and referential claims, is usefully encapsulated by Boyd's (1993) proposal that reference be understood in terms of the notion of 'epistemic access'. Epistemic access is a form of socially coordinated epistemic success, where the referential link between a term (c ref) and its referent is sustained by knowledge of a variety of material, causal connections (that is, p ref) between users of the term and examples of its referent, connections that are taken by the relevant community to be epistemically relevant indications of the existence of that referent. Boyd's definition is as follows:

> Roughly, a general term, T, affords epistemic access to a kind (species, magnitude, and so on), k, to the extent that the sorts of considerations which are (in the relevant historical context) rationally taken as evidence for statements involving T are, typically, indicative in an appropriate way of features of k.
>
> (Boyd 1993: 507)

For Boyd, reference is constituted by just this sort of epistemic access: 'it is correct to talk of a referent of a general term precisely in those cases in which the term affords substantial epistemic access to a single kind or, at any rate, to a family of closely related ones' (ibid.: 507).

Critical realism suggests that it is impossible to understand scientists as achieving non-accidental success without understanding them to be learning about (typically unobservable) causal powers and mechanisms which are transfactually active in the intransitive domain. It follows that, on a critical realist account, the sort of epistemic success that is characteristic of reference is possible only in cases where scientists' theoretical terms afford epistemic access to kinds which correspond to important causal features of the world. The objective of science is the task of ' "cutting the world at its joints' – the business of describing and classifying natural phenomena in ways which in fact correspond to underlying causal powers or mechanisms" ' (Boyd 1993: 511). Scientists' language and conceptual structures must be accommodated to the causal structure of the world if knowledge is to be possible. In particular, linguistically mediated epistemic access is possible only if language is accommodated to the world.

A corollary of the critical realist approach is that a distinction may be drawn between the task of establishing that *something* exists and the open-ended possibility of further investigation of *what it is* that exists. As Boyd (1993) has argued, referential continuity may be maintained throughout the process of accommodation. That is to say, a referent can persist as the focus of empirical research in the face of significant changes in the corpus of beliefs that the scientific community holds to be true of that referent. While reference to a referent is always secured under a description, once secured, reference can be sustained in the face of radical reconceptualisations. The display of an entity's causal powers upon which the causal criterion for existence hinges depends upon material practices for which only a weak notion like 'more or less adequate description' is required. Critical realism, then, is epistemically modest; it does not claim to achieve incorrigible existential claims, let alone infallibly true descriptions of the entities whose existence the causal theory of knowledge (fallibly) supports. Terms are seen to be representing reality without being representationally privileged.

Theory introduces terms with fixed senses. So, for example, the term 'gene' was introduced with the sense of 'the mechanism responsible for the transfer of acquired characteristics'. However, while the sense of the term (c ref) guides practical investigations (p ref), it does not determine what it is, in practice, that the term is used to refer to. As investigations proceed and the theory develops, the original sense of the term may be altered (for example, by replacing 'acquired' with 'inherited'), or it may even be decided that a term fails to refer (e.g., 'phlogiston'). The sense of terms is significant, not in tying one to an immediate, unyielding, and exhaustive description of the referent, but rather in providing epistemic access to a referent, which it is then the task of science to refine.

This perspective reveals that scientific investigation consists in the intersection of a cluster of material and cognitive practices. Science appears to be characterised by an accommodation between the fixed (in a given historical context) senses and denotations of terms, and the more flexible referential uses made of terms in investigative procedures. An examination of scientific practice suggests that it is accurate neither to say that 'Sense determines reference', nor to insist that 'Reference determines sense'. There is a dynamic, dialectic interaction between these two aspects of language: sense determines the possibility of reference, that is to say it directs a programme of search; reference, when achieved, effects a refinement of sense (Harré 1986; Boyd 1993).

However, granted that scientists' investigations are guided by the sense of theoretical terms, there remains the question of how such terms are to be introduced in the first place. According to critical realism, science entails attempts to describe hypothetical entities, relations, and mechanisms, some of which are as yet unobserved or even unobservable, the existence of which would explain the phenomena under investigation. New and potentially referring terms cannot simply be invented out of thin air; such newly coined terms, lacking any sense whatsoever, would scarcely be explanatory. It is therefore necessary to explain how the theoretical terms used in existential hypotheses to describe the putative referents of scientific theories can be introduced into a language so that they are both *intelligible* – that is, meaningful to a competent user of the language without recourse to further experience (novel observations, say) – and yet have novel meaning. The first requirement necessitates that the new terms be drawn from the body of terminology common to the language community, implying that the second requirement – novelty – be generated by a process internal to the language (Martin-Soskice and Harré 1982).

Furthermore, in the absence of a true description of the world 'as it really is', scientific language cannot simply be tied up to the true causal structure of the world through explicit and conventional definitions. Non-definitional procedures for reference-fixing are essential to the task of accommodating the language and concepts of science to the causal features of the world. Theoretical terms must be located within a semantic network in order to give them a sense and so allow intelligible, ordered investigation to proceed. However, it is important that the senses of terms are not rigidly defined if the theory is to be flexible enough to permit reference to entities whose essential properties are as yet unknown, and thus to facilitate the accommodation of linguistic categories to as yet only partially understood features of the world.

The interanimation theory of metaphor

We have seen that scientists require a way of introducing an intelligible theoretical vocabulary in order to conceptualise the hypothetical unobservable entities, mechanisms, and so on, governing the observable behaviour of their subject matter. The key to seeing how this takes place is an understanding of *generative* metaphor (Schön 1963, [1979] 1993). A generative metaphor is not merely an ornate expression of similarities and analogies its author was already aware of, but is the source of new perceptions of similarity and analogy, picking out similarities and analogies that were unknown until the metaphor pointed them out and thereby brought them to the author's attention. As we shall see, although the hypothetical unobservables postulated by scientists cannot be directly attended to and described, the use of generative metaphor allows scientists to conceptualise them in terms of (their knowledge of) other, more familiar entities, mechanisms, and so on. Generative metaphor enables the scientist tentatively to attribute, independent of any prior understanding of the unobservables, relations of similarity and analogy between those inadequately understood entities, mechanisms, etc., and the subject matter of some better-understood domain of scientific inquiry, so that knowledge about the latter can be used to structure an understanding of the former.[3]

Perhaps the most convincing explanation of generative metaphor is

Janet Martin-Soskice's (1985) interanimation theory, according to which metaphor is most appropriately characterised as *the figure of speech that allows us to speak about one thing in terms which are suggestive of another*.[4] Metaphor is a linguistic phenomenon; it is a form of language use (not necessarily oral) in which one thing (any object or state of affairs) is 'spoken' about in terms which a competent user of the language would conventionally associate with something else. The thinking underlying this definition will become clearer as we outline the theory.

Martin-Soskice's approach is a modified version of the work of I. A. Richards (1936). Richards distinguishes between the 'tenor' of a metaphor, its underlying subject, and the 'vehicle', the terms in which that subject is presented. Consider the following example: 'The brain is a computer'. The tenor is the working of the human brain, and the vehicle is the term 'computer'. Each term in the metaphor brings with it its own system of 'associated commonplaces', that is, a set of (other) words and thoughts that the original term evokes in the minds of members of the relevant speech community.

For Richards, the cognitive power of metaphor derives from what he calls the *interanimation* of words, which makes metaphor not just a matter of verbal displacement, of the substitution of one word for another, but 'a borrowing between and intercourse of *thoughts*, a transaction between contexts' (Richards 1936: 94). According to Richards:

> [W]hen we use a metaphor we have two thoughts of different things active together and supported by a single word or phrase, whose meaning is a result of their interaction . . . [W]e arrive at [the meaning] only through the interpretive possibilities of the whole utterance.
>
> (Richards 1936: 93, 55)

The distinctive cognitive content of the metaphor arises through the *interaction* of the two systems of associated commonplaces. Because metaphor works through the interaction of two different contexts – the two systems of associated commonplaces – it goes beyond mere comparison and is irreducible to any literal paraphrase. Metaphor has *emergent* cognitive content, portraying its underlying subject in a unique and novel way. For example, the word 'computer' occupies a different semantic field from the word 'brain', with a different set of associations conventionally predicated of it, so that the use of the term 'computer' allows the author to say something about brain activity that he would be unable to express simply by using the word 'thought' (Martin-Soskice and Harré 1982; Kittay 1987). For Richards, the full meaning of the metaphor results from the union of the tenor and vehicle, and cannot be ascribed to one of them alone: '[T]he vehicle is not normally a mere embellishment of a tenor which is otherwise unchanged by it but that vehicle and that tenor in co-operation give a meaning of more varied powers than can be ascribed to either' (Richards 1936: 108).

It is important to emphasise the point that the networks of associations are generated by particular *terms* in the metaphor, rather than by distinct subjects. This is the basis for Richards' intuition that a metaphor has just one underlying subject, and therefore that metaphor works not through the interaction of two distinct subjects, but through the interaction of *words*, the intercourse of *thoughts*. The intercourse of thoughts or interanimation of words which constitutes the working of the metaphor is not a comparison of two subjects. The metaphor has only one underlying subject, the working of the brain. The author of the metaphor is not speaking of both the brain and a computer. Rather, he is speaking about just one subject, the brain, in terms appropriate to the description of a computer.

The rationale for the definition of metaphor advanced earlier in the chapter is now apparent. Recall that metaphor was characterised as *the figure of speech that allows us to speak of one thing in terms which are suggestive of another*. In the example given above, the author of the metaphor is speaking of the brain in terms that are suggestive of a computer. We may use our analysis of this example in order to expand upon the definition, to say that metaphor is a linguistic phenomenon – an interanimation of terms – whose locus lies at the level of the complete utterance (a phrase, sentence or perhaps longer expression), set in a surrounding context. Metaphor is a 'form of language use with a unity of subject-matter and which yet draws upon two (or more) sets of associations' (Martin-Soskice 1985: 49) in order to say something which we can express in no other way, and it is in this capacity to express something which can be said in no other way that metaphor's unique cognitive role resides.

The unconventional use of terms encourages us to view the metaphor's tenor from a new perspective, suggesting new ways of thinking about the underlying subject. The vehicle organises our thoughts about the tenor in a new way, selecting and emphasising features of the subject matter different from those highlighted by conventional language, and even pointing out properties of the underlying subject that had gone unnoticed until the metaphor drew attention to them. The irreplaceable cognitive content of the metaphor arises because it does not merely express a previously describable state of affairs, but because it provides a description of the brain that is accessible only through the metaphor. The metaphor has identified and described the working of the brain in a unique and novel way; the metaphor is not an embellishment of what one already knows, but a vehicle for a new insight made available by the interanimation of terms.

In order to see more clearly how this occurs, it is necessary to consider the relationship between metaphor and scientific models.

Metaphors and models

Scientific thinking is characterised by its use of models (Hesse 1966). A scientific theory is an attempt to answer a question of the form, 'Why is the pattern of phenomena the way it is?' A theory answers this question by supplying an account of the constitution and behaviour of those things whose interactions with each other are responsible for the manifested patterns of behaviour. A theory is just a description of the nature and workings of a model.

An object or state of affairs is a *model* when it is viewed in terms of its resemblance, real or hypothetical, to some other object or state of affairs. Following Harré (1970: 38), a model will be described in terms of two features: its *subject*, what it is that the model represents; and its *source*, whatever it is that the model is based on. The relationship between the model source and the model subject can be used as a basis for dividing models into two broad categories: models which have the same subject and source are *homeomorphic* (for example, a scale model of an airplane); models in which the subject and source differ are *paramorphic* (for instance, the use of billiard balls to provide a model for the behaviour of gases).

Paramorphic models are fundamental to science, as conceived by critical realism. Science mostly uses paramorphic models, for the task of theory construction is generally to explain better what we do not yet fully understand, rather than modelling entities or states of affairs whose nature is clear to us. Paramorphic models draw on our under-standing of their source to suggest *existential* hypotheses about putative entities, relations, and causal mechanisms which might account for the behaviour of the subject; that is, they offer as candi-dates for existence putative entities, relations, and mechanisms which are as yet *unobserved*, challenging scientists to engage in the laborious practice of science to determine whether the hypothesised entities exist or not. In doing so, the paramorphic models provide the causal framework, as well as the theoretical terms and hypothetical entities, necessary for explanation.

Metaphor plays a fundamental role in the development of such paramorphic models.[5] Recall that metaphor is the figure of speech that allows us to speak about one thing in terms which are suggestive of another. Metaphor is a linguistic phenomenon. Recall also that an object or state of affairs is a model when it is viewed in terms of its resemblance, real or hypothetical, to some other object or state of affairs. The intimate relation between models and metaphors resides in the fact that the construal of a metaphor is characterised by its reliance on an underlying model; a model is what we have when we speak on the basis of a metaphor, for the metaphor suggests that its audience think of its subject in terms (that are suggestive) of something else (Martin-Soskice 1985: 55). That is, the metaphor *suggests* a model in terms of which the scientist can attempt to explain his subject matter. Put another way, when we talk on the basis of a model, we are talking metaphorically, for we are speaking of the subject of the model in terms (which are suggestive) of the model's source.

Metaphor, then, provides a model in terms of which the scientist can develop an understanding of the subject of his or her investigations. The important thing about metaphor in the context of scientific theorising – the task of which, according to critical realism, is the identification of the unknown entities and mechanisms responsible for observed behaviour – is that it does not prompt the routine renaming of otherwise identifiable aspects of its subject, but instead instigates and structures scientists' investigations by suggesting new interpretive categories and hypothesising new entities, mechanisms, etc. Metaphor is *prior* to analogy, describing similarities and analogies that were unknown before their existence was pointed out by the metaphor. Metaphor uses the known to express the unknown, in the case of science by providing a model (drawn from a comparatively well-understood domain of inquiry) in terms of which scientists can structure their investigations into the unknown mechanisms, etc., lying behind the observable behaviour of their subject matter. In using the metaphor, scientists do not merely rename otherwise identifiable features of the subject. On the contrary, the important point about scientists' use of a metaphor to suggest a model is that, because the model's subject consists of mechanisms, structures, and so on, that are as yet unknown, there is no way in which a literal description of the subject can be given in order to effect a comparison with the source. What happens instead is that the metaphor hints at potential similarities and analogies between the source and subject, thereby suggesting that scientists advance the entities, mechanisms and structures governing the behaviour of the source as putative analogues for the unknown entities, mechanisms, and structures underlying the behaviour of the subject. In this way, the metaphor generates existential hypotheses about putative entities, mechanisms, structures, and so on, which, if they were to exist, would explain the observable behaviour of the subject. Metaphor thereby facilitates scientists' attempts to explain their poorly understood subject matter. The task of scientific practice is then to investigate these existential hypotheses further, in order to refine them and to evaluate (corrigibly, of course) their explanatory power.

For example, the metaphor that scientists use when they talk of 'electric current' cannot be unpacked into an exhaustive list of literal comparisons of the form, 'In this and that respect but not these and those, electricity is like a current'. The truth is that scientists have no way of describing and understanding electricity other than as a current (Harré 1986). There is no literal vocabulary in which a description of electricity can be given in order to effect a comparison with a fluid. As Schön has written of geneticists:

> [W]e sometimes use metaphors as devices for explaining theory when they were actually essential to the formation of the theory. In discussing a theory of genes, the lecturer may say, 'Think of it, if you will, as a kind of code', when in fact he has no other way of thinking of it.
>
> (Schön 1963: 105)

Similarly, the 'fluid' metaphor is not just a heuristic which the scientist can dispense with once her theory of electricity is fully developed; the metaphor constitutes the substance of the theory, providing the only terms in which the scientific community can describe and explain electricity.[6]

We may differentiate theory-constitutive metaphors such as 'The brain is a computer' from what will be called 'metaphorically constituted theory terms'. The latter arise when, having derived a model of the human brain by means of a theory-constitutive metaphor ('The brain is a computer'), we go on to speak on the basis of such a model, attempting to explain the operation of the brain in terms of 'feedback', neural 'programming', and so on. In doing so, we are speaking metaphorically on the basis of the computer model, for the intelligibility of these terms depends upon their being related to the computer model of the brain. The computer metaphor initiates investigation into brain activity on the basis of an informed guess that there are important similarities or analogies between the computer and the brain. The metaphor is said to be open-ended because the research programme it initiates is incomplete; we do not know in what respects, if any, human cognition resembles machine computation. What metaphorical uses of computer terminology permit is that we introduce at a relatively early stage in the inquiry theoretical terms to refer to various plausibly postulated computer-like aspects of human cognition – for example, the suggestion that there exist processes such as 'programming' and 'feedback' in the brain that are analogous to the processes of programming and feedback in computers – which then become the objects of further investigation.[7] These metaphorically constituted theory terms provide an explanatory framework through which the scientist can understand his or her subject matter. Scientists who speak of 'neural programming', 'feedback', and the like rely upon the sense that these terms have in discussing the computer; but at the same time the speaker and the context of utterance make clear that they are speaking not of the computer but of the brain. The term 'neural programming' is given semantic placement in terms of the computer model on which it depends. While the construal of the term depends on the semantic network generated by the underlying computer model, the fact that in the context of the utterance of the metaphor, it is predicated not of a computer but of the human brain, indicates its extension to be different.

We can now see why, according to critical realism, metaphor plays such a crucial role in science. The interanimation theory shows how *generative* metaphor, with its capacity to say what cannot be said in any other way – its capacity to create a new vision and thereby to disclose for the first time similarities between objects hitherto regarded as dissimilar – might facilitate the creation of new meaning, independent of prior knowledge of the subject matter, thereby allowing scientists to postulate and describe the unobservable. Through metaphor, scientists' conceptual grasp of subject matter is enhanced by means of the displacement of a term from a well-established context of use in order to structure a different, less well-understood domain of inquiry (Schön 1963). A term used metaphorically is one familiar through its use in its established context, and which is used in a fresh context to express a belief for which there is no existing vocabulary. In this way, metaphor facilitates the creation of a new vocabulary – for the description of hypothetical unobservables – within the existing structure of language, thereby securing the intelligibility of the term in its new context of use.

In short, as the source both of a model and of an intelligible vocabulary in terms of which the theory based on that model can be expounded, metaphor supplies scientists with a set of conceptual and linguistic tools with which to order their thinking about their subject matter.

Metaphor and reference

We are now in a position to understand the role played by metaphor as a non-definitional mode of reference-fixing in scientists' attempts to depict reality. The terminology developed in the earlier section on reference may now be employed to refine our exposition of the interanimation theory of metaphor. Metaphorical reference is not reducible to the sense and denotation of the individual terms which compose the metaphor; rather, the speaker of a metaphor picks out a referent by means of the whole metaphorical utterance, taken in its context.

And it is because senses are important in making reference but not fully definitive of it that metaphor is so useful in the realist project of reality depiction. The way that the reference of the metaphorically constituted theory terms is secured has an essential dynamic and dialectic aspect. The senses of terms, by guiding the epistemic access that characterises reference, make reference possible, but do not determine it; it is not words that refer, but speakers using words in particular contexts who refer. Scientists who speak of 'neural programming', 'feedback', and so on rely upon the sense that these terms have when they are predicated of computers to render them intelligible, while simultaneously the context of utterance makes it abundantly clear that the scientists are speaking not of the computer but of the brain. Reference, once secured, effects a refinement of sense, for example, the discovery that preprogramming is not a feature of brain activity. The resultant changes in language use – for example, the fact preprogramming is not a predicate of 'brain activity' – reflect the dialectical process of the accommodation of language use to the causal structure of the world, and are characteristic of epistemic success, and hence of epistemic access and referential continuity.

Moreover, a corollary of the fact that epistemic access, and so reference, can be sustained in the face of significant changes in the beliefs that the scientific community holds to be true of the referent is that the use of metaphor can serve as a non-definitional mode of reference-fixing in circumstances where the scientists do not yet possess a definitive characterisation of the referents of the theory. We have seen that a referring expression may be factually inaccurate and yet still allow the audience to pick out its referent, so that reference may be obtained before the referent is fully comprehended. The metaphorically constituted theory terms generated by a metaphor may be seen as (partially) denoting (Field 1973, 1974), prior to definitive knowledge, putatively real entities. So, for example, understood in the context of computers, the term 'programming' leaves open the question of whether a machine is preprogrammed. Suppose now that the metaphorically constituted theory term 'neural programming' is used by scientists in an attempt to gain referential access to mechanisms operating in the human brain, referring to a hypothesised mechanism analogous to computer programming operating in the brain. Imagine that, as a result of the investigations of brain activity facilitated by such epistemic access, the scientists conclude that the brain is not preprogrammed. The sense of the term 'programming', understood in the context of brain activity, which facilitated scientists' attempts to secure reference to a hypothesised aspect of the working of the brain, has now been refined to rule out the possibility that the brain is preprogrammed. The scientific community's understanding of the referent, the brain, has been enhanced by the knowledge that cognitive processes are not preprogrammed.

It is just such developments as these that are marks of referential success. The partially denoting term 'neural programming' afforded scientists sufficient epistemic access to brain activity to facilitate the discovery of new and interesting features of the world, in this case the fact that the brain is not preprogrammed. The sort of linguistically mediated epistemic success which this example of knowledge-gathering exemplifies is the very core of epistemic access and so of reference. Metaphor can thus be seen to facilitate the scientific community's efforts at what Boyd has called the

> *accommodation of language to the causal structure of the world . . .* the task of introducing terminology, and modifying usage of existing terminology, so that linguistic categories are available which describe the causally and explanatorily significant features of the world. Roughly speaking, this is the task of arranging our language so that our linguistic categories 'cut the world at its joints'.
>
> (Boyd 1993: 483)

The very vagueness for which positivists condemn metaphor is a crucial ingredient in metaphor's contribution to scientific investigation. For it is the absence of strict stipulatory definitions of the metaphorically constituted theory terms that ensures that reference can be separated from unrevisable description so that, first, at the level of the use of general terms in science, one can metaphorically use terms to refer to little-understood features of the natural world without laying claims to unrevisable knowledge of them and, second and relatedly, the senses of terms can be revised so that linguistic usage is accommodated to newly discovered features of the world.

This echoes critical realism's insistence that all scientific models are open to revision and replacement if an alternative model with superior explanatory power is developed. An emphasis on the way that metaphor plays an indispensable cognitive role in science does not mean that the model derived from any given metaphor is privileged in any absolute sense. On the contrary, as we have just seen, a central aspect of metaphor's contribution to scientific theorising resides in the way that metaphorically based theory terms allow scientists both to gain access to poorly understood features of the world and to revise their terminology as their acquaintance with the world develops. So the indispensability of metaphor for science lies not just in the fact, acknowledged by idealists, that all scientific theories are based upon some metaphor, but also in the way in which theory-constitutive metaphors provide scientists with a non-definitional mode of refer-ence-fixing that enables them to accommodate their language to newly discovered features of the world. Idealism conflates the real world with the conceptual and linguistic resources in terms of which scientists conceive of it. Idealism therefore does not allow that scien-tists can gain even fallible, corrigible knowledge of the deep, structured ontology of the mind-independent world, and so leaves no place for the feedback from practical experimental activity – that is, from scientists' attempts at material intervention in the world – which is the stimulus for the refinement of scientific terminology. Idealism's failure to admit of the need to refine theoretical terminology in response to experimental evidence eliminates the need for metaphor's capacity to provide a non-definitional, and so revisable, mode of refer-ence-fixing, rendering idealism incapable of providing a comprehensive account of the vital part that metaphor plays in the development of scientific theories.

Conclusion

The major theme of this chapter has been that an understanding of how, according to critical realism, it is possible for scientists to gain access to the unknown, structured and intransitive objects of the mind-independent world requires a grasp of the part that metaphor plays in scientific theorising. Scientific metaphors are not merely linguistic ornaments that can be discarded in favour of literal descrip-tion. On the contrary, metaphors are essential to the conception, development, and maintenance of scientific theories in a variety of ways: they provide the linguistic context in which the models that constitute the basis for scientific explanation are suggested and described; they supply new terms for the theoretical vocabulary, espe-cially where there is a gap in the lexicon; and they direct scientists towards new avenues of inquiry, in particular by suggesting new hypothetical entities and mechanisms. Through metaphor scientists draw upon antecedently existing cognitive resources to provide both the model and the vocabulary in terms of which the unknown mechanisms, etc., governing observable behaviour can be conceived and so investigated. Metaphor thereby performs an indispensable cognitive role in scientific theorising.

Furthermore, a corollary of the fact that, on a critical realist account, metaphor plays an integral part in science is the poverty of the positivist and idealist approaches to metaphor, for it is only from the critical realist perspective that the full significance of the contribution that metaphor makes to scientific thought can be established. If it is the case that, as Bhaskar (1975) and Harré (1986) have argued, realism constitutes the most convincing explanation of the nature of scientific activity, and given that according to critical realism the crux of metaphor's role in science lies in the part it plays in the development of theories which facilitate access to the structures and mechanisms of an ontologically deep, structured mind-independent reality – that is, the very activity the possibility of which is denied by positivism and idealism – then it follows that the latter two philosophies yield an impoverished account which fails to bring out the true nature of metaphor's indispensability in scientific theorising.

So, in analysing the nature of metaphor's contribution to the development of scientific theories, the chapter has not merely filled a gap in the literature on critical realism. In addition, by clarifying the role of metaphor in scientific theorising – in particular, the importance of generative metaphor, and metaphor's function as a non-definitional mode of reference-fixing – the approach advanced provides the basis for a more focused critical realist critique of the positivist and idealist theories of metaphor and of the place of metaphor in science. A consideration of these issues suggests that it is only from a critical realist perspective that a full appreciation of metaphor's indispensability for scientific theorising can be had.

Notes

1 I would like to thank Jochen Runde, Tony Lawson, Steve Fleetwood, a number of anonymous referees, and participants in the Cambridge Workshop on Realism and Economics, for comments on earlier versions of this chapter. The usual disclaimer applies. Financial support from the ESRC (award R00429334205) is gratefully acknowledged.
2 Harré and Madden (1975).
3 According to a positivist interpretation of science, the problem of how scientists are in practice able to introduce intelligible theoretical terminology for the description of the unknown mechanisms etc. of a deep structured ontology does not even arise. It is unsurprising, therefore, that the theories of metaphor most closely associated with positivism, namely

the substitution and comparison theories, cannot explain how, on a realist account of science, *generative* metaphor plays a crucial part in the way scientists solve such a problem. According to the substitution and comparison theories, a metaphor such as 'The brain is a computer' is no more than a condensed or elliptic simile which may be replaced without remainder by a set of literal statements of the form, 'The brain is like a computer in the following respects . . . ,' where follows an exhaustive list of comparable characteristics. The similarities and analogies that form the basis for the comparison derive from literal descriptions given prior to and conceptually independent of the use of figurative language. The metaphor is not generative; it plays no part in the recognition of the similarities and analogies. All that the author of the metaphor does is compare two entities whose attributes she was already aware of before she coined the metaphorical phrase.

The implication of the substitution and comparison theories that metaphor is reducible without cognitive loss to a set of literal statements corresponds to positivism's insistence that reality can be described through the medium of a language that is accurate and unambiguous (in short, literal), so that the most significant cognitive role attributed to metaphor is that of a dispensable heuristic. However, if it is the case that, as Bhaskar (1975) has argued, critical realism provides the most explanatory adequate characterisation of science, then scientists make existential hypotheses about features of the world that are as yet unobservable, and in doing so they are not redescribing the properties of something they are already well acquainted with but attempting to describe something that is as yet unknown. A metaphor that does no more than re-express in a fresh garb a prior literal understanding is unable to help scientists in this task; if metaphor is confined to the realm of comparison, then, because comparison is rooted in the presentation of similarities of which the metaphor's author is already aware, the content of scientific assertions involving metaphor will be confined to subject matter that is already familiar and well understood. If metaphor is to be capable of fulfilling the role in science that, on a critical realist account, is required of it, it must suggest new perceptions of similarity and analogy in order to help scientists begin to understand their poorly understood subject matter. The substitution and comparison theories are unable to show how metaphor can do this. As we shall see, a theory of generative metaphor can.

4 The classic account of metaphorical creativity is Black (1962, [1979] 1993). Martin-Soskice's highly effective critique centres on the highly problematic notion of 'filtering' that forms the core of Black's interaction theory of metaphor.

5 A homeomorphic model need not be related to a metaphor, because such models need not be linguistic at all – one only has to think of a scale replica model car to confirm this. The term 'model' will hereafter be understood to refer to paramorphic models only.

6 In using the known to express the unknown, metaphor is sometimes described as serving a catachretical role in scientific investigation. *Catachresis* is the use of a term to fill a gap in the vocabulary. When a metaphor suggests a model which hypothesises the existence of previously unknown, and so hitherto unnamed, entities, relations, and mechanisms, it thereby introduces theoretical terminology where none

previously existed. This is Aristotle's 'naming that which has no name' and is a classic example of catachresis.

7 Metaphor's irreducibility to a literal equivalent is particularly important in its role as the source of a model and of metaphorically constituted theory terms. The metaphor that scientists use when they say that, 'The brain is a computer' cannot be unpacked into an exhaustive list of literal comparisons of the form, 'In this and that respect but not these and those, the brain is like a computer'. The 'conceptual open-endedness' or 'extensibility' of metaphor – the way that it yields a stream of theoretical terms and suggests potential areas of similarity and analogy between subject and source – is instrumental in hinting at the direction in which the scientist's thought should move next, how she should 'go on' in investigating her subject matter (Martin-Soskice 1985). Metaphor is indispensable for scientific explanation because it is only through metaphor that such avenues for further exploration come to our attention.

Bibliography

Bhaskar, R. (1975) *A Realist Theory of Science*, Leeds: Leeds Books.

—— (1989) *The Possibility of Naturalism*, 2nd edition (1st edition 1979), London: Harvester Wheatsheaf.

—— (1991) *Philosophy and the Idea of Freedom*, Oxford: Basil Blackwell.

Black, M. (1962) 'Metaphor', in M. Black (ed.) *Models and Metaphors*, Ithaca, NY: Cornell University Press.

—— ([1979] 1993) 'More about Metaphor', in A. Ortony (ed.) *Metaphor and Thought*, 2nd edition, Cambridge: Cambridge University Press.

Boyd, R. (1993) 'Metaphor and Theory Change: What is "Metaphor" a Metaphor For?', in A. Ortony (ed.) *Metaphor and Thought*, 2nd edition, Cambridge: Cambridge University Press.

Field, H. (1973) 'Theory Change and the Indeterminacy of Reference', *Journal of Philosophy* 70: 462–481.

—— (1974) 'Quine and the Correspondence Theory', *Philosophical Review* 83: 200–228.

Hacking, I. (1983) *Representing and Intervening*, Cambridge: Cambridge University Press.

Harré, H. R. (1970) *The Principles of Scientific Thinking*, London: Macmillan.

—— (1986) *Varieties of Realism*, Oxford: Basil Blackwell.

Harré, H. R. and Madden, E. H. (1975) *Causal Powers*, Oxford: Basil Blackwell.

Hesse, M. B. (1966) *Models and Analogies in Science*, Notre Dame: University of Notre Dame Press.

Kittay, E. F. (1987) *Metaphor: Its Cognitive Force and Linguistic Structure*, Oxford: Clarendon Press.

Lawson, T. (1997) *Economics and Reality*, London: Routledge.

Lyons, J. (1977) *Semantics: I*, Cambridge: Cambridge University Press.

Martin-Soskice, J. (1985) *Metaphor and Religious Language*, Oxford: Clarendon Press.

Martin-Soskice, J. and Harré, H. R. (1982) 'Metaphor in Science', in D. S. Miall (ed.) *Metaphor: Problems and Perspectives*, Brighton: Harvester.

Ortony, A. (ed.) (1993) *Metaphor and Thought*, 2nd edition (1st edition 1979), Cambridge: Cambridge University Press.

Richards, I. A. (1936) *The Philosophy of Rhetoric*, London: Oxford University Press.

Schön, D. A. (1963) *Displacement of Concepts*, London: Tavistock Publications.

—— ([1979] 1993) 'Generative Metaphor: A Perspective on Problem-Setting in Social Policy', in A. Ortony (ed.) *Metaphor and Thought*, 2nd edition, Cambridge: Cambridge University Press.

6

MONEY IS A SOCIAL RELATION

Geoffrey Ingham

There is no denying that views on money are as difficult to describe as are shifting clouds.

(Schumpeter 1994 [1954]: 289)[1]

Introduction

Money is a puzzle. The standard answer to the question of what is money derives from the late nineteenth-century functionalist account: money is what money does. Conventionally, it is a measure of value (or unit of account); a medium of exchange; a standard of deferred payment; and a store of value. However, there is, in fact, wide and at times quite vigorous disagreement as to what money does and which are the most important of the functions. Does the 'thing' have to perform all the functions in order to be money? Is 'credit' money? And so on. Further investigation reveals a quite surprising paradox: Money is one of the most important pieces of 'social technology' ever developed, but as an object of study in its own right it is neglected by the dominant or mainstream traditions not only in modern economics but also in sociology.

Surveying the economic literature on the nature and functions of money and looking at the more prominent recent disputes on the 'behaviour' of money, one is struck by the extent to which modern neoclassical economics remains dominated by the conceptual apparatus of the 'theoretical' school of economics that triumphed in the *Methodenstreit* (conflict over methods) around the turn of the century. At this juncture, historical and sociological perspectives on the 'economic' were expunged from the core of the discipline (see for example: Schumpeter 1994 [1954]; Machlup 1978; Swedberg 1987). Indeed, the most mathematically sophisticated and therefore most revered theories in neoclassical economics – broadly speaking, neo-Walrasian general equilibrium theories – have had great difficulty in

103

actually finding a place for money in their schemes. 'The most serious challenge that the existence of money poses to the theorist is this: the best model of the economy cannot find room for it' (Hahn 1982: 1). In these abstract models, money can, at best, only have the role of a pregiven *numeraire* – an accounting device in what is, essentially, a simple barter economy. A closely related approach in the broad neoclassical school has been to look on money as a rather special 'commodity', but one which, like all other commodities, must possess some utility for the rational maximising *individual*. (As we shall see, this basis for money has proved difficult to demonstrate with this methodological framework.) In general, in mainstream neoclassicism, money is, analytically, merely a 'veil' or a neutral 'lubricant' in a model of the economy, which is seen as comprising 'real' factors (Schumpeter 1994 [1954]: 227).

I shall argue that the difficulty in accounting for the existence of money and its role in actually existing economic systems is the result of the absence of anything resembling an adequate specification of its social structural conditions of existence. In 'critical realism's' terms, mainstream economics does not possess an adequate *ontological* theory of money (Lawson 1994). These comments apply mainly to neoclassical microeconomics. But modern macroeconomics fares little better, largely because it too proceeds from neoclassical rational choice assumptions, and, furthermore, conceptualises money simply as one of the statistically related aggregate economic 'variables'. (See Lawson's 'critical realism' perspective on economic methodology [Lawson 1995].) However, the initial partial break with economic 'classicism' in the first part of the century – most notably by Keynes – was, to some extent at least, an attempt to make sense of new, or more widespread forms of bank and state credit money in which, to some at any rate, the 'social' basis of money was blatantly obvious. Over the past few years, a distinctive 'post-Keynesian' macroeconomic school of monetary economics has been developed which, in opposition to neoclassicism, has taken up this aspect of Keynes's work and focuses on 'credit-money' (Wray 1990; Smithin 1994; Rogers 1989; Moore 1988). This work cannot be discussed in detail here; but, although it is undoubtedly an advance on orthodox thinking, post-Keynesian monetary theory is understandably embroiled in the problematics of academic economics in which the terms of discourse are partly dictated by the neoclassical and/or 'monetarist' conceptualisations it opposes. Hence, the preoccupation with 'endogeneity' and debates between 'horizontalists' and 'verticalists' conducted in terms of the strength of statistical relations between 'variables' (Cottrell 1994).[2]

Furthermore, there is a second aspect to the paradox in that

although money should be seen as having 'social' conditions of existence, sociology, with the notable exceptions of Weber and Simmel,
has contributed very little directly to the study of the actual social
production of money as a *system of social relations, sui generis*. This
contentious argument will be pursued in detail elsewhere; here we
may briefly note the basis for this judgement. In the division of intellectual labour between economics and sociology that developed in the first
part of the century money was placed under the jurisdiction of
economics (Swedberg 1987; Ingham 1996a). Moreover, partly as a consequence of this division, the major schools of sociology have tacitly
incorporated the orthodox conception of money from 'real' neoclassical
analysis. In Parsons' social theory, for example, money is taken to
symbolise underlying social relations; it is a generalised *medium* of social
interaction (Parsons 1937; 1951). (See the excellent discussions by
Ganssman [1988] and Dodd [1994].) Although Marx stressed the fundamental monetary structure of capitalism (M-C-M), he was primarily
concerned with showing that money was a 'mask' (or 'veil') over the
underlying 'real' social relations of the production of commodities.[3]
Institutions for the social production of money, such as banks, are not
seen as the essence of capitalism; rather, this is sought in the reality of the
capital–labour *relations of production* expressed in an alienated monetary
form. (To [mis]use Marx's terminology, I would suggest, rather, that
money should be seen as a 'force of production' which, as the post-
Keynesians correctly imply, has its own particular 'relations of
production'.)[4]

Obviously, money is socially produced in the sense that it does not
occur naturally, and it also mediates and symbolises social relations –
for example, capital–wage labour. However, I wish to go further and
argue that money itself is a social relation. By this I mean that 'money'
can only be sensibly seen as being *constituted* by social relations. I have
already hinted that this claim is most obviously sustained in the case
of credit-money as 'promises' to pay; but I shall argue that all forms of
money are social relations and consequently, for example, the conventional textbook distinction between 'money' and 'credit' is not merely
anachronistic, but is based on a conceptual confusion.

Money in orthodox 'real' economic analysis

Economic thought is marked by a long continuity of interrelated
disputes which involve surprisingly divergent conceptions of the
nature of money. The major differences have been between 'metallists'
and anti-metallists during the sixteenth and seventeenth centuries
(Schumpeter 1994 [1954]); the 'Currency' and 'Banking' schools and

105

more generally between 'materialists' and 'nominalists' in the first half of the nineteenth century; and the seesaw battle between 'monetarism' and various forms of Keynesian economics in the middle of the twentieth.

The two sides' differences with regard to the nature of money and how to 'manage' it are grounded in different conceptions of the scope and method of economics, which Schumpeter has referred to as 'real' and 'monetary' analysis. This was referred to earlier, but we now need to examine this distinction in a little more detail.

> Real analysis proceeds from the principle that all the essential phenomena of economic life are capable of being described in terms of goods and services, of decisions about them, and of relations between them. Money enters the picture only in the modest role of a technical device that has been adopted in order to facilitate transactions . . . so long as it functions normally, it does not affect the economic process, which behaves in the same way as it would in a barter economy: this is essentially what the concept of Neutral Money implies. Thus, money has been called a 'garb' or 'veil' of the things that really matter. . . . Not only can it be discarded whenever we are analyzing the fundamental features of the economic process but it must be discarded just as a veil must be drawn aside if we are to see the face behind it. Accordingly, money prices must give way to the exchange ratios between the commodities that are the really important thing 'behind' money prices . . . saving and investment must be interpreted to mean saving of some real factors of production . . . such as buildings, machines, raw materials; and, though 'in the form of money', it is these physical capital goods that are 'really' lent when an industrial borrower arranges for a loan.
>
> (Schumpeter 1994: 277)[5]

From the present standpoint two closely related features of this 'real' approach to money are most important. First, the almost exclusive concern is with money's *medium of exchange* function as a neutral 'lubricant' of exchanges between 'real' 'goods' or economic 'forces' or 'variables'. Money as a *measure of value/unit of account* is taken as given and *means of payment* is assumed to be covered by the medium of exchange function. Second, 'real' analysis is radically *a*historical and *a*social in the sense that particular forms of economic organisation are deemed to be epiphenomenal or merely 'contextual'; complex social structure – banks, productive enterprise, etc. – is reduced to purely abstract exchange relations between rational maximising agents.[6] For example, one of this century's most influential economists would have us believe that 'even the most advanced industrial economies, if we strip exchange down to its bare essentials and peel off the obscuring layer of money, we find trade between individuals and nations largely boils down to barter' (Samuelson 1973: 55. Quoted in Wray 1990: 3).[7]

The search for the 'micro-foundations' of money

'Real' monetary analysis derives from 'metallist' or 'commodity' theory, which argued that the function of the medium of exchange was dependent on its being a commodity with an exchange value independent of its form as currency. Thus, there could be an exchange ratio between the 'real' values of precious metals (or wheat or beans) in the form of money and other commodities. With the increasing use of 'worthless' token and credit-money in modern economies (i.e. non-commodity money), the basic logical structure of 'real' analysis was preserved in two ways. First, paper and base-metal could stand for and be convertible into a 'standard' of gold or silver. This formulation largely governed monetary policy to the early twentieth century and basically involved schemes which tried to make paper behave *as if* it were gold.

A second and more narrowly academic response in the wake of 'worthless' paper money argued that money was really no more than a 'token' or 'symbol' of 'real' goods. This line of reasoning found its most brilliant expression in Walras's system in which money is reduced to pure number – the *numeraire* – which enables the multilateral exchange of goods in instantaneously clearing markets in a world of virtual barter. As has frequently been noted, the presence of money makes no difference to the logical structure of such general equilibrium models. Abstract neo-Walrasian models are intentionally 'timeless' and as such do not imply or infer a history of monetary evolution. Money is not accounted for, rather it is simply introduced along with the 'auctioneer' in order to render the system operational.[8]

However, neoclassical economics in the English marginalist tradition did provide a rudimentary theory of money's 'origins'. Money evolved to overcome the inconveniences of barter which arise from the absence of a 'double coincidence of wants'.[9] The crudest formulations imply a teleological functionalism which Menger, for one, tried to avoid by arguing that rational transactors in a barter economy would realise the individual advantage in holding stocks of the most saleable commodity as a medium of exchange (Menger 1892).[10] Thus, as an unintended consequence of individual rationality, precious

metals, which in addition possess the convenient attributes of porta-
bility, divisibility, durability, etc., become money.

Unfortunately, the demise of commodity-money broke this explanatory link between individual rationality and collective or system
benefits. Hence Menger's paradox that institutions such as money
'make for the common interest, and yet . . . conflict with the nearest
and immediate interests of contracting individuals' in that an 'individual should be ready to exchange his goods for little metal disks
apparently useless as such, or for documents representing the latter'
(quoted in Jones 1976: 757). Modern neoclassicism's attempted resolution, which is consistent with the axiom of rational maximisation, has
been to update Menger and to assert that money reduces transactions
costs for the individual (Jones 1976; Ostroy and Starr 1974; Clower
1984). As we shall see in a moment from the implications of Hahn's
analysis, the very best that this axiomatic-deductive method can
demonstrate is that, *once in existence and widely accepted*, money can be
an 'individual' as well as a 'public' good.

'Money may slip through our fingers', Frank Hahn laments, 'unless
its role in transactions is made essential' (Hahn 1987: 42).[11] His
approach is instructive for two reasons. In the first place, the clarity of
the exposition throws a sharp light on the disabling consequences of
the 'primitive' terms of microeconomics. Second, the rigour of the analysis leads Hahn to consider abandoning, or at least seriously
modifying, these assumptions.

By modelling a money economy as a Nash equilibrium exchange
game, Hahn shows that it is indeed 'advantageous for any given agent
to mediate his transactions by money provided that all other agents
do likewise' (Hahn 1987: 26). Hardly a startling conclusion as he
acknowledges, but at least it presents a formal proof that money's
liquidity exists as a social convention. Surely, however, it is not so
much a question of whether it is advantageous to use money if others
do, but rather that agents *cannot* use money *unless* others do likewise.
To state the obvious: the advantage of money presupposes a monetary
system. We have here a typical example of the way in which the
rational choice explanations of neoclassical economics soon become
locked into slightly absurd circularities. Money is an advantage to the
individual only if others use it; but, according to the theory, they can
only rationally use it if it can be shown to be an individual advantage.

Significantly, Hahn admits that his purely deductive approach
cannot identify money as such: 'a barter economy might be a Nash
equilibrium as well' (Hahn 1987: 29). As he acknowledges, if barter
were 'the accepted mode of transaction', it would be risky and therefore disadvantageous to accept a promissory note. Of course, it is

simple to show that, in certain historical circumstances, the risk of accepting a promissory note that was embedded in a trustworthy network of banking families would be far less than transporting gold. But this is outside the methodological micro-foundations of economic analysis. Having pushed the spare principles to their limits, Hahn is left to ponder that 'it is open to argument how far the given transactions institutions . . . are part of the basic description of the economy' (Hahn 1987: 42). Armed with the set of axioms and assumptions he employs, one could never explain why a rationally advantageous monetary system, including credit, banks, and so on had not existed for all time.

The explicit aim of neoclassical 'real' analysis of money is to establish the *logical* preconditions for money's existence. However, it displays overwhelming theoretical deficiencies which, as a consequence of the methodological neglect of 'historical' and 'social' structure, are not remediable within the framework of its assumptions. In the first place, as I have already stressed, neoclassicism is mostly concerned with money as a cost-reducing medium of exchange for the individual. There is no attempt to account for the 'concept' of money as a *measure of value (or unit of account)* – or even to recognise that this might constitute an intellectual problem. Second, as Hahn inadvertently shows, money's general acceptability (or its liquidity) cannot be explained in terms of *individual* rational maximizing; this form of theorising becomes stuck and cannot proceed because it must presuppose that which it sets out to explain. Finally, the preoccupation with the medium of exchange in the hypostatic model of barter exchange *necessarily* involves the 'neutrality' assertion and the neglect of those monetary forms which are not only characteristic but also *constitutive* of capitalism's *production* of credit money.

Monetary systems are the result of the long-term historical development of a complex structure of social relations and practices which cannot be grasped by neoclassicism's methodology. In this respect, Smithin has observed that 'the micro-foundations of standard monetary theory have been left extremely weak' (Smithin 1994: 14). In fact, we need to go further: money cannot have 'micro-foundations' if these are sought exclusively in the formal deductive model of the individual agent's rational choice of holding a 'veil' or 'lubricant' as simple medium in a 'real' exchange economy.

Money as a structure of social relations

The dominance of neoclassical deductive methodology, in which money is a neutral veil, is the direct outcome of the triumph of the 'theorists' during the *Methodenstreit*. However, the ultimately vanquished 'historical school' in this struggle held to a theory of money's 'origins' which differed significantly from the one propounded by their opponents.[12]

The 'historians' (including some sociologists) held to a non-market theory of the origins of money and, in addition, stressed the essential role of the 'state' (or 'polity') in the reproduction of monetary systems.[13] In contrast to the theoretical economists' focus on the medium of exchange function, they sought the origins of money as a *measure of value/money of account* and (unilateral) *means of payment* of fines, tithes, taxes, compensations that is, debts between the political community and its members (see Schumpeter 1994: Chapter 4; Einzig 1966; Melitz 1974).

The expression of this approach in Knapp's *State Theory of Money* influenced Keynes's study of ancient near eastern currency and the methodology of *A Treatise on Money* (Knapp 1924; Keynes 1930). Here Keynes opens with unequivocal assertion that 'Money of Account, namely that in which Debts and Prices and General Purchasing Power are expressed is the primary concept of Theory of Money.' In what is probably an oblique reference to Menger's insistence that money has only the one function – as a medium of exchange, Keynes dismissively observes that: 'Something which is merely used as convenient medium of exchange on the spot may approach to being Money. . . . But if this is all, we have scarcely emerged from the stage of Barter' (Keynes 1930: 3). In this possibly unwitting endorsement of the German historical school approach, Keynes argued that the 'state or community' was the source of money of account (measure of value) and means of payment (ibid.: 4–5, 11–15).

A related divergence from the conception of money simply as a neutral medium of exchange is to be found in the work of those who, like Keynes, understood bank money as 'book money' – that is, an abstract money of account for recording debt. As I have indicated, post-Keynesian monetary theory focuses on the supposed distinctiveness of credit money's non-neutrality; but from the present standpoint I wish to emphasise the fact that the symbolic representation, or signifiers, of these debt-*relations* eventually became accepted means of payment and media of exchange. In other words, a particular social relationship – promise to pay – became money.

Thus, I intend to follow the 'historical school', Keynes (and the later Hicks) and see money primarily as a measure of value and a credit relation, and, furthermore, to argue that these attributes are to be seen as the structural properties of society.[14]

The social bases of money as a measure of value: state and society

Although the German historical school paid more explicit attention to money as a measure of value than the 'theorists', its origins were not fully explained beyond pointing to the need for the precise measurement of 'debts' of fines, tithes, taxes, etc. In this respect, although we might agree with Keynes's metaphor that the state or community claims not only to enforce but also to write the monetary 'dictionary' (Keynes 1930: 5), it should be pointed out that both activities presuppose the existence of a 'language' (Frankel 1977).[15] Independently of any economic analysis of money, the numismatist Grierson similarly decided 'on the test of money being a measure of value. Unless the commodities used for exchange bear some fixed relation to a standard, we are still dealing with barter' (Grierson 1977: 16). 'The parties in barter-exchange are comparing their individual and immediate needs, *not values in the abstract'* (Grierson 1977: 19, emphasis added).

But Grierson goes further and attempts to explain the origins of the *concept* of money as a measure of value:

> Behind the specific phenomenon of coin there is the phenomenon of money, the origins of which are not to be sought in the market but in a much earlier stage in communal development, when worth and wergeld were interchangeable terms.
>
> (Grierson 1977: 33)

Wergeld ('worthpayment') was widespread in premarket societies and comprised the scales and tariffs of compensation for injuries used as an alternative to socially and economically debilitating blood feuds and *lex talionis* (ibid.: 28).

It cannot be shown that *wergeld* actually pre-dates the use of media of exchange in more narrowly market transactions and Grierson accepts that the 'generalized application of monetary values to commodities could scarcely have come about before the appearance of market economies'. But Grierson is concerned with what Schumpeter refers to as 'logical origins' and argues that the *idea* of 'moneysworth' could not have been produced by the 'market'.

> The conditions under which these laws were put together would appear to satisfy much better than the market mechanism, the prerequisites for the establishment of a monetary system. The tariffs for damages were established in public

assemblies, and. . . . Since what is laid down consists of evaluations of injuries, not evaluation of commodities, the conceptual
difficulty of devising a common measure for appraising unre-
lated objects is avoided.

(Grierson 1977: 20–21)[16]

Grierson makes no use of sociological theory, but his argument could be
expressed as a Durkheimian hypothesis that money as a measure of value
is a 'collective representation' for which the analogue is the structure of
society. In taking this lead, we can develop our argument by noting that
wergeld expressed two meanings of 'worth' which derive from two
elements of basic societal structure: the utilitarian and the moral.

It is possible, but by no means easy, to construct reasonably objective
indemnity schemes for functional impairment caused by loss or
injury to individuals, social groups, or society at large.[17] However,
society's normative or moral order is inextricably bound up with
notions of functional 'worth' and, in this respect, *wergeld* was a matter
of both injury and *insult*. Payment for killing a king, for example, was
set at an absurdly high level that would have involved the selling into
slavery of the murderer's whole extended family. On a more trivial
level, it 'cost four times as much to deprive a Russian of his moustache
or beard as to cut off one of his fingers' (Grierson 1977: 20). Here, loss
of face was literally more important than at least some small loss of
function. Moreover, it is quite clear that the expiation of the culprit
was not intended to compensate precisely for destroyed functional
'value', but also involved punishment or vengeance for the transgression of the symbolic values of the 'sacred' social realm. The defence of
such values might have some utilitarian or functionally instrumental
consequences; but it is difficult to explain them entirely in these terms
(Elster 1989). Rather, the meaning of, say, insults and revenge must be
sought in society's system of values which, following Durkheim, is a
moral order *sui generis*. Of course, these arguments are simply a
restatement of the familiar sociological critique of the idea of the
primordial 'market'; that is, the theory of society based upon the
advantaged contractual interdependence of rationally calculating
maximising individuals.[18]

This is not the place to plough this already well-worked ground,
but perhaps it might be useful to illustrate the general argument, as
I have applied it to the 'origins' of money as a measure of value, by
looking at an analysis that proceeds along identical lines in its explanation of the 'logical origins' of inequality. Over thirty years ago,
Dahrendorf started from Durkheim's insistence that every society is,
fundamentally, a 'moral community' in the sense that both social posi-

tions and the performances of their individual incumbents are evaluated in relation to systems of norms and values (Dahrendorf 1968). These are supported by both material and symbolic sanctions – that is, punishments (including 'shame') for transgression; and rewards for exemplary conduct – especially 'honours'. The latter produces an inequality of status. Relatedly, *wergeld* symbolically represented society's two faces and involved, on the one hand, attempts to quantify the functional contribution of *social positions* by the imposition of tariffs for the impairment or loss of incumbents. On the other, such schemes, or *collective representations*, were the codification of the values and norms without which the evaluation of functional 'worth' would have remained *anomic*; that is, an unresolvable contesting of claims and counterclaims backed by coercion. There are then very good reasons for believing that the very idea of money originated outside the 'market', as this is conventionally construed in economics.

Credit money: banks and the state

Early intellectual opposition to the commodity-theory of money was largely founded on efforts to understand the theory and practice of new forms of state money and bank money other than as the mere representation of precious-metal money.[19] Money's transformation from, in Simmel's terms, 'substance' (commodity) to pure 'function' as an acknowledgement of debt (promise to pay) expressed in a money of account and issued by states and banks involved the realisation that money was *itself* a social relation.

The equivocal position of such views in economic theory is apparent in the difficulties that bank credit money has posed for orthodoxy. In so far as the actual *activity* of banks has been the subject of 'real' or narrowly neoclassical analysis, it has been seen as simple intermediation between savers and borrowers and in the reduction of transactions costs through the clearing of cheques, etc. However, from the fifteenth century, banking practice increasingly involved the '*manufacture*' of money as a social relation. Lending involved the creation of a deposit which stood in a relatively autonomous relationship to any approximate incoming 'balance' of deposits from other sources. The bank 'note' signified neither actual nor virtual goods and commodities, but simply a debt to the bank and promise of repayment. This difference has been expressed in a variety of ways; but perhaps most pithily in the distinction between the 'real' analysis conception of banking practice in which 'deposits make loans', and the converse 'credit' or 'monetary theory' view that 'loans make deposits'. The latter *act* of bank lending creates a deposit against which cheques may be drawn (Schumpeter 1994: 717; also Rogers 1989; Wray 1990).

The production of state-credit money is in principle the same process as bank-credit money. Since some Italian cities decreed, in the early seventeenth century, that their promises to pay their debts were legal tender, states have used this means of borrowing and increasing the money supply (Kindleberger 1984; Arrighi 1994). The acceptability of these promises depended, among other things, on the credibility of promises to repay debt. This was achieved by the gradual extension of long-term control over state finances by the creditors through the replacement of arbitrary and relatively untrustworthy monarchical rule by bourgeois democracy and constitutionalism. In effect, the rulers of the Italian bourgeois city–states – Genoa, Florence, Venice – guaranteed each other's debts. For similar reasons, the state's promise to pay became money relatively early and successfully in the Netherlands and England, but more unevenly and hesitantly else-where in Europe (Dickson 1967; Kindleberger 1984).

From the present standpoint two elements in this 'leap' in the social development of money are particularly important. First, the growing international bank 'giro' gave more prominence to 'the idea of a money of account which was defined by quantities of metal and which existed only as a bookkeeping device for facilitating large-scale trade and finance in a world of numberless and ever changing currency systems'. By the early seventeenth century, distinctions such as the one between *moneta immaginara* and *moneta reale* were being made (Schumpeter 1994: 296–297).

Second, it was the detachment of money, by banks and states, from being merely a signifier of commodities or deposits of commodity money that proved to be difficult to accommodate within 'real' analysis (Schumpeter 1994: 317–322).[20] This mode of monetary production involved the creation of debt and the acceptance of 'promises to pay' as media of exchange and means of payment. As promises, money is not a 'commmodity' which stands in a relatively stable relationship to other commodities, nor is it *merely* a reflection, symbolic representation, or signifier of an underlying existing 'reality' of economic relations. Rather, it is a social relation based upon definite and particular social structural conditions of existence involving, among other things, an institutionalised banking practice and constitutional legitimacy of the political authority in which the promises of banks and the states to pay gradually became currency (Dickson 1967; Hicks 1969, 1989; Weber 1981). The fundamental general social structural change that underpinned this critical step was the establishment, in custom and law, of the fungibility (transferability) of debt (Atiyah 1979:

135–138; Weber 1992 (1927): Chapter XX). This involved a second level of detachment in the transformation of social relations into 'money'. Not only was credit money separated from any direct relation to 'real' commodities, but also from particularistic (person-to-person) debt relations. The transformation of personal into impersonal trust (legitimacy) and, thereby, of IOUs into liquid money, was a long-term historical process which, like the concept of measure of value, cannot be deduced from the axioms of orthodox theory.

Considered in this way, banking practice, including state and 'central' banking, is *social practice*; that is, the social construction of credible rules of thumb that are considered prudent and legitimate by all concerned. It is not quite seventy years since Keynes attempted, in *A Treatise on Money*, to give a more secure theoretical foundation to the 'creation' of bank money:

> [I]t is evident that there is no limit to the amount of bank-money which the banks can safely create *provided that they move forward in step*. The words italicised are the clue to the behaviour of the system. . . . Each Bank Chairman sitting in his parlour may regard himself as the passive instrument of 'outside forces' over which he has no control; yet the 'outside forces' may be nothing but himself and his fellow-chairmen, and certainly not his depositors.
>
> (Keynes 1930: 26–27)[21]

The *theoretical* resistance to this view of bank money continues in a great deal of economics and is almost as mysterious as the production of money itself.[22] This subject would make a very interesting subject for the sociology of economic knowledge. It cannot be pursued here beyond the observation that the proximate reasons for the persistence of 'real' monetary analysis must lie in the dominant paradigm's conceptualisation of economic relations as those between individual agents and commodities or between economic 'variables'. But *bank money is debt, which is a social relation*. The theoretical explication, in economics, of the social process of the *production* of money remains underdeveloped for the simple reason that it would have drastic consquences for economic methodology as a whole (de Cecco 1987: 1–9). In this respect, it is important to note that after its rehabilitation into neoclassicism, most Keynesian monetary analysis devolved into the study of the 'portfolio' selection and 'liquidity preference' of rational maximisers. That is to say, mainstream macroeconomics became almost exclusively focused on money's least *specific* attribute – as a store of value.[23]

Is all money 'credit'?

Despite the fact that commodity money has long since ceased to have any significance, the distinction between 'money' and 'credit' persists in learned journals, textbooks, and everyday usage. The obvious empirical point that most money is now some form of credit money is not the one I wish to stress; rather, I would like briefly to argue that the reasoning behind the view that credit-money is a social relation be extended to all money, including its archaic 'commodity' forms. This general argument has been expressed most forcefully by the sociologist Simmel in his argument that the distinction between barter and money is sociological, not simply logical as in, for example, Clower's well-known formulation that money buys goods and goods buy money, but goods do not buy goods.[24] Consequently, Alfred Marshall's schoolyard barter or swaps of nuts for apples, for example, is to be seen as an essentially private transaction based entirely on the 'subjective' preferences and wants of the two individuals involved. For Simmel, however, money introduces a third factor:

> The pivotal point in the interaction of the two parties recedes from the direct line of contact between them, and moves to the relationship which each of them ... has with the economic community that accepts money ... [which] ... is only a claim upon society.
>
> (Simmel 1978: 177)

This mode of reasoning achieves two results. First, it draws attention to the fact that the 'real' model of *pure* barter can only be *bi*lateral exchange and cannot accurately refer to any historically real economic system of any complexity. Any move to multilaterality with heterogeneous goods would involve money at least as a unit of account, with or without acceptable tokens. Second, the distinction between 'money' and 'credit' is dissolved – both are promises to pay.[25]

> [M]etallic money is also a promise to pay and ... it differs from the cheque only with respect to the size of the group which vouches for its being accepted. The common relationship that the owner of money and the seller have to a social group – the claim of the former to a service and the trust of the latter that this claim will be honoured – provides the sociological constellation in which money transactions, as distinct from barter are accomplished.
>
> (Simmel 1978: 178)

Admittedly this does not take us very far and a large number of theoretical and empirical issues remain. And, it is not being suggested that distinctions between different forms of money should not be made; for example, commodity money, fiat money, promissory notes, cheques, credit cards, local exchange trading scheme (L.E.T.S.) tokens, etc. Each has its own particular conditions of existence; but *all* such conditions are essentially social, and the conventional economic distinction between 'money' and 'credit' can only obscure this simple but essential observation. Monetary relations are social relations and, consequently, all forms of money have a *fiduciary* character (Dodd 1994).

Conclusion

The position taken here is similar in all important respects to the 'critical realist' perspective in economics. Here it is argued that the essential methodological core, and fundamental error, of contemporary mainstream economics are its deductivist and/or empiricist methodology (Lawson 1994). This gives primary attention to the 'surface' phenomena of, on the one hand, individual calculations of utility as expressed in 'revealed preferences' and, on the other, to the statistical description of constant 'actual' event conjunctions. In consequence, mainstream economics rarely concerns itself with, and indeed cannot easily accommodate any role for, underlying social structures including, on one level, social relations. In this approach, 'social relations' or 'social structure' can be said to be conceptualised, at best, as the recognition that economic agents take each others' maximising strategies into account, as in game theory. At the same time, mainstream economists widely observe, and puzzle over, the difficulty of establishing an indispensable role for money in their theorising. My objective has been to demonstrate that money is itself a social relation in the sense that it cannot be adequately conceptualised other than as the emergent property of a configuration (or 'structure') of social relations.[26] Thus the inability of contemporary mainstream economics to accommodate money is a specific, and rather fundamental, manifestation of the sorts of failings that 'critical realist' and some sociological arguments have established more generally.

Notes

1 In general, writers on money tend to express perplexity. Marx admitted his difficulties, but apparently was mistaken in the attribution to Gladstone of the view that 'even love has not turned more men into fools

than has meditation on the nature of money' (see Ganssman 1988). Kindleberger begins a chapter on the nature of money with a long quote from *Dombey and Son* in which the former is defeated by the latter's question: 'Papa, what's money?' (Kindleberger 1984: 19). Robertson thought it appropriate to use quotations from *Through the Looking Glass* at the head of each chapter of his *Money*. In concluding a recent book on money, the sociologist Dodd was reminded of St. Augustine's remark that 'time' became more and not less elusive with close examination (Dodd 1994: 153).

2 See Ingham (1996a) for a brief discussion of the distinction between the economic 'aggregates' and 'variables' of macroeconomics and social structure seen as an 'emergent' property. I hope to address modern macroeconomic and post-Keynesian concepts of money, in more detail, in the future.

3 For Marx there are *two* veils: behind money lie 'real' economic 'forces' and, in turn, behind these lie the 'real' *social* relations that again, in turn, appear as monetary relations.

4 The tendency to analyse economies almost exclusively in terms of 'production relations' is pervasive within sociology. See, for example, Mann's attempt to write a 'total' sociological history from the standpoint of the gradual extension of 'infrastructural' and 'despotic' 'social power'. He devotes considerable attention to state finance, but nowhere is money as 'social power' *sui generis* given any specific treatment. 'Economic power' and 'economic organisation' are conceptualised entirely in terms of *production and exchange* (Mann 1986: 25).

5 The term 'real', as Schumpeter notes, is not very felicitous. Apart from the confusion, say, with 'real' and 'nominal' prices, 'real' analysis is distinctly 'unreal', as critical 'realism' would argue, from both historical and sociological standpoints!

6 This position on the relation between the 'economic' and the 'social' or 'historical' has recently been expressed succinctly by Oliver Williamson in a contribution to *The Handbook of Economic Sociology* (1994). He approvingly cites legal philosophy's distinction between the 'essentials' of the 'rational core' and the 'tosh' – that is, 'superfluous rituals, rules of procedure without clear purpose [and] needless precautions preserved through habit' (97–98).

7 Note also that Samuelson is not saying that it is heuristically useful to look on advanced industrial economies in this way, but that they actually 'boil down' to simple barter.

8 For example, one of Clower's early essays attempted to deal with this lacunae from within the neoclassical tradition and provide a pure theory of a money economy. However, the approach only serves to illustrate the impasse created by the neglect of history. By means of a purely formal analysis, Clower can only conclude that:

> A commodity is regarded as money for our purposes if and only if it can be traded for all other commodities in the economy. Correspondingly, a money economy is one in which not all commodities are money . . . money buys goods and goods buy money; but goods do not buy goods.
>
> (Clower 1967, in 1984: 86)

In short, the approach can proceed no further than providing a purely logical description of money as an 'object'.

9 Ever since Jevons's account in the late nineteenth century nearly all economic textbooks point out that barter requires a double coincidence of wants – that is, A has ducks but wants chickens at the same time that B has chickens but wants ducks. Not only does this approach tend to confuse, in Schumpeter's terms, 'logical' and 'historical' conception of 'origins'; it is also empirically suspect on two counts. First, there is considerable evidence to suggest that such barter economies never existed in the form assumed in 'real' analysis. (Heinsohn and Steiger 1989). Second, barter has occupied a wider role than is implied in the evolutionary–efficiency model. Historically, both barter and monetary exchange increased with the production of 'surpluses'; and, moreover, barter need not be as inefficient as is commonly thought (Braudel 1985; Melitz 1974).

10 Functionalism is bedevilled by logical problems. Teleology involves treating 'effects' (e.g. the systemic benefit of a multilateral exchange of heterogeneous goods) as 'causes' of origin; but there is also the difficulty of functional alternatives. Functionalism is unable logically to specify which items might fulfil any specific function; for example, Samuelson's analysis of the 'function' of money as an intergenerational store of value does not explain why money rather than another 'store' or 'asset' performs in this way (Samuelson 1966 [1958]). In short, the theory cannot adequately account for money's conditions of existence.

11 Hahn decisively dismisses the 'theoretical history' which explains money's appearance by its superior efficiency over barter: 'This Panglossian teleology lacks all merit until a process is described which brings about the superior outcome' (Hahn 1987: 24).

12 For a brief reference to the work of Roscher and Knies, see Einzig (1966). Despite his methodological critique of their work, Weber's analysis of money is heavily influenced by them and also Knapp (1924). Indeed, Menger's vehement and dogmatic insistence that money had only the one function as medium of exchange was probably as much a result of the intellectual enmity during the *Methodenstreit* as it was of scholarly conviction.

13 The state has no conceptual place in the 'real' analysis of money; the theoretical 'primitives' of this tradition do not incorporate social structure beyond the most elemental pure abstract exchange between utility-maximising agents. More recent neoclassically based analysis has attempted to explain the state's existence as a response to 'market failures' such as 'externalities', in the provision of 'public' and 'merit' goods, and in securing 'property rights'. But the state is accorded only a secondary or reactive role and older 'real' theories of money are readily accommodated in this framework. In a Mengerian account, for example, the market might yield the most saleable commodity as the medium of exchange; but the state can economise on transactions costs by being a more effective and trusted guarantor of that commodity's quality (Hodgson 1992).

14 Given Hicks's initial reaction to Keynes, it is perhaps a little ironic that he should reach exactly the same conclusion in the posthumously published *A Market Theory of Money*. After arguing that debt contract rather than spot payment was the most typical economic transaction and discussing the standard functions of money, he concluded: 'We seem thus

to be left with two distinguishing functions of money: standard of value and medium of payment . . . [and] money as a means of payment implies money as a standard' (Hicks 1989: 43). However, even though it appears that Hicks, in his very last work, was moving to a 'credit theory of money' (as opposed to a commodity-money theory of credit), he felt it necessary to take Keynes to task for defining money by its perfect 'liquidity'. Hicks's partial retention of the older style of theorising is evident:

> liquidity cannot be defined . . . except in terms of exchange-ability for money. So to define money as an asset with perfect liquidity is to argue in a circle. It is the other functions of money which are intrinsic; the liquidity property follows from them.
>
> (Hicks 1989: 42)

Obviously, money performs 'functions', but, as we have seen, their existence cannot be derived simply from their individual rationality or utility and that this applies especially to measure of value/money of account as an intersubjective, that is, social institution.

15 There is a long tradition of using a money/language analogy in economics and sociology. The former is traceable to Turgot and more recently is used by Tobin and Hahn who seem to imply that to indicate that they are aware that money is 'social' is all that is necessary to escape some of the restrictions of economics' 'methodological individualism'. This analogy obscures as much as it illuminates, but the argument cannot be pursued here.

16 There is considerable etymological support for this theory. In addition to Grierson, see Einzig: 'the word Geld is said to have originated from Vergeltung which . . . implies the settling of scores or revenge' (1966: 379); also Simmel (1978 [1907]: 357) notes that shilling is derived from 'skillan', meaning killing or wounding.

17 In their very important critique of neoclassical analysis of money, Heinsohn and Steiger (1989) follow Keynes in linking money of account to contracts and, thereby, argue that money has its origins in the institution of private property without which there cannot be contracts (see also Wray 1990). However, as Keynes, Hicks and Grierson argue, the measure of value is anterior to contract.

18 Sociology's development owed much to its rejection of the assumption to be found in 'real' economic analysis that there exists a 'natural' substratum of social and economic order that is 'in the nature of things' (Parsons 1937). Much of Durkheim's writing, for example, is devoted to an elaboration of this critique. Most notably he argued that economic institutions, which of course include 'money', could not be founded entirely on 'contracts' which supposedly expressed these natural interests. Durkheim insisted that the very idea of a contract presupposed an anterior social or moral order: 'all in the contract is not contractual . . . wherever a contract exists, it is dependent on regulation which is the work of society not that of individuals' (Durkheim 1964: 189, 194). Durkheim was not merely suggesting that contracts would be unworkable without norms of custom and practice and a degree of trust, but also literally unthinkable without the social construction of the idea of contract and procedure that, furthermore, could not have been generated by the immediate parties themselves.

19 The existence of state-issued precious metal coinage struck with the image or emblem of the ruler, as quality guarantee, can quite easily be incorporated in orthodox 'real' or neoclassical analysis (Hodgson 1992); but such treatments have tended to be at the expense of historical accuracy. While it is acceptable to present an *economic* analysis of the net benefits of the state's 'public goods' role in the provision of commodity money, it is misleading even to imply that this provides an adequate explanation of the emergence of the state's involvement. Even a cursory glance at the history of 'seignorage' and 'debasement' suggests that the exploitation of political advantage was at the centre of the struggle for the monopolisation of issue and that the outcome was contingent and not simply determined by any 'logic' of cost reduction for market transactors (Spufford 1988). Similarly, the brief references to the history of banking to be found in many economic textbooks merely perpetuate the misleading commodity-theory account of goldsmiths' receipts as the origin of banknotes (see for example, Begg *et al.* 1991: 404). To be sure, precious metals were deposited for safe-keeping and the receipts were often accepted as the *direct* representation of these commodities and thereby used as money; but this was probably one of the least important antecedents of modern capitalist banking.

20 Credit devices that originally facilitated trade, such as bills of exchange, also became 'detached' from any actual commodities that they might have directly represented and were issued by banks to serve as autonomous media of exchange and means of payment. It should be noted, however, that 'commercial-paper' as a medium of exchange that directly signifies actual goods is consistent with the idea in 'real' analysis of money as a neutral 'veil'. The conception of a purely paper credit barter economy in which a *numeraire* represents 'real' values is contained in the Walrasian model; and more recent theoretical developments, such as the 'New Monetary Economics', examine the possibility of large-scale 'cashless' barter systems based on advanced computer technology which can match traders and produce the necessary 'double coincidence of wants' (Smithin 1994: 14–16). See also the 'real bills doctrine' in relation to the Banking and Currency schools dispute (Smithin 1994: 4). However, in 'real' analysis, the equation between signifier (bill) and object (commodity) is either assumed or considered exclusively as a logical relation. 'Monetary' analysis points to the inherently problematic relationship that is the result of the relatively autonomous processes of the respective 'social' production of money and goods.

21 See the debate on the proposition that the money supply curve is horizontal at a given rate of interest (Moore 1988).

22 As late as 1921, no less an economist than Cannan, writing in the *Economic Journal*, used the 'real' analysis analogy that if a cloakroom attendant loaned out bags left with him this would not involve the 'creation' of bags and, moreover, before the owners of the bags could use them, they would have to be recovered from the borrowers (Schumpeter 1994: 1113–1114). But as Schumpeter explains, depositors and borrowers have simultaneous use of the 'same' money.

23 This most 'economic' of problems – that is, the value of money – is also, in part, a socially 'enacted' or 'accomplished' process involving, *inter alia*, economic theories of the 'causes' of inflation; financial journalism; accountancy theory and practice; central banks; ministries of finance, etc.

(see Mirowski 1990). In other words, the statistical relationships between the relevant macroeconomic 'variables' involved in the determination of the 'value' of money are the expression of underlying social and economic processes.

24 However, Smithin reports that shortly before his death, Hicks had abandoned any distinction between 'money' and 'credit' and maintained that 'the evolution of money is better understood if one starts with *credit*' (Smithin 1994: 25 , original emphasis). The evolution of Hicks's thought on money from his early orthodoxy of the 1930s ('Mr Keynes and the Classics', *Econometrica*, 5, 1937: 147–159) to the posthumous *A Market Theory of Money* (1989) and then the above statement displays, to this reader at least, a fascinating gradual movement to an inherently historical and sociological conception. This interpretation relies on some of his substantive arguments in this book rather than its explicit conclusions, with which they are frequently at odds in their adherence to both the logical and historical primacy of 'the market'. See also Schumpeter (1994: 321).

25 Simmel continues:

> This is the core of the truth that money is only a claim upon society. Money appears so to speak, as a bill of exchange from which the name of the drawee is lacking. . . . It has been argued against this theory that metallic money involves credit, that credit creates a liability, whereas metallic money payment liquidates any liability; but this argument overlooks the fact that liquidation of the individual's liability may still involve an obligation for the community. The liquidation of every private obligation by money means that the community now assumes this obligation to the creditor.
>
> (Simmel 1978: 177. See especially, 174–179)

Compare Schumpeter's formulation that 'money in turn is but a credit instrument' (1994: 320–321).

26 For a discussion of the distinction between social 'relations' and social 'structure' in relation to economics, see Ingham 1996(a), 1996(b).

Bibliography

Arrighi, G. (1994) *The Long Twentieth Century*, London: Verso.

Atiyah, P. S. (1979) *The Rise and Fall of Freedom of Contract*, Oxford: Clarendon Press.

Begg, D., Dornbusch, R. and Fischer, S. (1991) *Economics*, 3rd edition, Maidenhead: McGraw-Hill.

Braudel, F. (1985) *Civilization and Capitalism*, vol. I, London: Fontana.

Clower, R. W. (1984) 'A Reconsideration of the Microfoundations of Money', in D. A. Walker (ed.) *Money and Markets: Essays by Robert W. Clower*, Cambridge: Cambridge University Press: 81–89.

Cottrell, A. (1994) 'Post-Keynesian Monetary Economics', *Cambridge Journal of Economics* 18(2): 587–605.

Dahrendorf, R. (1968) 'The Origin of Inequality Among Men' in *Essays in the Theory of Society*, London: Routledge and Kegan Paul: 151–178.

de Cecco, M. (1987) *Changing Money: Financial Innovation in Developed Countries*, Oxford: Blackwell.

Dickson, P. G. M. (1967) *The Financial Revolution in England: A Study in the Development of Public Credit, 1688–1756*, New York: St. Martin's Press.

Dodd, N. (1994) *The Sociology of Money*, Cambridge: Polity Press.

Durkheim, E. (1960 [1893]) *The Division of Labor in Society*, Glencoe, IL: Free Press.

—— (1964) *The Division of Labour in Society*, New York: Free Press.

Einzig, P. (1966) *Primitive Money*, London: Pergamon Press.

Elster, J. (1989) *The Cement of Society*, Cambridge: Cambridge University Press.

Frankel, H. S. (1977) *Money: Two Philosophies*, Oxford: Blackwell.

Ganssman, H. (1988) 'Money – A Symbolically Generalized Medium of Communication? On the Concept of Money in Recent Sociology', *Economy and Society* 17(4): 285–315.

Grierson, P. (1977) *The Origins of Money*, London: University of London, The Athlone Press.

Hahn, F. (1982) *Money and Inflation*, Oxford: Blackwell.

—— (1987) 'The Foundations of Monetary Theory', in M. de Cecco and J. Fitoussi (eds) *Monetary Theory and Economic Institutions*, London: Macmillan: 21–43.

Heinsohn, G. and Steiger, O. (1989) 'The Veil of Barter: The Solution to the "Task of Obtaining Representations of an Economy in which Money is Essential"', in J. A. Kregel (ed.) *Inflation, Income Distribution and Capitalist Crisis*, London: Macmillan: 175–204.

Hicks, J. (1969) *A Theory of Economic History*, Oxford: Clarendon Press.

—— (1989) *A Market Theory of Money*, Oxford: Clarendon Press.

Hodgson, G. M. (1992) 'Carl Menger's Theory of the Evolution of Money: Some Problems', *Review of Political Economy* 4(4): 396–412.

Ingham, G. (1996a) 'Some Recent Changes in the Relationship between Economics and Sociology', *Cambridge Journal of Economics* 20(1): 243–275.

—— (1996b) 'The New Economic Sociology', *Work, Employment and Society* 10(3): 549–564.

Jones, R. A. (1976) 'The Origin and Development of Media of Exchange', *Journal of Political Economy* 84(4): 757–775.

Keynes, J. M. (1930) *A Treatise on Money*, London: Macmillan.

Kindleberger, C. (1984) *A Financial History of Western Europe*, London: Allen and Unwin.

Knapp, G. (1924 [1905]) *The State Theory of Money*, London: Macmillan.

Lawson, A. (1994) 'A Realist Theory For Economics', in R. E. Backhouse (ed.) *New Directions in Economic Methodology*, London: Routledge: 257–285.

—— (1995) 'The "Lucas Critique": A Generalization', *Cambridge Journal of Economics* 19(2): 257–276.

Machlup, F. (1978) *The Methodology of Economics and Other Social Sciences*, New York: Academic Press.

Mann, M. (1986) *The Sources of Social Power*, Cambridge: Cambridge University Press.

Melitz, J. (1974) *Primitive and Modern Money*, Reading, MA: Addison-Wesley.

Menger, K. (1892) 'On the Origins of Money', *Economic Journal* 2: 239–255.

Mirowski, P. (1990) 'Learning the Meaning of the Dollar: Conservation Principles and the Social Theory of Value in Economic Theory', *Social Research* 57: 689–717.

Moore, B. J. (1988) *Horizontalists and Verticalists: The Macroeconomics of Credit Money*, Cambridge: Cambridge University Press.

Ostroy, J. M. and Starr, R. M. (1974) 'Money and the Decentralization of Exchange', *Econometrica* 42(6): 1093–1113.

Parsons, T. (1937) *The Structure of Social Action*, New York: Free Press.

—— (1951) *The Social System*, New York: Free Press.

Robertson, D. H. (1928) *Money*, London: Nisbet.

Rogers, C. (1989) *Money, Interest and Capital*, Cambridge: Cambridge University Press.

Samuelson, P. A. (1966 [1958]) 'An Exact Consumption-Loan Model of Interest With or Without the Social Contrivance of Money', in J. Stiglitz (ed.) *The Collected Scientific Papers of Paul A. Samuelson*, vol. I, Cambridge, MA: MIT Press: 219–233.

Schumpeter, J. (1994 [1954]) *A History of Economic Analysis*, London: Routledge.

Simmel, G. (1978 [1907]) *The Philosophy of Money*, London: Routledge.

Smithin, J. (1994) *Controversies in Monetary Economics: Ideas, Issues and Policy*, Aldershot: Edward Elgar.

Spufford, P. (1988) *Money and its Use in Medieval Europe*, Cambridge: Cambridge University Press.

Swedberg, R. (1987) 'Economic Sociology: Past and Present', *Current Sociology* 35(1): 1–216.

Weber, M. (1981 [1927]) *General Economic History*, New Brunswick, NJ: Transaction Publishers.

Williamson, O. (1994) 'Transaction Cost Economics and Organization Theory', in N. J. Smelser and R. Swedberg (eds) *The Handbook of Economic Sociology*, Princeton, NJ: Princeton University Press: 77–107.

Wray, R. L. (1990) *Money and Credit in Capitalist Economies: The Endogenous Money Approach*, Aldershot: Edward Elgar.

Part II

DEBATE

7

SITUATING CRITICAL REALISM IN ECONOMICS

Steve Fleetwood[1]

Part II of this book is concerned with criticism and debate. Four chapters (Chapters 8 to 11) are concerned with challenges to the critical realist project in economics, emanating primarily from methodologists; these are followed by a response from Tony Lawson (Chapter 12). My purpose in this introducion is to provide something of the context of this interchange by situating critical realism within the broader subject field of economics and economic methodology.

On first glance a feature of the project of critical realism in economics that seems as striking as any is its propensity to attract the critical interest of economists who are dissatisfied with the mainstream position and are actively seeking alternatives.[2] And this phenomenon is at once suggestive of something rather fundamental about the nature and distinctiveness of the critical realist project in economics, its origins and orientations. For although in the last twenty years there has been a significant growth in contributions of an explicitly methodological kind in economics, most of these can be described as methodology for its own sake. Indeed, many of its protagonists seem primarily concerned with establishing, in effect, a sub-discipline of economic methodology. A distinguishing feature of the critical realist project is its concern *not* with methodology for its own sake, but with *underlabouring*[3] for an alternative economics, one that is intended to be rather more relevant and fruitful than the current mainstream.

The critical and practical orientation of the critical realist project motivates two further differences in particular between it and other recent contributions to economic methodology. First, critical realism is rooted more firmly in economics than in philosophy; and second, it focuses more consciously or explicitly upon ontology. Indeed it is specifically concerned with elaborating a sustainable socio-economic ontology. Let me expand upon these two observations.

Critical realism: rooted more firmly in economics

It is clear that the development of critical realism in economics has made use of recent achievements in philosophy of science and, in particular, the writings of Bhaskar (1978, 1989). But it should also be recognised that it is an autonomous programme and contribution in its own right.

In its critique of mainstream economics as well as its formulation of alternatives, the critical realist project goes beyond the insights deriving from philosophy of science, whilst remaining rooted in the writings of economists. In initially orienting itself this realist endeavour has focused upon tensions and inconsistencies that pervade the modern discipline of economics (Lawson 1997: Chapter 1). In formulating an alternative perspective (that avoids the identified problems of modern mainstream economics), critical realism has drawn critically upon the writings of a disparate group of largely heterodox economists.[4] The latter group includes Commons, Hayek, Kaldor, Keynes, Marx, Menger, Schumpeter, Shackle, Smith, and Veblen. Essentially, insights found in such writings have been systematised, rendered more explicit and consistent, and on occasion critically transformed.[5] Of course, transformative work of this sort has long been under way by, amongst others, economists working in the various traditions founded in the writings of the above noted group. And it is presumably because critical realism helps systematise the work produced within these heterodox traditions that it has enjoyed significant support amongst their modern practitioners.

Seen from this perspective, critical realism has some claim to being itself regarded almost as a methodological tradition within economics. Certainly it is rooted in the heterodox, critical traditions of economics. And this renders it quite distinct from other recent contributions to economic methodology. For example, in an introductory survey Backhouse (1994: 2) observes that many economic methodologists take, as their starting point, developments in the philosophy of science deriving, in particular, from the work of Popper, Lakatos Kuhn, and more recently the work of postmodern philosophers. In the main their objective is to recover the practice of (primarily mainstream) economists from the standpoint of philosophy in general, and epistemology in particular. In consequence, these methodologists tend to be preoccupied either with prescribing various epistemological rules, or, as with more postmodernist contributions, with (explicitly or implicitly) denying a role for methodological appraisal (cf. Blaug 1987; Caldwell 1991; Latsis 1976; McCloskey 1986; and Lawson 1997).[6] Backhouse's reading of the subject, and others like it who take their cue from developments in the philosophy of science, tend to neglect the more dominant methodological tradition in economics, stretching back through the heterodox economists noted above, a tradition which is primarily concerned to underlabour for a more relevant economics. It is within the latter tradition, in my view, that the critical realist project in economics must be placed.

Critical realism: the focus upon ontology

The critical realist project in economics focuses consciously, and explicitly, upon socio-economic ontology. This orientation can be seen as following straightforwardly from the dissatisfaction of its advocates with mainstream economics. For fundamental to this dissatisfaction is an awareness that the basic (deductivist) method of mainstream economics is inappropriate to its subject matter, to the nature of socio-economic reality, to socio-economic ontology.[7] Clearly any such awareness presupposes a prior analysis of the nature of social phenomena – as does any project of developing an alternative. Hence, for the critical realist project, socio-economic ontology figures centrally.[8]

In contrast, both mainstream economics and recent economic methodology tend to neglect ontology and emphasize epistemology.[9] Consider, first, the neglect of ontology in economics. Lawson, in fact, concludes that the main error of mainstream economics is the *epistemic fallacy*. This fallacy consists of the view that statements about being can always be reduced to, or analysed solely in terms of, statements about knowledge; that matters of ontology can always be re-phrased in epistemological terms. It is this misconceived epistemological reductionism that underpins the perseverance with (deductivist) formalistic modelling – an approach countenanced on epistemological considerations alone, and in the face of persistent failure.[10]

But explicit ontological reflection is also neglected in modern economic methodology. As Lawson notes in his preface to *Economics and Reality*:

> although the contributions of modern economic methodologists tend to be heavily rooted in the philosophy of science literature, it is questions of epistemic appraisal (i.e., epistemological questions concerning the rational basis for accepting or rejecting theories) that have dominated the economic methodology discussion.
>
> (Lawson 1997: xiv)

Now, as noted above, this 'discussion' draws primarily upon a small number of philosophers of science. Mäki sums up this situation by suggesting that a *'Popperian dominance*, a kind of Popperian mainstream in economic methodology has prevailed' (1993: 6). Whilst Mäki correctly identifies the epistemological orientation of recent economic methodology, his description of it as 'mainstream' elides a crucial point. The writings of heterodox, critical economists (past and present) are often steeped in methodological criticism even if those concerned do not always refer to their work as 'methodological' (even Lawson prefers to interpret his own output as *social theory*).

To appreciate the extent to which the heterodox, critical tradition in economics is rooted in methodology and specifically ontology we need only briefly consider the reasons provided by its central figures for their rejecting the mainstream. Thus, for example, Keynes writes of econometrics:

> If we were dealing with . . . independent atomic factors and between them completely comprehensive, acting with fluctuating relative strength on material constant and homogeneous through time, we might be able to use the method of multiple correlation with some confidence for disentangling their laws of their action.
>
> (Keynes, cited in Lawson 1997: 304)

Hayek writes of the mainstream methods of study:

> In the course of its slow development in the eighteenth and early nineteenth centuries the study of economic and social phenomena was guided in the choice of its methods in the main by the nature of the problems it had to face. It gradually developed a technique appropriate to these problems without much reflection on the character of the methods or on their relation to that of other disciplines of knowledge. Students of political economy could describe it alternatively as a branch of science or of moral or social philosophy.
>
> (Hayek 1982: 19–21)

Hayek notes, however, that by the mid-nineteenth century the term science had begun to connote a special rigorousness and certainty. Economists began to imitate it.

> Thus the tyranny commenced which the methods and technique of the Sciences in the narrow sense of the term have ever since exercised over the other subjects. . . . And, although

in the hundred and twenty years or so, during which this
ambition to imitate Science in its methods rather than its spirit
has now dominated social studies, it has contributed scarcely
anything to our understanding of social phenomena, [and
now serves] . . . to confuse and discredit the work of the social
disciplines.

(Hayek 1982: 19–21)

Veblen ridicules the continuing mainstream 'hedonistic' conception of
the human agent:

The hedonistic conception of man is that of a lightening calcu-
lator of pleasures and pains, who oscillates like a
homogeneous globule of desire of happiness under the
impulse of stimuli that shift him about the area, but leave him
intact. He has neither antecedent nor consequent. He is an
isolated, definitive human datum, in stable equilibrium except
for the buffets of the impinging forces that displace him in one
direction or another. Self-imposed in elemental space, he spins
symmetrically about his own spiritual axis until the parallelo-
gram of forces bears down upon him, where upon he follows
the line of the resultant. When the force of the impact is spent,
he comes to rest, a self-contained globule of desire as before.
Spiritually, the hedonistic man is not a prime mover. He is not
the seat of a process of living, except in the sense that he is
subject to series of permutations enforced upon him by
circumstances external and alien to him.

(Veblen 1919: 73–74)

Thinkers like Keynes, Hayek, Veblen and others[11] were clearly
prompted to reject mainstream economics on methodological grounds
– namely that mainstream economics rests upon a set of methods
which is inappropriate to the analysis of socio-economic reality. It
must be recognised, then, that economic methodology, as practised by
a range of heterodox, critical economists, has been with us for well
over a century; it is not something that began twenty years ago (*pace*
Backhouse 1994) with forays by economic methodologists into philosophy of science.

In summary, the ontologically oriented and practically conditioned
project of critical realism in economics is motivated to radically transform economic practice. It thus links up with the work of the many
heterodox economists also concerned to underlabour for a more relevant alternative. Indeed, it may be best to view critical realism in

economics not so much as an addition to the traditional alternative perspectives, but as an aspect of all of them.[12] Be that as it may, critical realism is distinct from the majority of recent projects in economic methodology which, under one or other of the banners of recovering practice, pragmatism, rhetoric, methodological pluralism, and so forth, offer some critical comment, but in the end leave the methods and practices of mainstream economics largely (at least in their fundamentals) untouched.

If this objective of facilitating a constructive transformation of the discipline is a distinguishing feature of critical realism, it, or the manner in which this objective is pursued, is an aspect of the project that itself attracts many criticisms. Indeed, critical commentary of this sort is clearly evident in the chapters included below. It warrants emphasis, however, that critical engagement with any aspect of the project has always been welcomed by its proponents; the project has striven throughout to be open-ended and non-dogmatic, aware of its own fallibility and likely transient nature (see Lawson 1997: Chapter 5). Indeed, in seminars and workshops organised under its epithet, criticism, including self-criticism, has been encouraged as fundamental. And of course it is precisely with the intention of facilitating further the critical input to, and the critically informed development/transformation of, this project, that the contributions to this second part of the book have been organised. I take it to be a sign of the recognised importance of the critical realist project, that scholars like Tom Boylan, Paschal O'Gorman, Wade Hands, Steve Parsons and Raj Kanth are willing here to engage with it. My hope is that the critical interchange which follows can mark a further facilitating, if critical, turn on a road that ultimately leads to a more relevant and fruitful economics.

Notes

1 For thoughtful comments on earlier drafts I wish to thank Paul Lewis, Mario da Graça Moura, Pat Northover, Steve Pratten, Jochen Runde and Nicos Siakantaris.

2 Including various Austrian, Evolutionary, Institutionalist, Marxists and Post-Keynesian economists. For an overview of those heterodox economists who make use of critical realism, or something like it, see Lawson (1997: Chapter 5, especially note 20). To this list, one might also add: Ahnstrom (1990), Assiter (1996), Fleetwood (1997a, 1997b); Lovering (1990); O'Neill (1995); Piore (1993) and Wilson (1991).

3 For a discussion of critical realism as 'underlabouring' see Lawson, Peacock and Pratten (1995).

4 In fact Lawson himself was developing the project back in the early 1980s, prior to his encountering Bhaskar's work, and drawing in particular on Keynes.

5 Examples of such re-appraisal include: Da Graça Moura (1997); Fleetwood (1995, 1997a, 1998); Kanth (1992); Lawson C. (1994, 1996); Lawson T. (1985, 1988, 1989, 1994b, 1997); Meikle (1995); O'Neill (1995); Peacock (1993); Pratten (1994, 1998), Runde (1997) and Wilson (1991).

6 For a discussion of these particular methodologists, and survey of recent projects in economic methodology see Backhouse (1994). Boylan and O'Gorman (1995: Chapters 1 and 2) also provide a useful survey.

7 For evidence of this, see Lawson (1997: 15–107) and his contributions to this volume.

8 This should not be misunderstood to imply that epistemology is somehow banned from critical realist discourse, or that epistemology and ontology conflict. On epistemological concerns in critical realism see Lawson (1997: part IV). For epistemological commentary that is not inconsistent with critical realism, see Lipton (1991); Ruben (1990); Ollman (1993); and Wilson (1991).

9 Virtually all other projects in economic methodology tend to neglect ontology. Most of the popular texts on economic methodology carry little or no discussion of ontology, and many do not even use the term at all. Cf. Blaug (1987); Boland (1991, 1992, 1997); Caldwell (1991); Hausman (1988, 1992); and Pheby (1990).

10 On deductivism see the exchange of views between Hands and Lawson in Part II of this volume.

11 We can also note that Marx's work too is littered with ontologically informed rejections of the methods used by 'vulgar economists', where the latter, in their method, seem not too different from the modern (deductivist) mainstream.

> It should not astonish us, then, that vulgar economy feels particularly at home in the estranged outward appearances of economic relations ... and that these relations seem the more self evident the more their internal relationships are concealed from it. ... But all science would be superfluous if the outward appearance and the essence of things directly coincided.
>
> (1984: 817)

12 Because, as a meta-theory, critical realism does not license any particular theoretical perspective, it is an 'aspect' of the perspectives just mentioned in the sense that it clarifies and occasionally transforms insights in them. See for example Lawson's (1994c) paper on the nature of Post-Keynesian economics – and Parson's (1996) critique.

Bibliography

Ahnstrom, L. (1990) *Economic Growth, Stagnation and the Working Population in Western Europe*, London: Belhaven Press.
Assiter, A. (1996) *Enlightened Women*, London: Routledge.

Backhouse, R. (1994) *Introduction to New Directions in Economic Methodology*, London: Routledge.

Bhaskar, R. (1978) *A Realist Theory of Science*, Brighton: Harvester Wheatsheaf.

—— (1989) *The Possibility of Naturalism*, Brighton: Harvester Wheatsheaf.

Blaug, M. (1987) *The Methodology of Economics*, Cambridge: Cambridge University Press.

Boland, L. (1991) *The Methodology of Economic Model Building: Methodology After Samuelson*, London: Routledge.

—— (1992) *The Principles of Economics: Some Lies My Teachers Told Me*, London: Routledge.

—— (1997) *Critical Economic Methodology: A Personal Odyssey*, London: Routledge.

Boylan, T. and O'Gorman, P. (1995) *Beyond Rhetoric and Realism: Towards a Reformulation of Economic Methodology*, London: Routledge.

Caldwell, B. (1991) *Beyond Positivism: Economic Methodology in the Twentieth Century*, London: Unwin Hyman.

Da Graça Moura, M. (1997) 'Schumpeter's Inconsistencies and Schumpeterian Exegesis: Diagnosing the Theory of Creative Destruction', PhD thesis, Department of Economics, University of Cambridge.

Fleetwood, S. (1995) *Hayek's Political Economy: The Socio-Economics of Order*, London: Routledge.

—— (1997a) 'Critical Realism, Marx and Hayek', in W. Keizer, B. Tieben and R. Van Zijp (eds) *Austrians in Debate*, London: Routledge.

—— (1998, forthcoming) 'Why Trade Union Models Are Inadequate: A Critical Realist Perspective', *LABOUR*.

Hausman, D. (1988) *The Philosophy of Economics*, Cambridge: Cambridge University Press.

—— (1992) *The Inexact and Separate Science of Economics*, Cambridge: Cambridge University Press.

Hayek, F. (1982) *Law, Legislation and Liberty*, London: Routledge and Kegan Paul.

Hume, D. (1978) *A Treatise of Human Nature*, Oxford: Clarendon Press.

Kanth, R. (1992) *Capitalism and Social Theory: The Science of Black Holes*, New York: ME Sharpe.

Latsis, S. (1976) *Method and Appraisal in Economics*, Cambridge: Cambridge University Press.

Lawson, C. (1994) 'The Transformational Model of Social Activity and Economic Analysis: A Reinterpretation of the Work of J. R. Commons', *Review of Political Economy* 6(2): 186–204.

—— (1996) 'Realism, Theory and Individualism in the Work of Carl Menger', *Review of Social Economy* LIV(4): 445–464.

Lawson, C., Peacock, M. and Pratten, S. (1995) 'Realism, Underlabouring and Institutions', *Cambridge Journal of Economics* 20(1): 137–151.

Lawson, T. (1985) 'Keynes, Prediction and Econometrics', in T. Lawson and H. Pesaran (eds) *Keynes's Economics: Methodological Issues*, London: Croom Helm.

—— (1988) 'Keynes on Probability, Uncertainty and Decision Making', *Journal of Post Keynesian Economics* 11(1): 38–65.

—— (1989) 'Abstraction, Tendencies and Stylised Facts: A Realist Approach to Economic Analysis', *Cambridge Journal of Economics* 13(1): 59–78.

—— (1994a) 'A Realist Theory for Economics', in R. Backhouse (ed.) *New Directions in Economic Methodology*, London: Routledge.

—— (1994b) 'Realism and Hayek: A Case of Continuous Transformation', in M. Colona and H. Hageman (eds) *Capitalism, Socialism and Information: The Economics of F. A. Hayek*, Aldershot: Edward Elgar.

—— (1994c) 'The Nature of Post Keynesian Economics and its Links to the other Traditions', *Journal of Post Keynesian Economics* 16(4), reprinted in D. Prychitko (1996) *Why Economists Disagree: An Introduction to Contemporary Schools of Thought*, New York: New York State University Press.

—— (1997) *Economics and Reality*, London: Routledge.

Lipton, P. (1991) *Inference to the Best Explanation*, London: Routledge.

Lovering, J. (1990) 'Neither Fundamentalism Nor "New Realism": A Critical Realist Perspective on Current Divisions in Socialist Theory', *Capital and Class* 42, Winter: 33–54.

McCloskey, D. (1986) *The Rhetoric of Economics*, Brighton: Harvester Press.

Mäki, U. (1993) 'Economics with Institutions: Agenda for Methodological Enquiry', in U. Mäki, B. Gustafsson and C. Knudsen (eds) *Rationality, Institutions and Economic Methodology*, London and New York: Routledge.

Marx, K. (1984) *Capital*, vol. 3, London: Lawrence and Wishart.

Meikle, S. (1995) *Aristotle's Economic Thought*, Oxford: Clarendon Press.

Ollman, B. (1993) *Dialectical Investigations*, London: Routledge.

O'Neill, J. (1995) 'Essences and Markets', *The Monist* 78(3): 258–275.

Parsons, S. (1996) 'Post Keynesianism, Realism and Keynes' General Theory', *Journal of Post Keynesian Economics* 18(3): 419–441.

Peacock, M. (1993) 'Hayek, Realism and Spontaneous Order', *Journal for the Theory of Social Behaviour* 23(3): 249–264.

Pheby, J. (1990) *Methodology and Economics: A Critical Introduction*, Basingstoke: Macmillan.

Piore, M. (1993) 'The Social Embeddedness of Labour Markets and Cognitive Processes', *LABOUR* 7(3): 3–18.

Pratten, S. (1994) 'Structure, Agency and Marx's Analysis of the Labour Process', *Review of Political Economy* 5(4): 403–426.

—— (1998, forthcoming) 'Marshall on Tendencies, Equilibrium and the Statical Method', *History of Political Economy*.

Ruben, D.-H. (1990) *Explaining Explanation*, London: Routledge.

Runde, J. (1997) 'Keynesian Methodology', in G. Harcourt and P. Riach (eds) *Keynes's General Theory*, second edition, London: Routledge.

Veblen, T. (1919) *The Place of Science in Modern Civilization and Other Essays*, New York: Huebsch.

Wilson, H. (1991) *Marx's Critical Dialectical Procedure*, London: Routledge.

8

CRITICAL REALISM AND ECONOMICS

A causal holist critique

Thomas A. Boylan and Paschal F. O'Gorman

Introduction

In the wake of the demise of logical positivism an increasing number of contending methodological positions have emerged in what is now a burgeoning literature reflecting a vibrant and multi-voiced discourse. This resurgence in economic methodology is linked to a complex set of interacting influences, both internal and external to the discipline. The development of the 'crisis' in contemporary economics followed from the breakdown of the post-war Keynesian paradigm during the course of the 1970s (Coats 1977; Bell and Kristol 1981). This resulted in a protracted period of theoretical reassessment which was matched by an intensive methodological interrogation of the discipline. The unsettled state of the discipline provides a plausible 'internal' explanation for the growth in methodological research which has been pursued relentlessly since then. The 'external' contributing factor arose from the 'crisis' in the related, but in the event extremely influential, domain of the philosophy of science. This latter crisis, which pre-dated the upheaval in economics, arose from the sustained critique of logical positivism and its variant, logical empiricism, which was launched in the 1950s. The ensuing decades have been characterised by the elaboration of alternative paradigms preoccupied with the role, status, and evolution of scientific knowledge in general and specifically the contribution of scientific theories. This has been a period of intense activity in the philosophy of science with implications for all the sciences, including economics. The major developments in economic methodology and its interaction with the philosophy of science have been the subject of a number of major surveys including Blaug (1980), Caldwell (1982, 1984, 1993), Hausman (1984, 1992), Redman (1991), Backhouse (1994).

In the post-positivist era the dominant position once occupied by logical positivism, and for a period during the Popperian interlude that of falsificationism, has been replaced by a range of increasingly exclusive methodological approaches. These reflect the influence of recent developments outside economics, including philosophy (both Anglo-Saxon and continental varieties), discourse analysis, and different strands of analytical theory. We have argued elsewhere that one of the most substantial and challenging philosophical positions to emerge during this period was that of realism (Boylan and O'Gorman 1995). More particularly, the form of realism, as expounded by Tony Lawson, and schematised as transcendental realism or in the context of social reality as critical realism, is the focus of this chapter. In an impressive array of publications, Lawson has provided a powerful case on behalf of transcendental/critical realism (1989a, 1989b, 1992, 1994a, 1994b, 1994c, 1994d). This perspective, Lawson has argued, 'can facilitate a more relevant economics than is currently available or is even possible within the confines of the (relatively unquestioned) explanatory norms and criteria of the contemporary economics discipline' (Lawson 1994d: 257).

The task of facilitating 'a more relevant economics' is a sentiment we share wholeheartedly with Lawson and our own efforts in this regard, what we termed causal holism, attempted to achieve the same objective. We also share with Lawson his rejection of the dominant approach to economic methodology, namely instrumentalism and in particular what he has termed 'predictive instrumentalism' (Lawson 1989a: 61). Critical realism is in our estimation a superior approach to economic methodology than the current orthodox position. Our approach in this chapter is, however, one of critical engagement with Lawson's critical realism. More specifically, it takes the form of a critical interrogation of certain aspects of the critical realist position. At certain junctures in the chapter we will invoke aspects of our own methodological position, causal holism, to provide the critical perspective within which our analysis and interrogation of critical realism can be most effectively facilitated.

The structure of the chapter is as follows. In the next section we examine the relationship between transcendental and critical realism. More specifically we question the commitment to specific modes of philosophical arguments, in this case transcendentalism, to guarantee the social ontology posited by critical realism. In the following section a number of issues are critically analysed including the critical realist account of explanation, the role of theory in economics, abstraction, and abductive inference. A short conclusion is provided.

138

From transcendental to critical realism

Transcendental realism has its origins in Bhaskar's neo-Kantianism where fallible science is subjected to a Kantian-type critique under the eye of Enlightenment pure reason. In this Bhaskarian setting pure reason is capable of furnishing a unique and incorrigible answer to the Kantian-type quest of specifying the necessary conditions of physical science in general or of specific scientific practices in particular. This necessary condition is the ontology of Lawson's transcendental realism, i.e. a world of structured intransitive objects. In contrast to transcendental realism, the philosophical sources of causal holism are very different. Causal holism has its origins in Quine's holism and van Fraassen's constructive empiricism (Boylan and O'Gorman 1995). Arising from these sources, causal holists see no need for any kind of neo-Kantian transcendental argument specifying how the world must be if science is to be possible. They are not attempting to privilege any one starting point in their philosophical endeavours. Any attempt to specify necessary conditions for the practice of science will inevitably be tainted by the historical location and presuppositions of our contemporary conceptual schemes. The transcendental quest for incorrigible necessary conditions is thereby abandoned.

In his recent exposition, 'A Realist Theory for Economics', Lawson attempts to qualify the full impact of Bhaskarian neo-Kantianism by pointing out that his claims of necessity are, 'like all cognitive claims, also fallible and corrigible' (Lawson 1994d: 271). Any 'must' arising from the quest for 'necessary' conditions must be placed in inverted commas. As causal holists we certainly welcome this qualification. It recognises Quine's point that philosophers have no privileged position from which to make their claims or theses. None the less the spirit, if not the letter, of Lawson's critical realism is that of neo-Kantian transcendental realism. In earlier work this qualification is not evident (Lawson 1989a).

How precisely does Lawson qualify Kantian transcendentalism? This is important in view of the fact that transcendental realism of some kind is still integral to his position. The transcendental question is explicated as follows; 'what claims about the nature of reality are viable in the sense that they render intelligible the generalized phenomena of experience taken as premises?' (Lawson 1994d: 272). We note that the term 'viable' now replaces the Kantian term 'necessary'. Many answers to this question may be found in the history of philosophy since the age of rationalism and empiricism. Lawson, however, gives us a choice between two and only two possibilities. One is a Humean empiricist view, explicated in particular in terms of a constant conjunction of events along with a dominant deductivist mode of explanation, and two is a transcendental realist view or some qualified version thereof.

As causal holists we share much of the critique of positivism as developed this century. While logical positivism may have played a pivotal role in the emergence of twentieth-century philosophy of language (with its focus on the literal meaning of sentences), within philosophy of science it has been subjected to a devastating critique. Numerous responses to this critique have emerged, one of which is transcendental realism. A number of other responses can be identified, including Feyerabend's epistemological anarchism, Kuhnian paradigms, Quine's empiricism without the dogmas, van Fraassen's constructive empiricism, causal holism, and a variety of non-transcendental realisms. A range of divergent views on such central philosophico-methodological issues such as the epistemological–ontological relationship, the role of theory in science, scientific explanation, and the aim of science may be found in these responses. Moreover, most of these responses do not see any advantage in starting with quasi-enlightenment or transcendental questions about conditions which render the phenomena of experience intelligible. They start with a different conception of rationality and in particular of the epistemological–ontological relationship. Quine, for instance, starts in the 'middle of things' with our ordinary enduring physical objects (Quine 1960). Similarly with van Fraassen, for him we are already in a world which pre-existed our arrival into it. Causal holists share this starting point. In terms of its informing influences, causal holism is holding some middle ground between logical positivism and Lawson's transcendental or 'transfactual' realism, with the latter living too much in the shadow of Enlightenment epistemology.

The question which arises from the above can be stated succinctly: what work is transcendental realism doing for Lawson's critical realism? Clearly critical realism is Lawson's end point. In critical realism, as well as agents and firms, the ontology includes social structures. These structures are not to be reified and, like Giddens, the focus is on their reproduction or transformation. Lawson tells us that, 'it is not difficult to reason that the transcendental realist perspective *must* carry over to the social realm' (Lawson 1994d: 269 [our italics]). However the 'must' here is not in inverted commas! Notwithstanding this, Lawson maintains that given the real choice which agents can and do exercise, 'economists are unable to reconcile this insight with their understanding of scientific explanation' (ibid.: 269). This may very well be the case but, as Donald Davidson points out, it is to Hempel's eternal credit that he resolved the difficulty of reconciling choice with the deductive-cum-probabilistic patterns of explanation (Davidson 1980). Moreover, Hempel's resolution, while saving deductivism-cum-probabilism, which is rejected by Lawson, does so without getting involved in ontological reductionist issues. We note this in order to indicate some possible weaknesses in the links of Lawson's chain of reasoning from transcendental to critical realism.

Let us return to the question already posed: what work is transcendental realism doing for critical realism? One obvious answer is that in the social realm it gives us Lawson's three realms of the empirical, the actual, and the 'deep', which are 'out of phase' with one another (Lawson 1994d: 263). While this is so, we are not at all convinced that transcendental realism 'carries over' to the full range of the ontological requirements of critical realism. As Lawson argues, social structures should not be reified; they are not like material objects. Like Giddens he uses linguistic structures (language) and their relationship to specific speech acts to illustrate how social structures function, especially how they are reproduced or transformed. In view of this, social structures are clearly not intransitive objects postulated by transcendental realism. The *modus operandi* of social structures are different from the structures of intransitive objects and consequently the ontology of critical realism does not coincide with the ontology of intransitive objects 'guaranteed' by transcendental realism.

As causal holists we fully acknowledge a complex range of indispensable causal roles to social structures. Like the later Wittgenstein we fully acknowledge that we live in a complex social world which is not a natural datum. Our social world, though contingent, has a long and intricate history. Some social structures are either posits or outcomes of this history. The institutions of law and politics, for instance, illustrate this, as does their network of interactions in real historical time with economic agents, other institutions, and resources. In general, we are, to use Quine's phrase, ontologically committed to extensive ranges of economic institutions, agents, and structures operating in real historical time. These ontological commitments are displayed in the vast variety of Wittgensteinian language games of modern life. We don't require Enlightenment or transcendental-type arguments to guarantee the existence of this ontology. In particular, social structures permeate our contingent network of Wittgensteinian forms of life. In short, our objection to critical realism is not to its social ontology, it is rather to its commitment to particular modes of philosophical argument *vis-à-vis* this ontology. Where substantive methodological differences occur is in the issues of the role of theory in economics and especially in the notion of economic explanation. We address these issues in the next section.

From ontology to methodology: issues for critical realism

Lawson's challenging discussion of the aim of science is developed in the context of his conception of science itself. Contrary to positivism, science 'is not . . . even dependent upon the seeking out of constant event conjunctions. Indeed, it is primarily concerned not with events at all' (Lawson 1994d: 264). Rather, in line with the ontology of transcendental realism, 'the concern is with identifying and illuminating the structures and mechanisms, powers and tendencies, that govern or facilitate the phenomena of experience' (ibid.: 264). Lawson draws our attention to the realist notion of tendency used here. When he uses the term 'tendency' he is not talking about long-run or average outcomes concerning events. On the contrary, he is referring to 'non-actual and non-empirical' powers which, if triggered, are exercised and are due to the essential nature of intransitive objects. A statement of a tendency is thus, 'a statement of natural necessity without qualifications attached' (ibid.: 265). In short, the aim of science is 'to illuminate structures that govern surface phenomena' and the laws of science 'express not event regularities but precisely such structures and their modes of activity' (ibid.: 265). Finally scientific explanation entails 'an account of those structures that have contributed to the production of, or facilitated, some already identified phenomena of interest' (ibid.: 264).

Lawson's account of the aim of science is perfectly consistent with his transcendental realism. This account carries over to the science of economics. In economics, however, he introduces two 'modes' of explanation. The first mode, 'pure or abstract' explanation, concerns 'the identification of underlying structures and mechanisms' (ibid.: 277). The second mode, 'applied or concrete' explanation, draws upon rather than reveals, 'antecedently established knowledge of relatively enduring structures and mechanisms', which explain the concrete phenomena which are the 'resultants of numerous countervailing tendencies' (ibid.). Finally the 'event-analogues of the social realm' are 'social activities' (ibid.).

We have a number of reservations about Lawson's critical realist account of economic explanation. We will attempt to discuss these by looking at his transcendental realist account of the aim of science and how this is transferred to economics. In the course of this discussion we will give an alternative account of these issues as developed within causal holism. In the first place transcendental realists, under the influence of their quest for intransitive objects, fail to give due recognition to the indispensable causal role of events in both the physical and social sciences. To take a standard philosophical example, the event of the short circuit in the electric system caused the fire. Similarly the event of frost over a number of nights caused the failure of the Brazilian coffee crop, or the event of the snow blizzard was a genuine causal factor for the absenteeism on that day. Events can and do play causal roles in both the physical and the human sciences, including economics. A difficulty with the 'standard' account of Humean empiricism is that it confines causality to events. Critical realism appears to go to the other extreme by failing to give due recognition to events as indispensable constituents of real causal webs in the economy. Science, contrary to critical realism, is sometimes primarily concerned with events.

Moreover, there is an obvious way in which events can include reference to entities. In many cases reference to events can be unpacked in terms of entities. For instance, what is the cause of John's illness? Is it the virus which has a specific biological make-up or is it the event that his lungs are infected by this virus? *Prima facie* it is both in that both are necessary. Critical realists, however, appear to rule this out in their over-restrictive account of the nature of science.

Finally we find the realist claim that science, 'is not . . . even dependent upon the seeking out of constant event conjunctions' too extreme and rather surprising. The source of our surprise is Lawson's earlier and perceptive realist reading of Kaldor's methodology (Lawson 1989a), where the role of Kaldorian stylised facts is fully acknowledged. The above claim also appears too extreme when viewed from the perspective that the seeking out of the constant conjunction of events is integral to some of Mill's famous methods for discovering causes and their ingenious statistical developments this century. Particularly in the case of econometrics, which critical realists associate with a Humean methodology, we fully acknowledge that it does not live up to the exaggerated claims made on its behalf. However, there is no reason why it cannot be uncoupled from this Humean association. When it is thus uncoupled, it would be an exaggeration to claim that it is of no use whatsoever to economists in their crucial task of discovering the real causes operational in the economy.

We now turn to our reservations about the critical realist's account of explanation. We concur with Lawson that the standard deductivist account of explanation is not adequate to the vast range of activities which fall within the extension of the term 'scientific explanation'. However, we do not concur with the transcendental realist account of scientific explanation. But before we discuss this, there is a more fundamental difficulty with the transcendental realist assumption about the central aim of science, namely explanation. In our opinion, this conception of the aim of science does not stand up to critical scrutiny. Our approach to scientific explanation is essentially Wittgensteinian; we look and see how the term is used in the various scientific forms of life. Frequently explanations are offered in answer to why-questions. The first point to note is that why-questions occur in specific contexts and that the context is crucial in determining the meaning of a why-question. For instance, the question 'why did Kate buy Peter a radio yesterday?' could, depending on the context, mean 'why did Kate, rather than Jane or Ann, buy Peter a radio yesterday?' Alternatively it could mean 'why did Kate buy Peter, rather than John or Paul, a radio yesterday?' or again, 'why did Kate buy Peter a radio, rather than a camera or a watch yesterday?', and so on. Indeed, one suspects that those adopting a rhetorical approach to the philosophy of economics are intuitively aware of the context-ladenness of scientific explanation. Certainly transcendental realists are not aware of the implications of this context-ladenness. One obvious consequence is that different explanations, all equally satisfactory, can be given to the same why-question, depending on the context in which it occurs. In other words there are numerous explanations, each one being completely satisfactory in context. In short, no one explanation has precedence over another; there is no such thing as *the* explanation. This, in our opinion, is the tacit presupposition of transcendental realism and, as we have just indicated, this presupposition does not stand up to critical scrutiny. We must take seriously the context-ladenness of scientific explanation.

This context-ladenness of scientific explanation is not limited to acknowledging the significance of tacit or explicit contrasts operational in specific contexts. Scientific explanation is context-laden in another sense: the professional interests of the relevant scientific experts influence the choice of explanatory factors in that these interests play a significant role in determining the relevant explanatory factors. Van Fraassen uses the example of an automobile accident to illustrate this contextual influence (van Fraassen 1980). The medical expert ascertains that the driver was drunk and thus isolates that as the relevant explanatory factor. Given the medical expert's professional interests, this is absolutely correct. The mechanic now arrives on the scene and, given his or her professional interests, he or she establishes that the brakes were faulty and again, quite correctly, identifies this as the relevant explanatory factor. Similarly the urban geographer, relative to his or her professional interests, identifies the corner where the accident occurs as dangerous and thus focuses on this as the relevant explanatory factor. The legitimate professional interests of the various scientific experts rule in certain factors as relevant and rule out others as irrelevant. Clearly this aspect of the context-ladenness of scientific explanation adds to the plurality of viable and acceptable scientific explanations. Enlightenment Metaphysics (with a capital M) may wish to privilege some one explanation over others. Our Wittgensteinian point is that the forms of life in which scientists use the term 'explanation' does not bear out this Enlightenment Metaphysical reading of scientific explanation. Critical realism with its inextricable links to transfactual or transcendental realism is, in our opinion, too closely associated with the spirit of this Enlightenment Metaphysical reading.

In particular, our thesis is not that science does not explain. On the contrary, we can and do identify numerous contexts in which science explains. These contexts require a vast variety of explanations. They affect the relevant explanatory factors chosen in such a way as not to privilege any one explanation. We see no reason why this does not apply in the social sciences in general and to economics in particular. This is clearly evident for instance in the multiplicity of explanations put forward for the very high unemployment figures in Ireland during the 1980s. In a number of major studies undertaken on this topic up to thirteen explanatory factors were identified including: increases in the Irish labour force; the growth rate in the United Kingdom; the levels of unemployment in the United Kingdom (the latter two factors reflecting the interaction between the Irish and UK labour markets); state of world demand; real interest rates; real exchange rates; existence of a large tax wedge (affecting the working of the labour market); changes in Irish Government expenditure; the replacement ratio (the ratio of average unemployment payments to average take home pay); changes in Irish output growth rates; high cost of labour relative to capital; emigration; hysteresis in the Irish labour market.

This in turn brings us to the issue of the role of theory in economics. In this connection Lawson, as already noted, focuses on 'pure' and 'applied' explanations. Among the crucial methodological concepts here are the notions of retroduction/abduction and abstraction. Lawson frequently associates abduction with analogy and metaphor (Lawson 1989a, 1994d) and identifies it as an essential mode of inference for the critical realist. He contrasts it to both induction and deduction. This is his general picture.

> If deduction is, for example, to move from the *general* claim that 'all ravens are black' to the *particular* inference that the next one seen will be black, and induction is to move from the *particular* observation of numerous black ravens to the *general*

claim that 'all ravens are black', retroductive or abductive reasoning is to move from the observation of numerous black ravens to a theory of a mechanism intrinsic to ravens which disposes them being black. It is a movement, paradigmatically, from 'surface phenomenon' to some 'deeper' causal thing.

(Lawson 1994d: 264)

Arising from the above we have a number of reservations. In the first place the concepts of deduction and induction as developed in logic, mathematics, statistics, and the other sciences are much richer, more complex, and diversified than characterised by Lawson. Over time the range of deductive inferences have been imaginatively pioneered and extended in both logic and pure mathematics. The same is also true for induction: applied mathematics (e.g. graphic representation), statistics, probability, and various specific sciences have over the years extended this domain. Critical realists may very well concede this but continue to insist on the indispensability of abduction as a crucial mode of scientific inference. However, in so far as abduction is linked to analogy and metaphor, it seems to us that it can be located within the inductive spectrum. Certainly arguments based on analogies between monkeys and humans in medicine, for instance, are in the inductive range. The issue of metaphor is, we concur, more complex. Metaphors can play a role in the construction of a new scientific concept. However, it is not the only factor involved. One has only to read Poincaré on the genesis of the notion of Euclidean space to see this. The genesis of fruitful concepts in theory construction involves numerous factors in no way related to metaphor.

Moreover, as we have argued elsewhere, we should not assimilate scientific theories or models too closely to metaphors (Boylan and O'Gorman 1995). The construction of both a theory and a model certainly depend on imagination, but scientific imagination should not be confused with either poetic or rhetorical imagination, central 'homes' of metaphor. As causal holists one of the central tasks of economics as a science is the construction of a theory which in turn furnishes economists with an extensive range of resources which they use in the construction of models of various aspects of an economy. Economists' epistemic aim is to ascertain whether or not these models are descriptively adequate, i.e. whether or not they furnish true or approximately true descriptions of the economy. The epistemic focus is on the descriptive adequacy of the theory which is ascertained by inductively investigating the range of models constructed from its resources. In this context the critical realist's abductive inferences fade into the background. It is not the central methodological mode of inference. Like any science the business of economics is the construction, not the discovery, of an economic theory which is descriptively adequate. At the level of construction, economists, like any other scientists, will use all the resources at their disposal, including metaphor. However, while a theory is in the process of being constructed or reconstructed, an associated task is the construction of models of different aspects of the economy such as models of corporate behaviour, models of inflation, models of pricing, models of income determination and employment, of growth and development and so on. Another indispensable task is to exploit the full range of our inductive procedures to ascertain the descriptive adequacy of these models. Like Kaldor we give priority to this inductive testing and again, like Kaldor, this inductive testing is 'non-monist' (Kaldor 1975: 348). If an economic theory is judged to be descriptively inadequate, economists must either reshape it or construct a new theory and then reiterate the above methodological blueprint. In this methodological blueprint abductive inference is subsumed under theory construction or model construction and here it is not privileged. Many inductive, deductive, and imaginative resources come into play. In the case of testing for descriptive adequacy its role is minimal.

We turn now to abstraction, about which we have a number of reservations, in particular the critical realist's abstractionist approach to economics. The notion of abstraction used, we are told, 'is quite consistent with' the traditional notion. This consists in 'focusing on certain aspects of something to the neglect of others' (Lawson 1989a: 68). For instance, I see a number of cats; one is black, the other is white, one is small, another is fat. I leave aside these differences in colour, size, and volume and I abstract out 'the essential' characteristic, i.e. they are cats. According to critical realism, 'on this realist view abstractions are made both in the initial analysis of economic phenomena and in the examination of the mechanisms which give rise to them' (ibid.: 68). However, given that in critical realism generative mechanisms are non-actual and non-empirical and are located on a different level to experience, how can abstraction access these? Recall that we are dealing with a notion of abstraction which is consistent with the traditional notion but, in this traditional notion, abstraction works on the level of experience; in our example above I see that the animals are cats. Generative mechanisms, however, are not on this level.

Second, what is the relationship between this process of abstraction and abductive inferences based on metaphor? Metaphor is at the creative end of the spectrum whereas abstraction is at the discovery

end. Are these two separate distinct ways of investigating the generative mechanisms and the tendencies of non-empirical objects? If so,
what if any is the relationship between them? Certainly abstraction
would give epistemic justification to the mechanisms and tendencies
abstracted, but how are these to be abstracted from the very complex
range of observable economic phenomena due to countervailing
generative causes? The analogy to cats breaks down here. We suspect
that mechanisms other than abstraction are at work.

Finally it is only fair to declare our hand here. Our philosophical
commitment is to a later Wittgensteinian approach to economic
language, where the focus is on the use of economic terms, both in the
language game of economics and in the vast variety of language games
of economic transactions. In this later Wittgensteinian approach there is
very little room for abstraction. Instead of giving an abstractionist
account of 'money' or 'capital' we look at how these words are used in
the various language games currently being played or those played in
the past. Thus the epistemic guarantee furnished by the traditional
notion of abstraction, especially the guarantee that one has correctly
abstracted the essences from the observable, is not available to us.

Conclusion

In this chapter we have examined a number of issues in critical
realism from the perspective of causal holism. The interchange
between critical realism and causal holism within the domain of
economic methodology reflects the larger discourse that has occurred
within twentieth-century philosophy of science. Scientific realism, the
progenitor within the philosophy of science of Lawson's critical
realism, has developed in direct opposition to the logical positivist
account of science, on the one hand, and relativist theories, associated
with Kuhn and Feyerabend, on the other hand, since the 1960s. It has
in the interim secured its position as the dominant philosophy of
science at the present time. However, a small number of dissenting
voices emerged in response to the dominance of scientific realism.
Two of these dissenting voices have been largely ignored in the philosophy of economics. The first is that of Quine, whose position is
counterintuitive to economists who think from the perspective of the
inseparability of economic theory and explanation. Quine challenges
us to reconsider this relationship and went on to demonstrate the
indispensability of theory at the descriptive level. The implications of
Quine's work, which is among the most sophisticated philosophical
analysis produced in this century, has radical implications for the
scientific realist account of science.

The second dissenting voice was that of van Fraassen. In the 1980s van Fraassen developed constructive empiricism in explicit opposition to scientific realism. Van Fraassen also challenges us to think about, rather than from, the influential picture which draws an inseparable connection between theory and explanation. The constructive empiricist alternative picture, like that of Quine's, is also counterintuitive to economists wedded to the dominant position in which explanation remains firmly rooted in the epistemic dimension of science. Van Fraassen argues for a radical relocation of explanation from the epistemic to the non-epistemic domain of science. In our work on causal holism we attempted to integrate, among other things, Quine's marriage of theory and description and van Fraassen's arguments for relocating scientific explanation in the non-epistemic dimension of science (Boylan and O'Gorman 1995).

As causal holists, then, our starting point is different from that of critical realism reflecting the larger philosophical discourse. While it is possible for us to identify a number of areas where we can and do agree with critical realists, we have chosen on this occasion, borrowing Husserl's idiom, to bracket these and instead to pursue a number of explicit differences which emerge between the two methodological perspectives. In our view, Tony Lawson has been the outstanding exponent of realism in economic methodology. He has produced a corpus of work, which given its intellectual scope and depth, must be seriously engaged by economic methodologists, philosophers of economics, and economists alike. In the course of this short chapter we trust we have contributed to that engagement.

Bibliography

Backhouse, R. E. (ed.) (1994) *New Directions in Economic Methodology*, London: Routledge.

Bell, D. and Kristol, I. (1981) *The Crisis in Economic Theory*, New York: Basic Books.

Blaug, M. (1980) *The Methodology of Economics*, (2nd edn 1992), Cambridge: Cambridge University Press.

Boylan, T. A. and O'Gorman, P. F. (1995) *Beyond Rhetoric and Realism in Economics*, London: Routledge.

Caldwell, B. J. (1982) *Beyond Positivism: Economic Methodology in the Twentieth Century*, London: Allen & Unwin.

—— (ed.) (1984) *Appraisal and Criticism in Economics*, Boston: Allen & Unwin.

—— (ed.) (1993) *The Philosophy and Methodology of Economics*, 3 vols, Aldershot: Edward Elgar.

Coats, A. W. (1977) 'The Current "Crisis" in Economics in Historical Perspective', *Nebraska Journal of Economics* 16: 3–16.

Davidson, D. (1980) *Actions and Events*, Oxford: Clarendon Press.

Hausman, D. M. (ed.) (1984) *The Philosophy of Economics: An Anthology*, Cambridge: Cambridge University Press.

—— (1992) *The Inexact and Separate Science of Economics*, Cambridge: Cambridge University Press.

Kaldor, N. (1975) 'What is Wrong with Economic Theory?', *Quarterly Journal of Economics* 89(3): 347–357.

Lawson, T. (1989a) 'Abstraction, Tendencies and Stylised Facts: A Realist Approach to Economic Analysis', *Cambridge Journal of Economics* 13(1): 59–78. Reprinted in T. Lawson, G. Palma and J. Sender (eds) (1989) *Kaldor's Political Economy*, London and San Diego: Academic Press. Also reprinted in P. Elkins and M. Max-Neef (eds) (1992) *Real Life Economics: Understanding Wealth Creation*, London: Routledge.

—— (1989b) 'Realism and Instrumentalism in the Development of Econometrics', *Oxford Economic Papers* 14(1): 236–58. Reprinted in N. de Marchi and C. Gilbert (eds) (1990) *History and Methodology of Econometrics*, Oxford: Oxford University Press.

—— (1992) 'Realism, Closed Systems and Friedman', *Research in the History of Economic Thought and Methodology* 10: 149–169.

—— (1994a) 'Critical Realism and the Analysis of Choice, Explanation and Change', *Advances in Austrian Economics*, 1(1): 25–35.

—— (1994b) 'Realism and Hayek: A Case of Continuous Transformation', in M. Colonna, H. Hagemann and O. F. Hamouda (eds) *Capitalism, Socialism and Information: The Economics of F. A. Hayek*, vol. II, Aldershot: Edward Elgar.

—— (1994c) 'Realism, Philosophical', in G. Hodgson, M. Tool and W. J. Samuels (eds) *Edward Elgar Companion to Evolutionary and Institutional Economics*, Aldershot: Edward Elgar.

—— (1994d) 'A Realist Theory for Economics', in Roger E. Backhouse (ed.) *New Directions in Economic Methodology*, London: Routledge.

Quine, W. V. D. (1960) *Word and Object*, Cambridge, MA: MIT Press.

Redman, D. A. (1991) *Economics and the Philosophy of Science*, Oxford: Oxford University Press.

van Fraassen, B. (1980) *The Scientific Image*, Oxford: Clarendon Press.

9

WHY THE 'TRANSCENDENTAL' IN TRANSCENDENTAL REALISM?

Stephen D. Parsons[1]

It is not the victory of science that is the distinguishing mark of our nineteenth century, but the victory of the scientific method over science.

Nietzsche

The Ideenkleid (the ideational veil) of mathematics and mathematical physics represents and disguises the empirical reality and leads us to take for True Being that which is only a method.

Husserl

Introduction

Through drawing upon the early works of Roy Bhaskar (mainly Bhaskar 1978; 1979), Tony Lawson had developed an interesting critique of certain assumptions which, it is claimed, underpin contemporary orthodox economics. Lawson characterises his approach as 'transcendental realism', contrasting it with the 'empirical realism' purportedly derived from Hume and adopted by mainstream economics.[2] The term 'transcendental' is invoked because 'the mode of reasoning employed here is basically Kantian' (1994: 124). The intention seems clear: Lawson will offer a Kantian-inspired transcendental argument in order to refute a Humean-based approach.[3] However, what exactly is meant by a transcendental mode of reasoning, and what is its relevance in rejecting a Humean approach?

What is a transcendental argument?

Initially, it may be useful to note certain arguments offered by a

151

different author to which the term 'transcendental' has been applied. Strawson (1959) claims that experience must be of spatial objects, and that I can only ascribe experiences to myself if I can ascribe them to others. Here, starting from some claim that is typically widely accepted ('I have experiences'), the argument attempts to show that other characteristics necessarily follow ('there is an external world', 'there exist other individuals'). Crudely put, these arguments purport to show that, given a widely accepted feature of the world, certain other features 'must', necessarily, be entailed. Consequently, transcendental arguments can initially be regarded as 'arguments that purport to establish certain *a priori* or necessary truths about the world' (Wilkerson 1976: 200). In Kant's case, the concern can be characterised as 'what are the necessary conditions of a possible experience' (Wilkerson 1976: 13) which are established through analysing 'the logical requirements for self-consciousness' (Bennett 1971: 303)?

With this, it would seem that the argument presented in transcendental realism will display the following form. It will start from premises that are widely accepted, and, through developing certain arguments, arrive at conclusions concerning certain necessary truths about the world. The actual description offered by Lawson is that the term 'transcendental' refers to the specific 'form of argument or reasoning' – i.e. to 'that species of retroduction which, following Kant, can be referred to as transcendental' (Lawson 1994: 124). The characterisation of the argument continues:

> The insights obtained, the support for the transcendental realist perspective sustained, have resulted from an analysis taking the form of an inquiry into the conditions of the possibility of certain especially significant generalized scientific practices and human capabilities that are experienced – scientific experimental practices in the natural realm as well as the capacity of human intentionality and choice in the social.
>
> (Lawson 1994: 124)

The argument advanced starts from certain premises (concerning scientific activities and human choice) and then, through a process of argumentation referred to as 'retroduction' or 'abduction', concludes with 'necessary conditions of a possible experience'. Presumably, as the premises from which the argument commences are (fairly) secure, the form of argument ('abduction') through which we arrive at certain conclusions from these premises is reliable, then the conclusions are valid. As the conclusions arrived at support the transcendental realist, not the empirical realist, case, then the argument for transcendental realism is vindicated.[4]

However, the relationship between the initial premise and the conclusions outlined is not as straightforward as the above would suggest. Thus it is admitted that 'the premises of (a) transcendental argument are always contestable' (ibid.: 124), and that the conclusions 'like all cognitive claims' are 'fallible and corrigible' (ibid.: 124). Consequently 'the results obtained must be recognized as conditional and hypothetical' (ibid.: 125). Despite this, it is argued that these caveats 'by no means undermine the realist project being defended' (ibid.: 125). Unfortunately, these caveats not only undermine the strength of the argument being advanced, they directly threaten the claim that a transcendental argument is being offered after all.

As noted earlier, transcendental arguments are concerned to establish certain *a priori* or necessary truths about the world. However, in the case of transcendental realism, the requirements of necessary or *a priori* truths are modified as follows:

> The transcendental argument to claims of 'necessity' . . . is, like all cognitive claims, also fallible and corrigible. . . . If, following Kant, (the results) are regarded as *a priori*, this cannot be understood in any absolute manner; merely in the sense of explaining the possibility of some other forms of knowledge.
>
> (Lawson 1994: 124–125)

What is to be made of the argument that the claim to have discerned certain necessary conditions of possibility is itself a contingent claim? We have:

Possibly, A is a necessary condition of B,

or

Possibly, A is a necessary truth,

where a necessary truth has the truth-value Truth in all situations. Clearly, if it is possible that A is a necessary condition of B, it is also possible that A is not a necessary condition of B. However, where exactly is the 'fallibility' in the argument creeping in? Either the initial premises selected are somewhat defective, or the mode of reasoning through which the conclusions are arrived at is deficient. Yet Lawson appears quite confident in the robustness of the initial premises:

The premises chosen as starting points for the transcendental argument are not only secure from the standpoint of current understandings but actually constitute central features of those accounts that, arguably, are most opposed to the theory of transcendental realism being supported here.

(Lawson 1994: 125)

The premises are not only widely accepted as 'valid', but significantly they would be acceptable to the opponents of transcendental realism. This entails that the only possible source of fallibility lies in the process of reasoning from these premises. Concerning this process, Lawson states that:

If deduction is, for example, to move from the general claim that 'all ravens are black' to the particular inference that the next one seen will be black, and induction is to move from the particular observation of numerous black ravens to the general claim that 'all ravens are black', retroductive or abductive reasoning is to move from the observation of numerous black ravens to a theory of a mechanism intrinsic to ravens which disposes them to being black.

(Lawson 1994: 116)

As noted, according to Lawson, the argument presented is transcendental precisely because it incorporates this process of retroductive or abductive reasoning. Consequently, in this case, from some widely acceptable premise ('ravens are black') we are arrive, abductively, at the conclusions that certain mechanisms must exist. Therefore, these mechanisms are 'necessary conditions' of the colour of ravens. Presumably this statement is 'fallible' because we might misidentify the 'correct' mechanism. In other words, 'fallibility' arises because of the fallibility of scientific knowledge.

It is now possible to discern the problem with Lawson's argument. Transcendental arguments involve claims about *logical* (or 'conceptual') necessities. Lawson's process of 'abduction' involves claims concerned with *causal* or 'natural' necessities. Transcendental arguments typically substantiate that, because X is logically necessary for Y, then X is a necessary condition of Y. In contrast, 'abduction' is concerned to substantiate that, because X is causally necessary for Y, then X is a necessary condition of Y: it seeks 'some "deeper" causal thing' (Lawson 1994: 117).

As transcendental realism is concerned with causal, not logical, necessities, then the status of the truths it claims to discover are also different from those pertaining to Kantian-inspired transcendental arguments. The latter seeks to establish what is logically, or *a priori*, true:[5] transcendental realism seeks to establish what is empirically, or *a posteriori*, true. Lawson admits that the '*a priori* truths' unearthed by transcendental realism are 'not absolute': however, he fails to realise that this is simply because they are not '*a priori*'. Consequently, the argument presented in transcendental realism is not transcendental in the sense ascribed to Kant, and if it is not transcendental in this sense, it is difficult to appreciate how it is 'transcendental' at all.

Of course, the arguments presented by Strawson, or Kant himself, may be mistaken. However, in these cases, the mistake is a philosophical failure to illuminate correctly, say, the logically necessary conditions of experience. With transcendental realism, the term 'mistaken' pertains to the empirical failure to elucidate the 'causally necessary' conditions of scientific phenomena. Lawson himself admits that: 'It is at least conceivable that other conceptions might (eventually) similarly derive support from (the same or alternative) accepted features of experience – facilitating different, perhaps competing, accounts equally qualifying for the label of "transcendental realism"' (Lawson 1994: 131, footnote 14).

Yet if we may arrive at different conclusions from the same premise, or different conclusions from different, equally viable, premises, then it is difficult to appreciate how we are being offered more than arbitrary inferences from arbitrary premises. Again, if the arguments are not concerned to establish logically necessary conditions, why are they termed transcendental?

The claimed 'Kantian source' of the argument becomes even more remote if one of the premises of Lawson's argument is recalled. Transcendental realism attempts to establish the (empirical) 'conditions of possibility' of scientific practices, and such practices thus constitute one of the premises of the argument. This premise is not found in Kant, who derives the basic concepts of experience from the premise of experience or self-consciousness, not any particular sphere of validity (e.g. scientific practices). This is significant because Kant's own 'transcendental deduction' assumes that 'the knowledge and use of the categories as *a priori* concepts presupposes neither philosophical analysis nor even the conscious pursuit of scientific knowledge' (Henrich 1989: 253). Henrich refers to this as the 'Rousseauian criterion': Kant justifies the claims of ordinary individuals to have well-founded experiences.

In contrast, transcendental realism legitimises the claims of *scientific* knowledge through assuming, from the start, the validity of scientific experiences.[6] The argument being advanced is, at best, regarded as neo-Kantian, not Kantian, in inspiration. This is because a certain type of knowledge and practices – scientific – are assumed to be 'valid', and thus ' "Transcendental realism" . . . is a repetition of a traditional Geltungslogik which assumes the validity of scientific realms' (Rose 1981: 212).[7]

In summary, a Kantian-inspired transcendental argument seeks to establish certain 'logical' or 'conceptual' necessities from specific widely accepted features of experience. Lawson's transcendental realism is concerned to establish certain empirical truths about the world, starting from the premise of scientific practices. As neither the form of the argument advanced, nor its starting point, can be attributed to Kant, then introducing the term 'transcendental' seems ill judged.

Justification of realism

However, it may be the case that the above merely indicates a certain amount of carelessness in formulating the nature of the arguments being advanced. Consequently, when the specific arguments are examined in detail, it may be the case that logical, not empirical, pre-requirements are exhibited. As noted, transcendental realism appeals to two premises, and the investigation is described as 'An inquiry into the conditions of the possibility of certain especially significant gener-alized scientific practices and human capabilities' (Lawson 1994: 124). From these two premises – scientific practices and (as yet unspecified) human capabilities – arguments claiming to be 'transcendental' will be advanced. The object of these arguments is to show that 'the Humean project in its economic guise . . . must be recognised as quite misguided' (ibid.: 123). However, unpacking this claim leaves it quite unclear who or what the specific target of criticism is. At times it seems to be Hume himself – 'But of course, as with Hume himself' (ibid.: 111) – at other times contemporary methodologists or philosophers influenced by Hume – hence references to 'Humean analysis' (ibid.: 111) – and at yet other times 'the Humean . . . conception of science' which, it is claimed, 'is uncritically accepted in much of contemporary economics' (ibid.: 112). Criticism thus appears to be directed at (i) Hume; (ii) the 'Humean project'; and (iii) the Humean conception of science.

Unfortunately, the arguments directed against Hume himself display a lack of sensitivity to the subtleties and complexities of Hume's own analysis. For example, it is argued that Hume denied 'The possibility of establishing the independent existence of things' (Lawson 1994: 111). Compare this to Hume himself: 'As to what may be said, that the operations of nature are independent of our thought and reasoning, I allow it' (Hume 1978: 168). Similarly, we are told that positivism 'is rooted in the writings of Hume' (Lawson 1994: 111) and 'presupposes an ontology . . . (which) comprises atomistic events and their (supposedly ubiquitous) constant conjunctions' (ibid.: 112). However, Galen Strawson has argued that Hume's claims were specifically epistemological, not ontological. That is, Hume claimed that all we can ever *know* concerning causation is regular succession, not that causation is regular succession (Strawson 1989). If the arguments are directed at Hume himself, then – as with the claimed 'Kantian foundation' – considerably more care is warranted.

Given this, it would seem advisable to move to the next target, and construe the arguments as targeted at the 'Humean position' or 'Humean conception of science' termed empirical realism. The main difference between empirical and transcendental realism is summarised thus:

> According to transcendental realism the world is conceived first of all as constituted not only by phenomena interpretable as events and states of affairs and our impression or experience of them but also by (possibly irreducible) structures, mechanisms, powers and tendencies that, although perhaps not directly observable, nevertheless do underlie actual events and govern them.
>
> (Lawson 1994: 114–115)

Whereas the empirical realist only admits to events and states of affairs, transcendental realism seeks to substantiate the truth of the claim that there are various structures and mechanisms which 'underlie' and 'govern' them. Modesty is certainly no virtue here, as apparently 'there is no comparably viable alternative theory of ontology on the scene' (Lawson 1994: 131, footnote 14) – a claim that seems somewhat premature as only a purported 'Humean ontology' is subject to critique.

The argument concerning scientific practices derives its initial premise from what is claimed to be the 'Humean view', committed to a belief in event regularities. Consequently, the transcendental argument takes event regularities as the initial premise, asking 'Under what conditions are the sought after event regularities of Humean science actually obtained?' (Lawson 1994: 119). The transcendental argument thus runs from the premise of event regularities sought by science, and will attempt to justify the claim that the world is indeed in the form argued for in transcendental realism. If the argument is indeed a Kantian-inspired transcendental argument, then it must be indicated how a commitment to event regularities logically necessitates a commitment to transcendental realism. The relevant argument can be broken down thus:

1   outside of astronomy, most constant conjunctions of events only occur in experimental conditions;
2   however, the resulting 'law-like' claims are frequently successfully applied outside the experimental situation;
3   the constant conjunction view of laws leaves the question as to what governs events outside of the experimental situation unanswered and unaddressed;
4   consequently, events must be governed by mechanisms.

As the statement that 'most constant conjunctions of events only occur in experimental situations' logically entails that constant conjunctions of events occur, then it might be more advantageous to take this as the premise of the argument. This is because it is claimed that the empirical realist accepts that constant conjunctions of events occur, although may not accept that such conjunctions only occur in experimental situations. Thus from the premise that constant conjunctions of events occur, the argument concludes that thus 'powers and tendencies ... underlie actual events and govern or produce them' (Lawson 1994: 114–115). The argument boils down to this. A Humean analysis concerned with establishing causal relations searches for constant conjunctions of events. However, this fails to recognise that such conjunctions only occur in experimental situations. If only the Humean analysis acknowledged this, it would be forced to recognise that any such events must be governed by mechanisms.

One problem consists in the relationship between the premise that constant conjunctions occur and the next stage of the argument. If opponents of transcendental realism believe that constant conjunctions of events are 'ubiquitous' in non-experimental situations, then why should they accept the thesis that they are not? This problem is not trivial. If constant conjunctions of events do not occur outside of the experimental situation, why should science be interested in producing them? Further, if constant conjunctions only occur in experimental situations, and yet the scientific findings so obtained can be applied outside of the experimental situation, what exactly are these findings applied to? An answer to these questions may be forthcoming if we ask: does transcendental realism accept the initial premise of their own argument – that constant conjunctions of events occur?

The answer seems straightforward enough – they occur in experimental situations, and only rarely outside. Unfortunately, this answer gives two different, competing accounts as to what the causal relation relates, and two competing accounts as to what a law refers to. As constant conjunctions of events do not readily occur in an open system, then any causal relations or laws outside the experimental situation cannot refer to such events. Consequently, when experimental findings are applied outside of the experimental situation, they are applied to events, where 'events . . . are multiply determined by various, perhaps countervailing, factors' (Lawson 1994: 115).

Given this, then the causal relation relates mechanisms to events. For example 'the autumn leaf pass(es) to the ground . . . underlying such movement and governing it are real mechanisms such as gravity' (Lawson 1994: 115). This implies that the main problem with 'empirical realism' lies with the understanding of the causal relation. According to empirical realism, the causal relation relates events: however, according to transcendental realism, the causal relation relates an event and a mechanism or mechanisms. Thus, say, there is an event (the falling of a leaf) and a 'causal' mechanism (gravity) plus (in an open system) mechanisms (countervailing forces). As transcendental realism differentiates between the 'ontological levels' of mechanisms and states of affairs or events, then a causal relation relating mechanisms to events cannot also relate events to events, and the empirical realist understanding of the causal relation is wrong. Consequently, for transcendental realism, in an open system, a law 'must express not event regularities but . . . structures and their modes of activity' (ibid.: 117).

However, what of the situation under experimental activity? Here, 'event regularities that have been elaborated have been restricted in the main to situations of experimental control' (Lawson 1994: 120). Consequently, 'Outside astronomy at least, most of the constant event conjunctions that are held *as significant, as laws*, only in fact occur under the restricted conditions of experimental control' (Lawson 1994: 119, emphasis added). Here, laws refer to constant event conjunctions, not event/mechanism relations. However, if scientific activity produces constant event conjunctions then, in the experimental situation, causal relations would seem to relate events, and laws refer to constant event conjunctions. Indeed, why would science produce such conjunctions, unless the causal relation relates events? Consequently, in the experimental situation, laws refer to constant event conjunctions, and the causal relation relates events.

There appears to be some confusion here. In an attempted clarification, take the following examples offered of the relationship between 'surface phenomena' and 'governing mechanisms':

- skin spots and viruses;
- puppies turning into dogs and genetic codes;
- relatively slow productivity growth in the UK and the British system of industrial relations.

(Lawson 1994: 115)

According to transcendental realism, the 'actual' level is that of events and states of affairs, which are governed by mechanisms. However, each of these causal relations can be stated simply in terms of events or states of affairs, such as:

State of affairs A caused state of affairs B

If all of the given examples can be so rephrased, then the transcendental realist *is*, necessarily, committed to the view that the empirical realist's constant conjunctions of events do occur outside the experimental situation, this directly contradicting the original argument. Transcendental realism accepts that the above three examples occur in an open system, and the empirical realist would be quite happy to accept this also, identifying them as examples of causal relations between events. Of course, the causal relation is asymmetric: however, it cannot be concluded that, therefore, this asymmetry pertains to an asymmetry of 'ontological levels'. Consequently, whatever transcendental realism is objecting to, it does not now seem to be the empirical realist argument that the causal relation relates events or states of affairs. This is because transcendental realism:

1 bases its analysis of causality upon precisely such relations in experimental situations;
2 implicitly assumes that such relations occur outside of the experimental situation (in so far as all the examples offered can be redescribed in terms of states of affairs).

However, if transcendental realism cannot produce an argument as to why the causal relation does not relate events and states of affairs, then any reference to the 'deep' level appears completely superfluous. Consequently, it seems necessary to clarify what the difference between transcendental realism and empirical realism essentially consists in. Following Tooley (1987), someone advocating a realist interpretation can be identified in terms of answers to the following two questions:

1 Do the theoretical terms in theory T have a denotation?

2   Is it possible to analyse or reduce all statements about such enti-
    ties to statements about the observable properties and relations of
    observable objects?

Transcendental realism would give an affirmative answer to question
(1), thus opposing instrumentalism. However, in the present context,
question (2) is the more pertinent. Whilst the transcendental realist
would give a negative answer to (2), the empirical realist would give
an affirmative answer to the same question. The transcendental realist
objection to empirical realism is that the latter demands that all statements must refer to observable properties and objects. The objection is
that, in 'Humean analysis', 'reality is essentially defined as that which
is given in experience' (Lawson 1994: 111). As transcendental realism
asserts the existence of mechanisms that are 'perhaps not directly
visible' (ibid.: 115), then such entities would not be admissible to the
empirical realist.

Consequently, whilst the empirical realist is interested in event
regularities, transcendental realism is interested in discovering laws
that 'express' (unseen) mechanisms: 'Laws, or law-statements, must
express not event regularities but precisely such structures and their
modes of activities' (Lawson 1994: 117). There is a further, related,
objection to empirical realism in its 'Humean guise'. Hume argued
that causal relations are contingent, whereas transcendental realism
claims they are necessary. Therefore, the transcendental realist is
concerned with establishing laws 'expressing' mechanisms, not event
regularities, and causal relations as necessary, not contingent.
However, there is a major problem with the strategy pursued by transcendental realism:

> Even if it turns out to be true that laws are not reducible to
> regularities, it will still be the case that there is no *observable*
> difference between a world that contains certain regularities,
> and a world that contains both regularities and underlying
> laws. This means that for any nomological statement there
> will be an experientially equivalent statement that refers only
> to the corresponding, Humean regularities. . . . In the case of
> causal terms . . . it will still be true that there is no *observable*
> difference between a world in which all of the non-causal facts
> are as they would be if states of affairs were causally related,
> and a world in which the states of affairs in question really are
> causally related.
>
> (Tooley 1987: 28, emphasis in original)

There is thus no observable difference between the world as it appears to the transcendental realist and the world as it appears for the Humean analysis. Therefore, we cannot somehow 'read off' from the way the world is, that one or other position is correct. Consequently, the transcendental argument must, necessarily, fail. If it starts from a premise about experience or the world that the Humean analysis would accept, then these features of the world will look the same whatever explanation is 'really true'. This is why the transcendental realist argument states that the world is not 'really' the way the empirical realist sees it (i.e. constant conjunctions of events do not occur).

The transcendental realist is thus caught in a dilemma. If the premise of the transcendental argument refers to observable features of the world that the empirical realist would accept, then these features can be appealed to in support of either position. However, if the argument is 'loaded', as it were, and observable features are appealed to that the empirical realist would not accept, then the initial premise of the argument would simply be rejected. A transcendental argument that starts from a premise concerning observations acceptable to both parties cannot establish natural necessity.

It is now possible to relate this result to the targets of transcendental realism, starting with Hume himself. In the course of his analysis of causality, Hume states that:

> Here is a billiard-ball lying on the table, and another ball moving towards it with rapidity. They strike; and the ball, which was formerly at rest, now acquires a motion. This is as perfect an instance of the relation of cause and effect as any which we know, either by sensation or reflection.
>
> (Hume 1978: 649)

As this relation between billiard-balls is a 'perfect example' of cause and effect, and if, as transcendental realism claims, Hume based his analysis of causality on the constant conjunction of events, then Hume clearly believed that the billiard-ball example is an example of the constant conjunction of events. The transcendental realist can now adopt either one of the two strategies outlined above. One strategy is to argue that Hume is mistaken in identifying these occurrences as a constant conjunction of events, as such events only occur in the experimental situation. Not only would this be rejected by Hume, it would destroy the claim that Hume does base his analysis on a constant conjunction of events.

Alternatively, it may be argued that something about the observations Hume is making necessarily commits him to the transcendental realist position. However, as Hume's whole argument, as transcendental realism acknowledges, is that nothing he observes so commits him, then he would again reject the argument. If Hume is committed, as transcendental realism claims, to the view that only events and states of experiences that can be experienced can claim legitimacy, then he would not be convinced by any appeal to unobservable entities. Whatever strategy is adopted, the argument fails.

What if attention is now directed at a contemporary 'Humean position'? Two key components of this position will be taken as:[8]

- given the problems in establishing causal relations as 'necessary', there cannot be entailment-licensed predictions;
- causal relations involve relations between events however described, and causal explanations relate propositions, not events.[9] As causal relations 'hold' no matter how described, the analysis can proceed through using a purely extensional language. This allows for substitution of co-extensive terms without affecting truth value. For example, if falling from the ladder was the cause of Fred's death, and 'Fred' and 'the oldest man in Manchester' refer to the same individual, then falling from the ladder was the cause of the death of the oldest man in Manchester.

As the causal relation holds no matter how described, then a singular causal judgement does not require any reference to a 'law': 'A singular causal statement entails that there is a relevant law, but does not entail the relevant law' (Bennett 1971: 309; see also Davidson (1980)).[10] What this means is that if a singular causal judgement is made of the form 'Jones's fall from the ladder caused his death' this statement is not somehow defective because it does not refer to some 'law'. Further, this causal statement specifies the whole cause of the event of Jones's death, even if it does not wholly specify it. Consequently, from the perspective of the 'Humean position', a singular causal judgement does not require any reference to a 'law', and is not defective because of this omission.

Of course, the concern here is with singular causal judgements, not constant conjunctions of events. However, as one arm of the transcendental realist argument is to deny that these occur outside the experimental situation, criticism can hardly be levelled on this account. Further, as there are no observations that the transcendental realist can indicate to persuade the advocate of the 'Humean position' why any statement must be law-like, then transcendental realism cannot explain why a singular causal judgement in the above form does not specify the whole cause of an event.

The problem with the argument against empirical realism again goes back to the misunderstanding of a transcendental argument. A Kantian-inspired transcendental argument is concerned with logical necessity, and commences from a widely accepted premise. In contrast, transcendental realism attempts two strategies. It either commences from a premise unacceptable to the empirical realist – that event regularities only occur in experimental situations. Here, it accepts such regularities, yet argues that, because of the manner of their occurrence, mechanisms do exist. Here, as with the empirical realist, the causal relation appears to relate events, and nomological statements refer to event regularities. Alternatively, it argues that the empirical realist misunderstands the nature of the causal relation and nomological statements. However, both claims involve the positing of unseen natural necessities which, as unseen, would not be accepted by the empirical realist. Consequently, there is nothing within the observational set shared by the transcendental and empirical realist which would force the latter to accept the claims of the former. However, as the argument is not concerned with logical necessities, then there is nothing that would logically force the empirical realist to accept the required claims. Consequently, the argument has neither observational nor logical force, although these are two criteria which would be acceptable to the empirical realist.

Summing up so far. The argument advanced by transcendental realism is neither transcendental nor Kantian. The position of Hume is oversimplified and, when the Humean causal relation is explored, transcendental realism misses the mark. It must conclude either that Hume did not see what he claimed to see, or misinterpreted what he saw. It is quite unclear why Hume should accept either of these claims. In the case of a contemporary 'Humean position', transcendental realism does not appear equipped to deal with the relevant arguments. However, this still leaves another 'transcendental argument' awaiting exploration.

The argument from human capabilities

Again, what is required here is an argument which commences from some aspect of human capabilities, and results in the claim that the world must be of the form claimed in transcendental realism. The argument can be broken down as follows (Lawson 1994: 121–122):

1 choice is real;
2 this 'presupposes that the world is open and actual events need not have been';

164

3   this in turn 'entails that agents have some conception of what they are doing';
4   'all agency . . . is inherently transformational';
5   therefore 'there are real material causes which proceed (sic) it';
6   consequently 'agents must have knowledge at least of the conditions that render their intended acts . . . feasible';
7   this 'knowledge presupposes sufficient endurability in the objects of knowledge to facilitate their coming to be known';
8   however, 'event regularities, or at least significant ones, do not, as widely reported, generally occur in the social realm';
9   consequently 'the enduring objects of knowledge must then lie at a different level – at that of structures which govern, but which are irreducible to, events'.

This argument can also be briefly summarised. As agents make choices, they must have some awareness of the world within which these choices are made. Such knowledge, in turn, is only possible if the 'objects of knowledge' are (relatively) enduring. Therefore, there are (relatively) enduring structures that govern events. The key problem is clearly how the 'therefore' follows from the previous statements. Consequently, for brevity's sake, the arguments from 1 to 4 will only receive minimal attention, as the key problem lies with 7 on.

Hume or a contemporary Humean would not accept the reference to a 'material cause' in 5. However, if the argument that transformational action requires something that can be transformed, and if the transcendental realist wishes to term this a 'material cause', so be it. So if arguments 1 to 7 are accepted, the main problem is with 8. This time, the problem is that argument 8 bears absolutely no relationship to 7, and thus conclusion 9 simply does not follow. The argument illicitly moves from an argument concerning enduring objects, to one concerning event regularities, with no connecting arguments to support this move. Even if knowledge presupposes enduring objects, why does an argument concerning the occurrence or otherwise of event regularities have any relevance in this context?

In attempting clarification, the statements from 7 onwards appear to consist in an attempt to reformulate an argument initially advanced by the philosopher Strawson, derived from Kant, and modified by Davidson. According to Strawson, there is only a limited possibility of identifying events without reference to objects, as objects provide 'a single, comprehensive and continuously usable framework' of reference (Strawson 1959: 46ff.). In other words, identifying something as an event presupposes relatively enduring objects. If Strawson's argument is accepted, it does show that identifying *events* requires enduring *objects*. Davidson (1980: Chapter 8) has further argued that 'events often play an essential role in identifying a substance' (1980: 175). However, neither of these arguments remotely substantiate the claim that, therefore, objects are 'underlying structures', or 'generative mechanisms'.

Identifying events may require (relatively) enduring objects, and events may facilitate the identification of objects. However, none of this entails that the 'objects' in question are the 'objects of knowledge' that transcendental realism is concerned with. The argument, quite illicitly, *redefines* a Humean or empirical realist 'object' as a transcendental realist 'object of knowledge' – i.e. a 'structure'. Not only is it difficult to appreciate why anyone should find this even remotely convincing, it seems to result in absurdity. If any action is an event, and if all events are governed by mechanisms, then all actions are so governed. However, if all actions are governed, how are they the result of choice, an assumption that forms the initial premise of the argument?

If the argument is scrutinised in the context of transcendental arguments generally, it can be seen where the confusion arises. Arguments 1 to 7 could be identified, in the manner of Strawson, as an attempt to establish certain 'logically' or 'conceptually' necessary truths. Thus, it is logically necessary, in order that individuals can make choices, that any objects pertaining to these choices are (relatively) enduring. However, arguments 8 and 9 are not concerned with logical necessity at all, but with *causal* necessity. Consequently, the argument breaks down at the very point that a confusion about 'necessity' surfaces. The argument moves from a concern with logical necessity to a concern with causal necessity, yet remains oblivious to the distinction between these two understandings of necessity, even though this confusion completely breaks the back of the argument.

Conclusion

What conclusions follow from the above analysis as far as economics is concerned? According to transcendental realism:

> Social structure can only be present in an open system. In consequence, it would seem, any economic laws must usually be manifest merely as tendencies and only rarely . . . as empirical regularities, so that the Humean project in its economic guise must . . . be recognised as quite misguided.
>
> (Lawson 1994: 123)

All this appears to say is that the economic system is an open system, and thus strict economic laws are not discoverable. This statement does not require any reference to Hume, Kant, positivism, 'Humean analysis', or anything else. If economists agree that the economic system is an open system, then some form of aid may be forthcoming from transcendental realism. However, I suggest not before the following questions have been answered.

- What does a causal relation relate?
- What does a law-like statement refer to?
- Why is natural science interested in event regularities?
- If the economic system is an open system where any closure is impossible, then what is the relevance of the mechanisms apparently detectable under closure in natural science? The social sciences generally would appear to be incapable of correctly identifying any mechanisms purportedly existing, so what is the relevance of the natural sciences here?
- If constant conjunctions do not occur in open systems, then why does this happen – 5555555 – when I repeatedly press the '5' key on the keyboard?

Notes

1 This paper is partially based on a presentation given at the Post Keynesian Study Group, London, 1995. The author would like to thank participants for comments.
2 Lawson also characterises the approach he is arguing against as 'positivism'. I regard this characterisation as misleading.
3 As Lawson's position with regard to transcendental arguments is clearly set out in Lawson (1994), I shall restrict the following comments to this article.
4 Following Lawson, I will use 'empirical realism' and 'Humean inspired', or 'Humean approach' interchangeably, with term used depending upon context.
5 Unlike Strawson, Kant bases his argument on what he terms 'transcendental logic'. However, this difference does not effect the similar status of their respective arguments.
6 In the case of Bhaskar himself, it is argued that 'it is a condition of the possibility of scientific activities (A) and (B) that the world is stratified and differentiated, X and Y' (Bhaskar 1979: 7). In a footnote to his article, Lawson himself states that 'The question posed is: what claims about the nature of reality are tenable in the sense that they render intelligible the generalized phenomenon of experience taken as premise?' (Lawson 1994: 131, footnote 14). However, a transcendental argument from the premise of 'generalised experience' is not presented.
7 A 'Geltungslogik' is a neo-Kantian logic of validity.
8 See Beauchamp and Rosenberg (1981), Bennett (1971), Davidson (1980)

9 Thus Bennett states that in 'the "Humean view" the causal relation holds between events' (Bennett 1971: 311).
10 Strawson weakens this assumption even further:

> At the level of ordinary causal explanations of particular events and circumstances, the level at which we employ the common vocabulary of description rather than the technical vocabulary of physical theories, there is no reason to think that our explanations presuppose or rest upon beliefs in the existence of general, exceptionable, and discoverable laws.
>
> (Strawson 1985: 132–133)

Bibliography

Beauchamp, T. L. and Rosenberg, A. (1981) *Hume and the Problem of Causation*, New York: Oxford University Press.

Bennett, J. (1971) *Locke, Berkeley, Hume: Central Themes*, Oxford: Clarendon Press.

Bhaskar, Roy (1978) *A Realist Theory of Science*, 2nd edn, Hassocks: Harvester Press.

—— (1979) *The Possibility of Naturalism*, Brighton: Harvester Press.

Brueckner, A. L. (1983) 'Transcendental Arguments I', *Nous*, 17.

—— (1984) 'Transcendental Arguments II', *Nous*, 18: 197–225.

Davidson, D. (1980) *Essays on Actions and Events*, Oxford: Clarendon Press.

Henrich, D. (1989) 'The Identity of the Subject in the Transcendental Deduction', in E. Shaper and W. Vossenkhil (eds) *Reading Kant: New Perspectives on Transcendental Arguments and Critical Philosophy*, Oxford: Oxford University Press.

Hume, D. (1978) *A Treatise of Human Nature*, Oxford: Clarendon Press.

Lawson, T. (1994) 'Why Are So Many Economists So Opposed to Methodology?', *Journal of Economic Methodology* 1: 105–134.

Parsons, S. (1996) 'Post Keynesian Realism and Keynes's General Theory', *Journal of Post Keynesian Economics* 18(3): 419–443.

Rose, G. (1981) *Hegel Contra Sociology*, London: Athlone Press.

Strawson, G. (1989) *The Secret Connexion: Causation, Realism, and David Hume*, Oxford: Clarendon Press.

Strawson, P. F. (1959) *Individuals*, London: Methuen.

—— (1985) 'Causation and Explanation', in B. Vermagen and M. B. Hintikka (eds) *Essays on Davidson: Actions and Events*, Oxford: Clarendon Press.

Tooley, M. (1987) *Causation: A Realist Approach*, Oxford: Clarendon Press.

Wilkerson, T. E. (1976) *Kant's Critique of Pure Reason*, Oxford: Clarendon Press.

10

EMPIRICAL REALISM AS META-METHOD

Tony Lawson on neoclassical economics

D. Wade Hands

Introduction

Tony Lawson has, over the last few years, established a reputation as the economics profession's staunchest and most prolific defender of Roy Bhaskar's transcendental realist philosophy of science. In a series of papers beginning in the late 1980s Lawson systematically defended Bhaskarian realism as a general philosophical framework for understanding scientific knowledge – both natural and social – while at the same time using this philosophical perspective as the springboard for a sustained critique of the theoretical and empirical practice of mainstream economists.[1]

The breadth of Lawson's realist programme provides his critics with a potentially wide range of possible targets for critical examination. Detractors might contest: realism in general; Bhaskar's transcendental realism in particular; Lawson's own reading of realism, Bhaskar, or any other aspect of his philosophical discussion; the Lawson/Bhaskar reading of the primary alternative to transcendental realism (called empirical realism); or even the particular application of transcendental realism to the social sciences (called critical realism).[2] While the following discussion will provide a critical commentary on Lawson's project, it will not focus on any of these philosophical issues; in fact, there will not be any attempt to criticise Lawson's (or Bhaskar's) realist position at all. My decision not to challenge any of these core philosophical notions should not be interpreted as a statement that such issues are uninteresting, or not legitimate fodder for critical discussion, or that Lawson's Bhaskarian philosophy is beyond reproach. It simply means that this is not the place or the time for debating philosophical realism; the critical focus in this chapter will be on economics and economic methodology.

The following discussion will focus exclusively on *Lawson's reading of neoclassical economics*, or to be more specific, *his argument that the philosophical underpinning of modern neoclassical (mainstream) economics is empirical realism*. Lawson's reading will be challenged directly – by looking at the type of theoretical activity that actually occurs within mainstream economics – and also by examining what various philosophers and economic methodologists have said about the defining characteristics of neoclassical theory. The bottom line of this discussion will be that Lawson's claims are way off base – that neoclassical economics is not in any sense the empirical realist-inspired inquiry that Lawson makes it out to be – in fact, it seems to be more consistent with the type of transcendental realism that he himself endorses.

The chapter is arranged as follows. The first section briefly reviews transcendental realism, empirical realism, and Lawson's reading of mainstream economics. The next section briefly examines the theoretical practice of economists and demonstrates that while it may not be clear exactly what mainstream neoclassical theory is, it most clearly is not an exercise in empirical realism. The following section briefly examines the history of methodological discourse in economics and demonstrates that the vast majority of commentators have not found economics to be consistent with empirical realism (and that is often seen as a problem) and that it is actually closer to transcendental realism (and that, for many, is also a problem). The conclusion offers some comments about the implications (and irony) of Lawson's particular reading of modern economic theory.

Empirical realism and neoclassical economics

Roy Bhaskar's philosophy of science was presented in a series of books and articles over the last twenty or so years.[3] His general approach has been to uncover a number of fundamental tensions within the positivist-inspired view of scientific knowledge and to posit his own transcendental realism as an alternative (and solution) to these problems. Bhaskar is in many respects a very contemporary philosopher of science; by this I mean that he (like so many recent philosophers) tries to walk a middle ground between the traditional concerns of *philosophers* (as opposed to historians or sociologists) of science and the contemporary recognition of the social, and perhaps even socially constructed, nature of the scientific enterprise. While Bhaskar seems to be quite contemporary in his approach, he is not a philosopher that gets much attention from the general philosophical community – this is in spite of the fact that his arguments often have much in common with various other philosophers (Cartwright 1989, for example) who do get discussed in the philosophical literature. Bhaskar's main impact has been – and this is in part due to the work of individuals such as Tony Lawson – in the philosophy of social science.

Bhaskar's approach, unlike most philosophers of science, is *ontological*. He argues that any theory of knowledge, any epistemology, necessarily presupposes some (perhaps implicit) ontological commitment regarding the objects of that knowledge. Empiricist epistemology, the epistemology of mainstream philosophy of science, inspires an implicit ontology of *empirical realism*, which makes the objects of scientific investigation the same as the objects of sense experience. Since those things that can be observed, the objects of sense experience, are most often empirical event regularities, event regularities become the objects of (the only objects of) scientific inquiry. As Lawson characterises the situation, science becomes concerned exclusively with identifying regularities of the form 'whenever event (type) x then event (type) y'. Bhaskar refers to this view as the *epistemic fallacy*: the fallacy of reducing matters of ontology (existence or being) to matters of epistemology (knowledge).

This epistemic fallacy generates an *ontological tension* (Bhaskar 1989: 18) in at least two different ways. First, it generates a tension between the standard philosophical characterisation of scientific knowledge and the ontological presuppositions of practising scientists. Practising scientists actually look for the underlying, hidden, causal mechanisms that generate the empirical regularities they observe, and consider these underlying causes, not the empirical regularities themselves, to be the proper objects of scientific inquiry. A second, related, tension emerges within the experimental practice of science. Successful experimental practice always entails structuring the environment so that the effect of a single causal mechanism can be isolated; it requires the artificial structuring of the experimental context so as to eliminate or neutralise the impact of all other causal mechanisms other than the one under consideration. The empirical regularities that are supposed to be at the heart of science can only be observed in the closed and human-constructed environment of experimental systems; implying, of course, that there is nothing 'natural' about the domain of natural science.

The necessity of experimental closure doubly vindicates realism. On one hand, the 'facts' of science are clearly a social product; the observable facts of science 'are real; but they are historically specific social realities' (Bhaskar 1989: 61). This means that if, as empiricism suggests, the 'laws of nature' are factual regularities, then 'we are logically committed to the absurdities that scientists, in their experimental activity, cause and even change the laws of nature!' (ibid.: 15–16). On the other hand, in order to apply science outside the environment of the laboratory one must presuppose that the same causal mechanisms that were empirically revealed in the closed experimental context will continue to act in the more complex open environment outside the lab, again suggesting that something must be going on other than the constant conjunction of empirical events. All of this adds up to an extremely problematic situation for empiricist philosophy of science; Bhaskar offers transcendental realism as a solution to these problems.

Transcendental realism starts with an ontological distinction between the underlying causal laws (generative structures, capacities, causal powers, mechanisms, etc.) and the observable patterns of events (empirical regularities). These underlying causal mechanisms are the *intransitive* objects of scientific inquiry, while the empirical regularities are the *transitive* products of scientific investigation. These causal laws are tendencies which may or may not exhibit themselves empirically in any particular situation. In the complex and open world outside the experimental environment there are many causal forces at work, many *tendencies*, and that which becomes empirically manifest is co-produced by the interaction of these multiple causal factors. These empirical manifestations are more likely to be observed within the context of a closed experimental environment, but that is the purpose of the experimental set-up; the 'experimental activity can be explained as an attempt to intervene in order to *close* the system, in order, in other words, to insulate a particular mechanism of interest by holding off all other potentially counteracting mechanisms' (Lawson 1994a: 268, emphasis in original). The process of scientific development is the process of uncovering ever deeper layers of these causal forces; the intransitive domain of these causal forces exists independently of our scientific investigation, but the scientific investigation is itself a transitive and historically contingent social process. Transcendental realism simultaneously sustains the claims that: (1) the object of science is to uncover non-observable causal laws that exist independently of our theorising about them, and (2) that science is socially produced and its empirical domain does not exist independently of our theorising.

> Now I have argued . . . that constant conjunctions are not in general spontaneously available in nature but rather have to be worked for in the laboratories of science, so that causal laws and the other objects of experimental investigation must, if that activity is to be rendered intelligible, be regarded as ontologically independent of the patterns of events and the activities of human beings alike; and that, conversely, the

concepts and descriptions under which we bring them must, if *inter alia* scientific development is to be possible, be seen as part of the irreducibly social process of science. Thus experiences (and the facts they ground), and the constant conjunctions of events that form the empirical grounds for causal laws, are social products. But the objects to which they afford us access, such as causal laws, exist and act quite independently of us.

(Bhaskar 1989: 51)

As Lawson and others have emphasised, Bhaskar's transcendental realism has particularly strong implications for the social sciences. For one thing, social systems are inherently open, which makes it particularly difficult to find useful empirical regularities within the social context; an implication of this openness is that human science will be much more concerned with explanation than prediction. For another thing, the social nature of 'fact production' is even more significant in the social sciences where the (social) process of science is more clearly, and more inseparably, intertwined with the (social) object domain. For Bhaskar, the human sciences are clearly 'sciences', but they have their own unique characteristics and he does not in any way support their reduction to biology or physics.

To sum up, then, society is not given in, but presupposed by, experience. But it is precisely its peculiar ontological status, its transcendentally real character, that makes it a possible object of knowledge for us. Such knowledge is non-natural but still scientific. As for the law-like statements of the social sciences, they designate tendencies operating at a single level of the social structure only. Because they are defined only for one relatively autonomous component of the social structure and because they act in systems that are always open, they designate tendencies (such as for the rates of profit on capitalist enterprises to be equalised) which may never be manifested. But they are nevertheless essential to the understanding and the changing of, just because they are really productive of, the different forms of social life.

(Bhaskar 1989: 87)

Lawson wholeheartedly endorses Bhaskar's transcendental realist critique of empirical realist-based philosophy of science (termed 'positivism' by Lawson)[4] and also the application of his view to the discipline of economics (critical realism). But for Lawson critical realism is the way that economists *should* think about economics; it is *not the way that economists actually do think about their discipline.* According to Lawson, modern neoclassical economics is not concerned with identifying the underlying, intransitive, causal mechanisms that generate economic phenomena, or in characterising the tendency laws that are in operation in the background of economic life; instead it is driven by the search for the type of constant conjunctions and event regularities that characterise the positivist approach to scientific knowledge. Not only is empirical realism the philosophical vision that undergirds economic theorising, this empiricist vision is also, according to Lawson, the main reason for the discipline's many failures. Both the substantive claims and the heuristic practice of mainstream economics are a product of the positivist approach to scientific knowledge and its associated 'deductivist' approach to explanation.

> Now it is not merely the case that these two positivistic results or features – the event regularity conception of science and a social theory based upon the atomistic individual – are widely accepted in contemporary economics; they are, I suggest, definitive of it. Together, they determine both the structure of orthodox analysis as well as its material form.... For such reasons, if to repeat, I suggest that these two results, along with the positivistic perspective from which they derive, be recognized as essentially definitive of the orthodox project. I know of no other interpretation that can account for the sweep of orthodox analysis so readily.
>
> (Lawson 1994c: 113)

Two things need to be emphasised about Lawson's reading of the relationship between empirical realism and economics. First, this is a very *strict version* of empiricism. It is the radical empiricism of David Hume, and not one of the much weaker forms of empiricism endorsed by the logical empiricists or the early Popper (or by contemporary philosophers of science). Second, Lawson is asserting much more than the familiar claim that orthodox economists pay lip-service to positivism; he is arguing that positivist ideas really do effect both the form and content of mainstream economic theory. This is not simply about positivist rhetoric in economics; it is a much stronger claim about the causal power of positivist ideas in determining the conduct of modern economic inquiry.

Regrettably the intensity of Lawson's commitment to this empirical realist reading of contemporary economics is not matched by either the quantity or the quality of the evidence that he garners in defence of his reading. In fact, Lawson offers very little evidence to support his claim that positivism has an overarching impact on modern economics. He frequently makes statements such as 'I do not think it is contentious to observe that deductivism so understood character-izes contemporary economics' (1994a: 260) or that it is 'the misguided adherence to this conception of science, ... including accepting the universal applicability of the deductivist form of explanation, that constitutes the fundamental problem in the economic scientific project' (1995: 18), but there is seldom any real defence of these state-ments. Lawson does not provide any serious case studies in the history of economic thought, or any detailed investigations of the theoretical practice of economists; in the end his argument amounts to little more than proof by repeated assertion.[5] Let us try to provide this missing link; let us consider neoclassical economics more carefully and see if empirical realism is as influential as Lawson claims in these repeated assertions.

What neoclassicism is not: economic practice

Recall that according to empirical realism only atomic sense experi-ences exist, and to explain something entails deducing it from a set of initial conditions and a universal law (event regularity) of the form 'whenever event (type) x then event (type) y'. In particular, according to the positivist view, science is not concerned with the identification of the underlying structures and causal mechanisms that govern the phenomena of experience or to explain this phenomena in terms of such structures or causal mechanisms. Is this what mainstream economists do, or attempt to do?

Since 'mainstream' (or 'orthodox' or 'neoclassical') economics could arguably entail a wide range of different theoretical and/or empirical activities, and it is not clear how far back into the history of economic thought one might go and still find 'mainstream' economics, let me simply examine the one case that Lawson himself considers: Walrasian general equilibrium theory circa 1970.[6] Lawson obviously considers this particular research programme at this particular time to be an example (perhaps the paradigm example) of what he means by main-stream economics. To be more specific let us consider the canonical text of the genre: Arrow and Hahn (1971).

Arrow and Hahn's first content chapter is Chapter 2. In this chapter the authors provide a simple existence proof for the general equilib-rium price vector (p^*) in a Walrasian economy characterised in terms of continuous aggregate excess demand functions. Their main concern is:

the description of situations in which the desired actions of
economic agents are all mutually compatible and can all be
carried out simultaneously, and for which we can prove that
for the various economies discussed, there exists a set of
prices that will cause agents to make mutually compatible
decisions.

(Arrow and Hahn 1971: 16)

Where is the event regularity that this exercise is supposed to explain?
Such existence proofs show that certain things are *possible* in certain
hypothetical worlds (worlds that are admittedly far simpler than
ours). Such proofs provide, as Daniel Hausman has argued, a type of
'theoretical reassurance'; such demonstrations of existence 'give one
reason to believe, in Mill's words (1843, 6.3.1), that economists know
the laws of the "greater causes" of economic phenomena' (Hausman
1992: 101). This is a transcendental realist role, not an empirical realist
role, for such existence proofs. We want our economic theories to
isolate the underlying 'greater causes' of the phenomena that we
observe, and one way that we can obtain the 'reassurance' that we
have in fact isolated these greater causes is to see if it is *possible* that
such causes would be consistent with the type of coordinated activity
that seems to prevail in a market economy. Existence proofs provide
us with some reassurance that we are 'on the right track' (Hausman
1992: 101) in this essentially realist endeavour. Perhaps the closest that
anyone has come to linking such proofs to something like event regularities was in Roy Weintraub's early work on the history of general
equilibrium theory, and even in that case the linkage was indirect and
very weak. Weintraub (1985) argued that existence proofs were part of
the hard core of a Lakatosian research programme in general equilibrium theory and that the protective belt of that programme included
many different applied theories that did have empirical implications.
The fact that even this very weak empirical linkage was severely criticised (and abandoned by Weintraub in later work) only demonstrates
how ineffective an empiricist vision is in explaining the primary theoretical activity of Walrasian economics (proving existence).

Other aspects of Arrow and Hahn's second chapter are equally
inexplicable in event regularity terms. Even the aggregate excess
demand functions themselves – something that might conceivably be
observable – are not. These excess demand functions are:

an *ex ante* concept; it is hypothetical in the sense that the
actual purchases and sales may differ from those that the

theory of the decisions of agents tells us would be the
purchases and sales regarded as proper by the agents at p.

(Arrow and Hahn 1971: 19)

In other words, even these excess demand functions are not in any
sense empirical; they are hypothetical demands representing what
(abstractly well-behaved) agents would want to buy if in fact they
could sell what they wanted to sell (and buy the other things they
wanted to buy) at the price vector p, but of course unless the price
vector is the equilibrium price vector (unless p = p*), that is, unless
that which we are trying to prove the existence of has already come to
pass, then these hypothetical demands will not be 'demands' at all
(even in this pristine Walrasian world). Finally, it should be noted that
these excess demand functions are assumed to satisfy both Walras'
law (W) and zero degree homogeneity (H), two assumptions that are
almost never found to hold on empirically estimated aggregate
demand functions.[7] All of these things certainly suggest that whatever
is driving the theoretical activity in Chapter 2 of Arrow and Hahn it is
most certainly not the positivist-inspired search for event regularities,
and if Hausman's argument is accepted, it looks much more like (at
least one aspect of) a search for the actual causal mechanisms behind
the phenomena of the competitive market.

Chapter 3 is about production. In this chapter single-output firms,
with knowledge of all technically possible relationships between their
output and all the various combinations of inputs that they could
possibly have access to, engage in timeless ('inputs and outputs are
contemporaneous' 1971: 53) production. It is not exactly clear what
status such a firm might have in a positivist world where the only
meaningful propositions are those involving sense experiences or the
purely analytic propositions of logic and mathematics, but it certainly
seems that the latter would be more likely than the former. These
firms maximise a continuous profit function defined over a bounded
and strictly convex production set that admits free disposal. These
firms are shown to generate an aggregate supply correspondence that
is continuous. We find ourselves at the end of Chapter 3 and we did
not encounter a single event regularity, or even anything that might
strictly be considered observable.

Arrow and Hahn's Chapter 4 is entitled 'Consumer Decisions and
Efficient Allocations'. The 'households' in this chapter each have well-
ordered preferences (transitive, continuous, non-satiated, etc.) which
can be represented by a 'continuous, semi-strictly quasi-concave
utility function' (1971: 87) – an assumption that seems to be radically
at odds with the ostensibly constitutive mandate that only those

things that are empirically observable can be considered (or even exist). The main result in the chapter is the demonstration that a competitive equilibrium for a pure exchange economy composed of such consumers is *Pareto efficient* (1971: 93). Pareto efficiency is of course a normative notion; it has to do with making one person 'better off' without making someone else 'worse off'. In a positivist world composed exclusively of sense experience and event regularities such notions are *simply meaningless nonsense* (literally non-sense). They are meaningless propositions derived from a hypothetical economy composed of agents whose only defining characteristic is a mathematically well-behaved but unobservable (and thus nonsense) utility function. There doesn't seem to be much empirical realism in Chapter 4 either.

Well, I could go on, but the point seems to be pretty clear – whatever is happening here it certainly does not appear to have any direct relationship to the positivist conception of scientific theorising. I should also add that things get even worse (if that is possible) in later chapters. Chapter 9 is about uniqueness – the restriction that there exists only one equilibrium price vector – how could uniqueness be observable? Non-uniqueness could perhaps be observable, but not uniqueness. Chapters 11 and 12 are about stability, that (clearly) transcendental realist concept of a 'tendency to equilibrium' (1971: 263). The final chapter is an attempt to analyse a Keynesian model with money, expectations, and the possibility that Walrasian (target) demands are not active in determining the course of economic activity; this chapter is best interpreted as another attempt to get at the real causal mechanisms at work in a market economy. It seems impossible to conceive of a theoretical construction that is less directly inspired by the Humean radical empiricist view of scientific knowledge than Walrasian general equilibrium theory. Perhaps other parts of 'mainstream' economics are slightly more inspired, but general equilibrium theory (particularly Hahn's version) is Lawson's most cited example.

What neoclassicism is not: methodology

Even a brief look at the literature on economic methodology would indicate that the lack of fit between Walrasian general equilibrium theory and the rather extreme version of empiricism that Lawson calls empirical realism is more the norm than the exception in economics.[8] The development of economic theory from Adam Smith to that which appears in the most recent theoretical journals has never been guided, much less constituted, by a pristinely Humean notion of what constitutes legitimate scientific knowledge. Of course this is not to suggest that 'the facts' do not matter at all, or to claim that economics is not empirical in some rough and tumble sense – and it is also not to deny the role, and persuasive power, of focused empiricist rhetoric in the history of economic thought (as both Samuelson's operationalism and Friedman's predictivism clearly demonstrate) – but it is to deny any significant causal role to the type of radical empiricism that Lawson calls empirical realism. Finally, this also does not assert that the history of economic thought is totally devoid of individuals who were guided by radical empiricism on some particular topic (Henry Ludwell Moore and Wesley Clair Mitchell come immediately to mind), only to assert that it has ever been the driving force behind most of what has appeared in mainstream economics. The history of methodological discourse in economics clearly bears this out.

Positivist ideas had their first serious impact on methodological discourse with the publication of Terence Hutchison's book in 1938. Hutchison was reacting specifically to Robbins (1932), but at that time Robbins simply represented the most recent version of the Millian tradition in economic methodology. From Hutchison (1938) through Blaug (1992) economists committed to empiricism have argued persuasively that while economists pay lip-service to empiricism (they preach it), they do not in fact behave according to its precepts (they do not practise it).[9] Now neither Hutchison nor Blaug subscribe to the type of radical empiricism that Lawson considers to be the guiding spirit of mainstream economics – both are Popperian falsificationists – but this is precisely the point. Even those methodologists who advocate a much weaker form of empiricism than that which Lawson attributes to mainstream economics have argued systematically and persuasively that empiricism has not played a very important role in the evolution of economic theory.[10] If the enervated empiricism of Hutchison and Blaug has not been constitutive of economic theorising, then how could Lawson's empirical realism play such a role?

The history of methodological discourse not only demonstrates that radical empiricism has played very little role in the development of economic thought, it also demonstrates that the Millian tendency law view that Lawson advocates has played a rather significant role. The argument that economics is a separate science that cannot – because of the type of mechanisms that govern economic phenomena – be conducted in strict compliance with the empiricist method of natural science, has been an influential perspective in the history of economic methodology. In fact, this is, much more than positivism, the *traditional* (and perhaps even the dominant) characterisation of the method of economic science (by both supporters and critics). Versions of this argument appear of course in Mill, but also in Cairnes, Neville Keynes, Robbins, and most recently in Hausman (1992). This is not to say that all of these authors endorse the exact same philosophical perspective (particularly Hausman), but they do all argue that a strictly Humean approach to economic science is impossible, that it is impossible because of the essential nature of (the underlying causal forces at work in) the subject matter of economics, and that some version of a tendency is the only reasonable way to think about 'laws' in economic science. Lawson even seems to agree that this has been the traditional view of economic method; he not only cites Mill as an advocate of this view, but also Neville Keynes (1989a: 63). He must also believe that tendency laws dominated the practice of economic science, at least until the middle of the twentieth century, since he cites Mill, Marx and Marshall (1989a: 62) all as practitioners of this view.

Hausman's position is particularly relevant to this discussion about the philosophical vision behind contemporary mainstream economics. Hausman presents what is basically the Millian view that economics is an 'inexact and separate science'. He argues (following Mill and Cartwright 1989) that causal laws 'are not mere correlations among features of human action', but that 'tendencies are the causal powers underlying the genuine regularities that inexact laws express' (1992: 127). He then discusses four separate notions of tendencies and the associated concept of an inexact law (1992: 127–131). None of these four notions exactly captures the way that Lawson uses the term tendency, but the point is that for Hausman, like Lawson, the 'laws' of economics are tendency laws. Hausman later goes on to argue that such laws can be rationalised in (weakly) empiricist terms, but he never abandons the basic Millian view. Much more important than his argument that such tendency laws can be reconciled with some version of empiricism is the fact that Hausman consistently argues that *the Millian view is the best characterisation of what economists actually do in their science* – not just Mill, Marx and Marshall, but contemporary mainstream (even general equilibrium theorists) as well.

> This [Mill's] vision of economics as a separate science, although not often expressed in this terminology, remains, . . . central to contemporary microeconomics. The whole project of microeconomics and general equilibrium theory presupposes that a single set of causal factors underlies economic phenomena and determines their broad feature. Other relevant causal factors are regarded as disturbing causes.
>
> (Hausman 1992: 225)

Thus not only do we see that contemporary mainstream economics is not driven by the philosophy of empirical realism, it is driven by roughly the same Millian tendency law vision that Lawson advocates. This is clear from our examination of the type of theoretical work that mainstream economists actually do, as well as what the best method-ological commentators have said about that economic practice.

Conclusion

I believe that I have made a solid case against Lawson's interpretation of neoclassical economics and I will leave it to the reader to speculate about how this criticism impacts Lawson's more general philosophical programme. I have just two concluding points to make about this misreading.

First, Lawson tries to make a strong case that the transcendental realist framework will serve as solid ground for a *critique* of main-stream economics. In Lawson (1989a) the argument is packaged as a way of helping us understand (as legitimate) Kaldor's criticism of Walrasian general equilibrium theory; more specifically, Lawson argues that if we understand transcendental realism (Kaldor's philo-sophical position) we will understand why Kaldor thought that the abstractions of general equilibrium theory were of the 'wrong kind'. This argument does not work; transcendental realism does not help with such matters. The practical problem with transcendental realism – the practical problem with any such Aristotelian or essentialist philosophical framework – is that it provides almost no information about how one practically chooses between two theories. It is an ontology, a theory of the nature of being, and not a theory that provides any practical guide to determining what the nature of being actually is. Trying to use such an ontological framework to choose between two ostensibly scientific theories is a type of 'ontological fallacy' that is essentially the reciprocal of the 'epistemic fallacy' that Bhaskar discusses. The fact that Lawson can consider the economic theories of Mill, Marx, Marshall, Kaldor, and Hayek (1994b) to all be consistent with transcendental realism is testimony to the fact that such an ontological view does not help us choose between or among theories in any practical sense. When Lawson argues that 'Clearly assumptions such as universal perfect competition, linear expected profit functions, Cobb-Douglas production functions, etc. are not intended to capture the mode of operation of real economic mecha-nisms' (1989a: 74), he is simply asserting his own view of what is *real*. Many neoclassical economists *really do* view such conditions as the conditions that *really are the relevant underlying* conditions in a competitive market economy (at least as Hausman would say 'inexactly'). Lawson and the neoclassical economist can have exactly the same view of the type of things (real underlying causes) that one should be looking for in economic science, and yet disagree totally about what those real underlying causes are. Attempting to find some common ground for deciding which are, and which are not, the real underlying causes is of course how Western intellectual life came to be obsessed with epistemology; mere ontological frameworks don't help, and when one tries to use ontology for such purposes all one ends up doing is reproducing their own beliefs about what is and what is not legitimate knowledge (Kant is a case in point).

Second, there seems to be a certain irony involved in Lawson's view about mainstream economics. The irony is that Lawson appears to have applied the same epistemological realism at the meta-level that he criticised so harshly at the scientific level. To see this incongruity consider the question of how a good realist of the sort that Lawson endorses would go about explaining the theoretical behaviour of the economics profession. It seems that such a realist would look for the real underlying causes, the generative mechanisms, behind the (transitive) phenomena of day-to-day professional life in economics. The fact that most economics papers have econometrics and other 'empirical results', and the fact that the rhetoric of the discipline (what economists say they are doing) is all about testing, prediction, and operationally meaningful propositions, would not be the main interest of such a realist. All this is surface phenomena, event regularities on the surface of economic professional life; the transcendental realist would not stop here. What the realist would want to do is to *explain* this surface phenomena of empirical 'results' and econometric 'tests' – to find the underlying causal mechanism that generates this empirical phenomena of disciplinary empirical practice. There are of course many possible stories about what the relevant generative structures might be, but the point is that *Lawson never really asks the question*. He seems entirely content to stop at the empirical level and assume that economists really are doing exactly what their surface behaviour suggests they are doing – trying to describe accurately the event regularities in economic life. One would expect a transcendental realist to look deeper.

Notes

1 A partial list of this work would include Lawson (1989a, 1989b, 1994a, 1994b, 1994c, 1995 and 1997). Lawson also discussed realism and instrumentalism in his earlier work (1981 and 1983 for instance) but his argument was different than (and perhaps even the reverse of) the one presented in his later, Bhaskar-inspired, writing.

2 I will follow Lawson and others in using the term 'transcendental realism' for Bhaskar's general philosophical position, and 'critical realism' for the application of that programme to the social sciences by Lawson and others (see Collier 1994 and Jackson 1995).

3 Bhaskar (1978, 1987, and 1989); also see Collier (1994).

4 I will follow Lawson in freely substituting the term 'positivism' for the combination of Humean empiricist epistemology and empirical realist ontology. This does not imply that I endorse Lawson's use as the only, or even most appropriate, use of the term 'positivism'.

5 The one mainstream economist that is repeatedly cited as evidence for this positivist reading is Frank Hahn. It is not clear why Lawson considers Hahn to be an authority on the philosophical foundations of neoclassical economics. Hahn obviously made a number of very important contributions to 1960s' and 1970s' general equilibrium theory, but he has never demonstrated anything more than passing interest in the issues relevant to the epistemological appraisal of economic analysis. This, combined with the dismissive attitude exhibited in the few places where Hahn has mentioned methodological issues, makes him a particularly unreliable source for philosophical evaluation (and he is effectively Lawson's only source). One could learn from Debreu's comments about the Bourbakian programme (Weintraub and Mirowski 1994) or from Thomas Mayer's (1995) discussion of monetarist methodology, but not from Frank Hahn's miscellaneous methodological musings.

6 Lawson frequently mentions Walrasian general equilibrium theory as an example of mainstream or orthodox economics, but his primary discussion is contained in one of his earliest papers employing the Bhaskarian language (Lawson 1989a).

7 See for example Deaton and Muelbauer (1980), Gilbert (1991), or Keuzenkamp and Barten (1995).

8 Of course it may be that such (Humean) empiricism has never represented the guiding principle behind any type of scientific activity, natural or social, but that is a separate issue.

9 One could add that empiricists in other social sciences also have the same criticism of economic theory (Green and Shapiro 1994, for example).

10 In fact Hollis and Nell (1975) appears to be the *only* book on economic methodology in the last twenty years (and there have been many such books during this period) that *does* agree with Lawson about the type of empiricism that dominates economics – and even Hollis eventually seemed to change his mind on the matter. Hollis (1996) presents four basic approaches to social science (empiricist, post-empiricist, realist, and interpretative) and neoclassical economics is clearly listed as 'an example of explanatory realism' (p. 367), not as empiricism.

Bibliography

Arrow, K. J. and Hahn, F. H. (1971) *General Competitive Analysis*, San Francisco: Holden-Day.

Bhaskar, R. (1978) *A Realist Theory of Science*, 2nd edn, Brighton: Harvester.

—— (1987) *Scientific Realism and Human Emancipation*, London: Verso.

—— (1989) *Reclaiming Reality*, London: Verso.

Blaug, M. (1992) *The Methodology of Economics*, 2nd edn, Cambridge: Cambridge University Press.

Cartwright, N. (1989) *Nature's Capacities and Their Measurement*, Oxford: Oxford University Press.

Collier, A. (1994) *Critical Realism: An Introduction to Roy Bhaskar's Philosophy of Science*, London: Verso.

Deaton, A. and Muelbauer, J. (1980) *Economics and Consumer Behavior*, Cambridge: Cambridge University Press.

Gilbert, C. (1991) 'Do Economists Test Theories?', in N. De Marchi and M. Blaug (eds) *Appraising Economic Theories*, Aldershot: Edward Elgar, 137–168.

Green, D. and Shapiro, I. (1994) *Pathologies of Rational Choice Theory: A Critique of Applications to Political Science*, New Haven, CT: Yale University Press.

Hausman, D. M. (1992) *The Inexact and Separate Science of Economics*, Cambridge: Cambridge University Press.

Hollis, M. (1996) 'Philosophy of Social Science', in N. Bunnin and E. P. Tsui-James (eds) *The Blackwell Companion to Philosophy*, Oxford: Blackwell, 358–387.

Hollis, M. and Nell, E. J. (1975) *Rational Economic Man: A Philosophical Critique of Neo-Classical Economics*, Cambridge: Cambridge University Press.

Hutchison, T. (1938) *The Significance and Basic Postulates of Economic Theory*, London: Macmillan (reprint, New York: Augustus M. Kelly, 1960).

Jackson, W. A. (1995) 'Naturalism in Economics', *Journal of Economic Issues* 39: 761–780.

Keuzenkamp, H. and Barten, A. (1995) 'Rejection without Falsification: On the History of Testing the Homogeneity Condition', *Journal of Econometrics* 87: 103–127.

Lawson, T. (1981) 'Keynesian Model Building and the Rational Expectations Critique', *Cambridge Journal of Economics* 5(4): 311–326.

—— (1983) 'Different Approaches to Economic Modelling', *Cambridge Journal of Economics* 7: 77–84.

—— (1989a) 'Abstraction, Tendencies, and Stylised Facts: A Realist Approach to Economic Analysis', *Cambridge Journal of Economics* 13(1): 59–78.

—— (1989b) 'Realism and Instrumentalism in the Development of Econometrics', *Oxford Economic Papers* 41(1): 236–258.

—— (1994a) 'A Realist Theory for Economics', in R. E. Backhouse (ed.) *New Directions in Economic Methodology*, London: Routledge, 257–285.

—— (1994b) 'Realism and Hayek: A Case of Continuing Transformation', in M. Colonna, H. Hagemann and O. Hamouda (eds) *Capitalism, Socialism and Knowledge: The Economics of F. A. Hayek*, vol. I, Aldershot: Edward Elgar, 131–159.

—— (1994c) 'Why Are So Many Economists So Opposed to Methodology?' *Journal of Economic Methodology* 1: 105–133.

—— (1995) 'A Realist Perspective on Contemporary "Economic Theory"', *Journal of Economic Issues* 29(1): 1–32.

—— (1997) *Economics and Reality*, London: Routledge.

Mayer, T. (1995) *Doing Economic Research: Essays on the Applied Methodology of Economics*, Aldershot: Edward Elgar.

Mill, J. S. (1843) *A System of Logic*, London: Longman, Green & Co., 1949 printing.

Robbins, L. (1932) *An Essay on the Nature and Significance of Economic Science*, London: Macmillan.

Weintraub, E. R. (1985) *General Equilibrium Analysis: Studies in Appraisal*, Cambridge: Cambridge University Press.

Weintraub, E. R. and Mirowski, P. (1994) 'The Pure and Applied: Bourbakism Comes to Mathematical Economics', *Science in Context* 7: 245–272.

11

AGAINST EUROCENTRED EPISTEMOLOGIES

A critique of science, realism and economics

Rajani Kanth

Introduction

The time is perhaps ripe now, at this juncture of the near-total triumph of the capitalist mode, and the apparent capitulation of the erstwhile 'socialist' bloc, to re-examine the corpus of 'science' that capitalism has arrogated to itself, not least in the form of 'economics'. It should be obvious that not only is capitalism defended today as the best of all possible worlds[1] (it being usually taken for granted that the matter is now empirically resolved beyond contention, in a Darwinian mode of argument, à la the so-called Alchian Thesis),[2] both politically and economically, but also as the only system guaranteeing plural values alongside the rigour of a positive, objective science that is universally applicable. In fact, the so-called 'scientific' world view is often blithely equated with the European capitalist revolution historically, as though the Egyptian, the Indian, and the Chinese, to speak only of a few non-capitalist, and/or extra-European, scientific traditions, never existed.[3]

Perhaps this much was to be expected; after all, since Europeans had pretty nearly conquered the world, they had earned the 'right' to rewrite history on their own, self-congratulatory terms.[4] And that is, in fact, exactly what happened. However, success in this sphere was not entirely univalent for the votaries of capital, given the emergence, coeval with the European conquest of the world, of a European working-class movement whose most famous, if not always most faithful, representative was to be Marxism. The Marxist, generally, did not question the fairytale of the Capitalist enlightenment as the great European boon to humankind, but she did suggest that, in many regards, this revolution was inadequate, incomplete, and indecent. For its part, Marxism claimed to have achieved a sort of sublation of capitalist philosophy, being ready in its own way to go beyond it, though carefully building on its pre-existing foundation. Thus Marx visualised his political economy as fulfilling the failed promise of the Ricardians, that is as completing a 'search' process (for the holy grail of surplus value) begun, supposedly awkwardly, by Petty, Smith and Ricardo.[5]

Perhaps the best document that illustrates the critical ambivalence of Marxism *vis-à-vis* capitalist modes is the *Manifesto*,[6] which is, astonishingly, as much a ringing paean, celebrating the capitalist revolution in lyrical terms not even approached by capitalist ideologues in their most zealous moods, as a critique of it. Accordingly, in all dialectical, if dubious, relish, Marxism celebrates the accomplishments of capitalism prior to rejecting it (the rejection itself being an inescapable verdict imposed by historical 'forces' immanent in the womb of the order) as an inadequate social formation.

The burden of my critique here is to show that there is little in capitalism (or in erstwhile 'socialisms', for that matter), and the crown jewel of its hegemonic ideology – 'economics' – that warrants any such celebration; and that *human emancipation demands the almost total rejection of European capitalist institutions ('science', and 'economics', included) if we are to survive as a (decent) human species in a hospitable ecological environment.* I will also argue that this is not merely an *argument*, in a rationalist mode (where *debate* is the end-all), but a vital *moral* imperative (where *deeds* count for more) as well. Finally, I will, however summarily, evaluate the claim of realism to have set right the agenda of science and (socialist) emancipation on a philosophically sound footing.[7] Given that this chapter is written for an *economics* readership (may their tribe decrease!!), many of the examples, and some arguments, are taken from that arena, to the neglect of the many other (and vastly more interesting) dimensions of social life.

Science

Too often, in intellectual discourse, we take meanings as given. And quite often, for that reason, we capitulate unwittingly to the ideological kernels that inhabit the domain of words, to the disarming spell of everyday 'reverie' as Bachelard[8] so very eloquently put it. Science is one such word that has been sacralised by capital (as much as by its socialist enemies), its myriad profanities notwithstanding. Even Marxists and Anarchists, generally contemptuous of most conventional social contrivances, none the less genuflected readily, and uncritically, before this vengeful goddess – if only for needing its blessed anointments for the easier dissemination of their ideas.

The capitalist revolution separated the state from the church (at least formally). It immediately conjoined the state with the new deity of science, however, thereby giving this new tradition a power boost that put it almost beyond the reach of social discipline.[9] The mythology of religion was soon to be replaced by the mythology of science, as science itself blessed the state and sacralised the world-view(s) of capital. Physics led the way in this beatification of formal knowledge (Newton being the ruling demiurge in this cosmos), and physics-envy naturally was to become the obvious bane of all the sciences, economics being no exception.[10]

Stated simply, science, in economics at least, became identified with quantification *per se*, with qualitative analyses sinking into a low second place as inferior (if not wholly irrelevant) modes of analysis.[11] The apparent rigour of mathematics[12] was recruited avidly by neoclassicism to justify and defend its truistic, axiomatic, and almost infantile, theorems that deeply investigated but the surface gloss of economic life. Indeed, for the longest time, Marxists (in the US) had to live in the academic dog-house for not being familiar with matrix algebra, until keen (if not always scrupulous) Marxist minds, with academic tenures at stake, realised the enormous (and inexpensive) potential of this tool for restating Marxian ideas in formalised language and instantly acquiring the gloss of high science, the latter-day pundits of repute here being Roemer in the US and Morishima in England, who were of course soon emulated by a host of lesser lights to whom this switch in language alone promised hours of (well-funded) computerised fun and games.

Of course, all the formalisms did not advance a critical understanding of the *organon* of Marxian system, and its many difficulties, one iota; but it did succeed in generating grudging respect for the Marxist by the even more facile and shallow savants of neoclassicism. The enemy was being forced to speak their language; capitulation could not but be far away.

The point should be clear; henceforth, the aura of science would perforce hallow all social projects deemed necessary by (and to) the governing élite. Mathematics could now step in in place of traditional forms of mumbo-jumbo to keep the lay audience in a comfortable trance of mystification – from which it was hoped they would (and need) never awake. *And yet the facts of social life have always stood in truculent, if silent, testimony against this meretricious scientism.*[13] Indeed, to ask the questions, what is economics a science of, and what qualifies it as a scientific discipline, is to invite a revelatory education into the inherent charlatanism of economic ideology. The issue here is not so much the validity of economic theory (problematic enough in any economic discourse), but rather its deceptive wrap of *scientism*. The fact is that even if economic theory were true, and its 'science' valid, in some acceptable sense, *it would still represent only one manner of interpreting the myriad facts of social life*; and it would not, *ipso facto*, have the right to impose its special discernments, such as they are, on other traditions by force. In simple terms, science is only one tradition amongst many, with no epistemic prior claim to apodeictic knowledge; it succeeds in capitalist society not because of any demonstrable cognitive superiority but because, with the blessing of state power, it has managed to rig the game in its favour, monopolise research funds, and drive its competition out of the market. But it is time, indeed, that its erstwhile competitors were resuscitated and revived, and generally brought back into being, so science can (as in medieval times) learn all over again to humbly *work* to prove its platitudes, rather than to simply pontify from the commanding heights of power and privilege.

Economics

What is economics a science of? Interestingly, diverse intellectual traditions have provided diverse answers. For Smith, economics was the science of the *production* of wealth, for Ricardo *distribution*, for Jevons *exchange*, etc., faithfully reflecting the various historical moments of capitalist evolution in Britain,[14] and their own location within it. Contrary to the selective emphases in the foregoing, and speaking more generally, economics is simply an examination of all those varied moments of the economic life. But how shall we study such 'systems'? Mainstream economics, classical or neoclassical, has approached the 'economy' wearing the raiment of the very select premises of capitalist society, i.e. with the specification of self-directed, Hobbesian, individuals armed with material passions, seeking requital only in a deluge of privatised consumption.[15] *All the realist problems of mainstream economics can be traced to this fundamental epistemic error, of supposing 'maximising' behaviour (apart from assuming it to be 'rational') to be unmediated by cultural norms.*[16] Indeed, we can ask some rather simple questions at this stage which help underscore the gross vapidity of the discipline. First, how do we know these highly select behavioural traits to be true (even within its own domain of market society)? Second, how do we know them to be *universal*? Economics, of course, has customarily argued these postulates by *assumption*, through the fable of 'inspired introspection' as in Ricardo's choice parlance.[17]

This is, surely, a fantastic feint. One can now assume economic truths to be self-evident and move on, which is in fact what economics did, and still does, with someone like Friedman[18] 'methodologically' (i.e. *spuriously*) placing these alleged axioms securely beyond critical review.[19] Few sciences, other than wholly sham ones like economics, could dare to make such incredible claims! But economics is the ruling ideology of the capitalist system, embodying its flagship *logos*, so to speak, and so it can do just that, with impunity; indeed, with its highly specious pretensions being sacralised by the wholly gratuitous bestowal of a Nobel Memorial prize. Thereby, one tendentious way of *interpreting*, and apologising for, the economic society of capitalism, can now come to be seen as the only, axiomatic way of *doing* things in the material sphere; and economics, appropriately, has become, ever so safely, in all craven cowardice, an *axiomatic* science at one pole, and a *'praxiology'* (as Lange[20] put it percipiently a long time ago) at another. Even the ever sceptical Karl Popper[21] could hardly make headway against this crown jewel of capitalist ideology: how can one, in all reason, falsify axioms?[22]

Mainstream economics has thrived on this absurd (but smugly self-validating) set of premises, with the thoughtful (if naive) amongst its ilk occasionally venturing out in brief, if usually unsuccessful, empirical forays into 'reality', supposedly to 'test' the axioms. But, of course, that's dissembling, in regal style; to borrow a leaf from bourgeois philosophy itself, no amount of empirical evidence[23] alone (supposedly) can 'prove' that a proposition is 'universal' – the time and space constraints of the observer being far too finite for any such inference. On the other hand, if evidence was (more plausibly) preponderantly against its axioms, economics could switch gears and argue that its universal laws were merely 'statistical laws' that didn't always hold, and so on.[24] So, in fact, economics simply legislates, magisterially, how the world *should* be, and then presumes (turning its back squarely on reality forever) that that is how it *really* is; the world, meanwhile, plods on, innocent of any of the sins of 'theory'. I have never met a successful businessman who knew a single theorem in economics (I know a lot of unsuccessful ones who do know a lot, by the way!); similarly, I can't think of a single major business school anywhere that could last a day if they took the theorems of economics seriously.[25] Being practically minded, they investigate the world as it appears to them, rather than through any absurd filter of *a priori* premises. And appearances, however evanescent as they may be, are just a step closer to reality than tendentiously 'inspired' introspections! At any rate, I know of no practical science that enjoys this extraordinary status of near total irrelevance in the realm of applications! To state the moral: *the entire enterprise of neoclassical economics is rigged to show that laissez-faire produces optimal outcomes*, but for the disruptive operation of the odd externality (a belated correction) here and there.[26] The fact that economics has had to stand reality on its head to 'demonstrate' this thesis only shows the extent to which zealotry can go to defend a material interest.

But how does one seriously tackle a *science of assumptions*? Not empirically, because 'evidence' is always a contextual affair, neither abstract, nor general; rather, one needs only, I argue, a coherent set of *counter* assumptions. That is, indeed, all it would take to deny and ignore mainstream economics. Set up premises directly *contra* the premises of economics and we have, presto!, a different economic system (if as imaginary as the one dear to neoclassical dreams)! A counter economics is no more (or is it no less?) 'real' than the economics of our professors, of course, but is as legitimate as theirs for being based on the same airy nothingness (and we can then safely cite no less an authority than Nobel Laureate Friedman to the effect that the 'realism' of our fundamental assumptions are quite irrelevant to their scientific value!).

So, for sake of argument, I could legislate a new set of premises,[27] where social groups (not individuals) are the prime economic 'agents', deemed fundamentally altruistic, systematically avoiding self-interest in favour of group interest, thinking that less is better, and so on. Lo and behold, we would then erect a new economic theory with a new set of 'laws'[28] (instead of indifference curves, of course, we might now craft sinuously hooped curves of social affection, behaving quite perversely!). But why then does this new, and entirely possible, 'economics', not have a ready patron? Because such postulated traits simply do not answer to the behavioural needs of capitalism. Period.[29] And, to assume what needs to be proved is, of course, an old artifice in the fine art of dissembling. At any rate, contrary to the pretensions of both mainstream and Marxians, truth is that there are potentially as many 'economics' as there are culturally derived value systems in human society.

Classical Marxism, converted by academic opportunists into a vulgar antipode of neoclassical 'economics', fares little better; the 'assumptions' needed to make Volume One Analyses, specially value theory, 'work' are more than equally as heroic as neoclassical ones, and deserve to be just as securely martyred.[30] Worse, in many respects, Marxian economics internalises many of the philosophical premises of mainstream economics (attesting to their shared *materialism*, where the *primacy* of economic motivations in the general sphere of social conduct is readily granted),[31] to its lasting discredit. The question might then well be raised: what is it that Marxists say and do, *qua* economists, that neoclassicists don't?[32] I argue that there is a radical difference in their *ontological* assumptions about capitalism,[33] though the gulf is often exaggerated, and is much narrower, in actual *academic* practice than frequently assumed; the very fact that non-Marxians like Robinson or Kalecki[34] can accept so many of the macro statements of a Marxian 'economics' sustains the fact that liberal theory (such as the so-called 'Cambridge School') can appropriate much of Marxist 'economics' safely without prejudice to its interests. And the fact that an arch conservative like Schumpeter,[35] directly or indirectly, supported so many of Marxian views on capitalist growth is another indication that the two domains are perhaps not that far apart. *Indeed, the premises that Smith and Marx shared in common – faith in science, belief in 'progress', and a shared metaphysic of materialism* vis-à-vis *human motivations – quite outweigh their otherwise significant differences.* It is worth noting, in this context, that *all materialist visions of emancipation are, inherently, self-immolating;* only moral critiques carry the immanent promise of transcendence. In this important regard, viewed from a non-Eurocentred perspective, capitalism and socialism are only the two (equally ugly) faces of Janus.

All paradigms carry three inescapable attributes; a set of *'assumptions'* constituting the infrastructure; a corpus of *'theory'*, or a more or less cohering set of propositions based on those assumptions; and a definite *'policy'* imperative (apparently) flowing from the theory. Of course, it would be naive to imagine the scientific process as a sequence moving in that (logically) schematic, if satisfactory, order, from initial assumptions to final policy; the truth is exactly the obverse: *it is policy that guides the selective choice of assumptions, with 'theory' a mere rationalisation of the former.*[36] Easy to see why Marxists have never had the heart to seize upon the vacuity of the fundamental neoclassical assumptions about economic behaviour; because Marx's assumptions, about an idealised 'capitalism', in Volume One of *Capital*, are equally untenable.

Let me state the matter now succinctly. *There is no such thing as an 'economics' (construed as a set of deductive propositions from arbitrary 'assumptions'),* whether it is neoclassical, Marxian, or Martian for that matter, stripped aside from the containment of its many social veils. There is a material dimension to social life, to be sure, but it is one completely encapsulated in a cultural matrix, where the 'economic' moment arises as an *interdependent resultant,* so to speak, rather than as a prime mover.[37] There is a social economy; but there is no 'economics'. The truths of the economic life (*being concrete and contextual, in the main*) have to be gleaned, quite regardless of the paradigm involved, by direct, patient, careful observation – by *induction,* so to speak not by abstract 'theorising'[38] *(sober reflection suggests there is no other way in any form of knowledge-gathering activity, natural or social: even realism, at its best, is not the gift of an empyrean inspiration, soaring above us all, and falling upon a few, like manna from heaven, but a brilliant derivation from the exoteric, empirically sullied, facts of the social life).* In this regard, unlike the fields of botany and zoology, regrettably, the voyage of the *Beagle* in Economics has not even begun.

But even were it to begin now, it would be too late, for some rather important reasons. Unfortunately for emergent economic theorists, it is only a spontaneously evolved capitalist economy, competitively subject to an unfettered 'market', operating 'behind our backs', so to speak, that allows for specific economic outcomes to be 'theorised' and speculated about – unlike, say, the more self-conscious systems such as medieval European feudalism and/or state socialism, where the key economic parameters are 'set' quite transparently by human agents, acting more or less publicly and 'voluntarily'. In this day and age of state and corporate direction, and near-global macro 'management', the spontaneous urgings of a 'blind', self-propelling, economy (if indeed such an entity ever existed) are considerably held in check; and, as such, today's capitalisms are getting more and more like those other modes of production where the key agents and players are identifiable, and broad trajectories of most key variables are wholly the premeditated assignations of controlling agencies with determinate strategies. Unintended consequences still operate, of course, as they must; but a far better guide to the macro dynamics would flow from a *political* analysis of the state and its major corporate allies, as opposed to any, old-fashioned, 'economic theory'.[39] *Corporate empires, today, are run simply like other empires;* theories of administration, management, and war games are, appropriately, far closer to the ground (particularly in the penumbra of 'prediction' so dear to the Friedmanite) than the antiquated mechanics of an 'economic' theory self-consciously embedded in the archaic fable(s) of simple competition.

Realism

The economic science of capitalism is not absurd because it is *irrealist* (any more than, say, the near-abstract Volume One analysis of Marx, which gratuitously disregards entire chunks of capitalist ontology);[40] rather, it is simply *irrelevant* for being a fantasy world of an ideal, rational, capitalism where all motions are mutually equilibrating,[41] in a Newtonian co-ordination of the elements. Gerard Debreu won a Nobel prize for his work on the speculative robotics of General Equilibrium;[42] by that token, any one who can devise an ideal model of the nature of, say, a Martian topsoil hypothesised as ideal for the growing of Martian rutabagas should equally qualify for a similar award; economic theorising always scores high marks where reality and relevance are not important![43] Any realist questioning, in fact, leaves the science completely befuddled, and ever so bemused. It is true that the vulgar (but conscientious) practitioners, closer to the ground in a manner of speaking, keep looking (morosely) for empirical confirmation of their theoretical absurdities[44] (such as wages equalling labour's marginal product, for example); but the great ideologues, e.g. Walras in the past, or Debreu, in the present, leave such coarse terrain completely alone. *In all ideologies*[45] (Marxism included), the naive empiricist is seen as the indelicate boor who fails to leave the workings of idealist fantasy alone. Let them eat their empirical confirmations, is the prevalent attitude! And yet, we cannot speak of a 'science' that can exist (and thrive!) in sovereign defiance of empirical application and testing! *Asserting the fact that the empirical domain is only one dimension of reality, and perhaps not the critically 'generative' one, is far from implying that it is either irrelevant or unimportant.* A critique of empiricism is highly plausible, even necessary; but a nihilist critique of simple empirics is absurd. At their worst, both neoclassicism and vulgar Marxism have shared this enduring taint of leaping lightly over the simple world of 'appearances',[46] to avoid decisive refutation.

The dodges employed by neoclassicism to defend against simple empirical refutation are Homeric in scope. The laws of demand, for example, allow for quantity demanded to rise, fall, or remain stationary, as price changes, because there are normal and perverse customers much as there are normal and perverse 'goods'. *This means, of course, that almost anything is possible*[47] (although neoclassicism cannot face up to this fact, realism should teach us that, at the level of individual behaviour, which is the chosen domain of the neoclassical, *it is emphatically true that 'anything goes'*: only aggregates display clear patterns – the individual, on the contrary, is 'free')! And yet Samuelson could contentedly claim that the law of demand is the most verified 'law' ever 'discovered' in economics[48] (naturally, since it allows for all possibilities!). Truth is that economics is incapable of *discovering* anything, since its genius lies in facile fabrications, such as the marginal productivity 'theory' of distribution, where the market allocates just desserts to all factors according to their 'productivity'.[49] The greatest empirical defeasance of realism, in capitalist economics, consists in its viewing production and consumption as individual rather than social activities, such that externalities and interdependencies are, at first blush, assumed away. Of course, the added fact that consumption may itself depend upon the nature of production makes the equations even more indeterminate.[50]

Can 'Critical Realism', of the Bhaskarian kind,[51] be brought in as a useful critique of the misplaced ontological assumptions of neoclassicism?[52] I think the answer is in the affirmative, for it easily cuts the ground from under the latter's dissimulating methodological fiction of an *individualist* ontology residing paradoxically within the *social* order of capital. More generally, merely to state (the fact) that an institution such as the 'army' is not simply the plural of soldier, is sufficient to implode the pretensions of that high, if misguided, rule of scientific method (at another remove, the so-called 'paradox of thrift' is where Keynes comes close to understanding the radical limitations of 'methodological individualism'). More importantly, critical realism goes well beyond the schoolboy stage of correcting epistemic errors (of the neoclassical world view), to the more fascinating task of discovering the *generative mechanisms* that produce the phenomenon of neoclassicism itself. In fact, herein the signal, *a priori*, philosophical superiority – in terms of depth – of critical realism: that its protocols demand that we not merely criticise the irrealism of a model, but also *explain* why the putatively unreal and the erroneous arise, and persist, as social forms despite their repeated violation(s) of reality. As such, for instance, a Realist Marxism can (and must) explain the 'errors' of neoclassicism as much as why the erroneous thinking still endures (be it as 'false consciousness', 'ruling class tool', 'fetishism', or whatever); neoclassicism, however, is unable to offer any such symmetrical explanation as to *why* Marxism exists as a counter ideology (though it may well deny the validity of Marxian theorems on a different plane). Neoclassicism, therefore, simply lacks the social analysis *(for not being a serious social science at any stage of its monotonous evolution!)* to describe such a phenomenon. In this way, and on this scale, even vulgar Marxism is, warts and all, irrefutably superior, as an *explanatory* system (neoclassicism chooses not to explain, being content only to *prescribe* acceptable capitalist behaviour, in keeping with its status of a political *ideology of control*) to any version of mainstream economics (despite the fact that it is worse than useless in teaching us how, for instance, to operate a bank, even under socialism!).

But critical realism actually goes one better. As I read it, the greatest realist discovery to date is the ontological hiatus between society and the individual or, speaking of economics, the 'gap' between the macro and the micro, reflected in their mutual antagonism and incompatibility. *I argue that it is an ontological truth extant in both nature and society that the domain of the macro is always subject to apparent regularities – 'laws' and 'controls' and so forth – while the micro sphere is always 'free', erratic, and capable of unpredictable movements* (even in physics, the debate between the relativists and the quantum theorists revolves around the not always appreciated distinction between the respective *logos* of the part and the whole). In this sense, no macro and micro theory, Marxist or neoclassicist, can ever be brought into synch; *it is a property of reality that the twain can never meet.* Of course why this should be so is as unclear as why matter should be possessed of gravity; it just is. At any rate, the consequences of this realist discovery are profound for all the sciences and will definitely affect their internal development once the idea is generally disseminated and absorbed. And only one important derivative of this insight is the fact (I pose the matter enigmatically here, but I have devoted a book to the subject) that what we call social change is both cause and consequence of precisely this hiatus between the two dimensions.[53]

It is generally assumed (indeed, an article of faith in Anglo-American economic traditions) that philosophy and methodology, being 'soft core' forms of knowledge (as Joan Robinson expressed the idea once: methodology is a 'bastard' science!), can proffer no *substantive* truths (whether in economics or in any other discipline), only formal propositions. But the foregoing point gives the lie to that sentiment directly; the discovery of the conflict and incompatibility between the macro and the micro domains is a substantive ontological discovery immanent in critical realism, of obvious importance to the sciences generally. I treat this as Bhaskar's greatest contribution to philosophy, although he seems not always aware of the importance of his own discovery.

On the other hand, it is also clear that critical realism, by itself, cannot offer a parallel economics; it can only correct where correction is due, and by and large this rectification will be visited upon Marxian political economy, which has always been in serious need of a non-positivist philosophy of science to check its expansive and effusive proclivities, particularly when it comes to airy speculations about the nature of the communist utopia. The fact that society is an *open*, not a closed, system is enough, for instance, to require amendments of all inexorable Marxian 'laws of motion'; there are no such things, *only tendencies and counter-tendencies* (as brilliantly described by Marx in his great, but misunderstood, chapter on the falling rate of profit, possibly Marx's most sophisticatedly *'realist'* analysis of all!) *with the outcome left wide open*, subject only to conjunctural, situational, determinisms (in the plural). Class struggle, for instance, is real enough; but its outcome, on Marxist lines at any rate, is no historically given certainty. Nor can the so-called 'economic' be the determining element in the putative 'last instance': there is, simply, no such last instance except perhaps on the day that the globe blows up. In the same vein, (material) bases cannot 'determine' so-called (ideological) superstructures, as in hoary Marxian *dicta; rather, there are many sites of social practices, each with its own 'base', and its own rationalising justifications.* Religious practice, for instance, is as real as economic or political practice, and generates its own set of illusions. Similarly, the fabled distinction between absolute and relative autonomy, that has dominated discussions of the state in Marxian political theory, is simply inutile; there is nothing, no stationary *centre*, to be autonomous from![54]

Clearly, then, critical realism 'opens up' Marxism, and surgically excises its laggard deficiencies; and it does so by offering a more sophisticated social theory than Marx (though building upon the latter's intuitions).[55] We can now confidently situate the great Marxian revolution in the history of ideas: *Marx was, simply, the first Realist on the royal realist road to science,* vested with all the raw genius of a precursor. It is quite unnecessary to dwell on the implications of critical realism for neoclassicism, given that it spells nothing short of sudden death for the latter's somewhat neolithic philosophical posturings (wavering, clumsily, and quite carelessly – for an ideology in power suffers from no need for justification – between a traditionalist, hard-bitten positivism, and a 'new wave' of post-modernist hermeneutics, *à la* McCloskey) – *if it is taken seriously* (of course, it won't: I had one of the most pre-eminent economists, and philosophers, of our time, assure me, quite blithely, that he could not fathom it at all).[56]

Against Eurocentricism

It is clear then that critical realism[57] can sharpen the tools of science, and serve as a critique of all schools of economics that specialise in airy 'model' building. For models, if totally accurate in what they depict, are superfluous; and if they are not, they are quite useless! *Their real social functions, in the social sciences, are as ideological constructs to help recruit and consolidate scientific communities (i.e. they are 'policy' tools).* But the real unasked question is whether, and why, 'we' need 'science' (critical realism included) and 'economics' at all? The *subject* (i.e. the 'do-ers') of the scientific enterprise is often left quite anonymous; though it is clear, materially speaking, that this terrain is populated by the governing techno-scientific élites that serve as His Corporate Majesty's interpreters, soothsayers, and sycophants. What is taken for granted in almost all of scientific discourse is the *legitimacy* of the academy and the scientific process, as though the university, and the effete élites it nurtures, are charitably endowed with only a public-spirited scientific curiosity about the world and nothing else.[58]

Nothing, of course, could be further than the truth; *the scientific establishment is as corrupt, and in much the same ways, as the general state of corruption in a capitalist society* (sharing the egregious ills of socialism, similarly, when located therein).

The modern university presupposes an organised scientific establishment, itself serving as a loyal instrument of state. Indeed, *science is simply another name for the systematic record-keeping and surveying requirement of a predatory system built upon unlimited greed wedded to virtually limitless power.*[59] The corporation and the state are the Trustees of this carefully controlled scientific process, whose object is a varying mix of profiteering and control over subject populations (workers, women, minorities, tribals, etc.).[60] The largely co-opted intellectual class that dominates this process is arguably both parasitic and undemocratic, posing as great a threat to the liberty and freedom of the vast populace as imperialist armies regularly do to weak and/or small states of the Third World.

Who is it, then, that is in need of the science of 'economics'? Whom will critical realism serve, once understood, and digested? Is it at all likely that scientific understanding will be appropriated by ordinary people who stand outside the process (though serving regularly as 'insiders' in the form of victims,[61] experimental subjects, and so forth)? Hardly. The scientific urge, in the modern era, is a *corporatist* one; ordinary, hapless people are its subject population, usually denied their rights, rituals and practices, in the name of science and the higher wisdom of the masters of the polity. *Stated succinctly, science is become now simply the master tool of corporate enslavement,*[62] no less in socialism as in capitalism; getting better at it, or even more scientific at it, is still no guarantee that the resulting process/products will either extend, or even preserve, the domain of freedom for humbler people.

It is this disconsolate fact, in this period of world mastery of capital, that dictates an attitude of extreme caution with regard to scientific paradigms, *en général*. Given the infamous history of the twentieth century, in the area of the *abuse* of science (a history all but suppressed, forgotten, and apparently unknown even to many radicals), it would be entirely safe to venture that the less science we have, the better off we possibly might be; the less economics, the better off, and so on. Very much in this vein, critical realism is no amiable friend of the people, and not just for being ever so wilfully inaccessible – I personally know top notch scholars, both in and out of economics, who quite *literally* don't understand a word of it – but because it looks upon the world with unfailingly corporatist eyes. It is arguably superior to the established ideologies of the already rich and powerful in its insights, but it probably craves that very same power; and what if such power were to come its way? Millions had to suffer unthinkable horrors so we may now know that Marxism is a flawed guide to political practice; how many victims will critical realism claim, when it gets its hour under the sun? The question is worth pondering, lest we forget . . .

In this spirit of populism – and I take the personal position *that freedom is a far higher order value than science*[63] – I reject and distrust critical realism as much as the economics and philosophies it opposes and lays bare. I know, from the acuity of experience, that critical realism is no palliative when toothache strikes; it can neither feed, house, clothe, nor warm, nor nurture, those whom it touches. It is, in the European vein, just another bright idea. Frankly, I think that we of the non-European cast (as much as women and minorities living *within* European domains), have had enough of such hollow stimulations. It is high time we turned away from these perilous snares to discover some of our own bright ideas (slowly coming to light today in a myriad of fields: in agriculture, in nutrition, in healing, in co-operative co-existence, etc.; not bright perhaps, I think, so much as *warm* – their purpose being not to exude the cold, harsh, glare of intellectual illumination but the far gentler, more ambient glow, of human warmth?); I rather suspect that their time, not that of critical realism or economics, is nigh.

My western Realist comrades will have to forgive me; but this is a statement of an enlightened apostasy. Supposedly scientific mantras ('freemarket', 'communism', etc.) have, in our own times, and often with our own unthinking participation, destroyed countless lives and threatened the very survival of this fragile planet. What we need now is not newer mantras, or better methodologies, but far simpler *logics of resistance* to the plans of the rich and the powerful. *Contra Bhaskar, scientific knowledge is neither a necessary nor a sufficient condition for human emancipation.*[64] The latter stems from a moral, spiritual, and personal resolve to struggle against iniquity, injustice and oppression. Ordinary people such as rubber-tappers in Brazil, workers in Poland, and peasant women in India, amongst innumerable others, have heroically shown the way (repeatedly) to resist the depredations of capital and the state without consulting the manuals of science, or visiting the in-salons of the hip intelligentsia; *it is they that stand between us, today, and the realm of Flash Gordon.* For science, today, is the regrettably co-opted province of an emergent, engulfing, *Technofascism* based on the unscrupled harnessing of the icy hoards of instrumental reason. Since the time of the capitalist Enlightenment, western Science has been a cruelly misanthropic, misogynist, and warlike force that has fostered only the terrifyingly oppressive climate of Big Brother and Organised Intolerance – *an adjunct of imperialism, an accessory to racism and genocide, an accomplice of Stalinism and fascism, and a dire threat to workers, women, minorities, 'other' cultures, other species, and the wretched of the earth, generally.*[65] Philosophical realism, as a form of Counter-rationalism, can and will, I am afraid, offer only a loyal, effete, opposition to that grim, colourless, and despotic world; what we need, however, in stark contrast, most desperately, and urgently, is an *Exit*, an affective escape from its noxious exactions.[66] It is time – indeed, it may already be too late! – to bid a fervidly passionate farewell to all the regime(s) of corporate (and materialist) reason devolving from the great European Enlightenment. Let critical realism, brimming over with its blinding intelligence, *interpret* the world, by all means; we wish to remain busy, henceforth, in the much more modest task of trying to *save it.*[67]

Notes

1 The clearest statement of this triumphalism may be found in Francis Fukuyama (1989).
2 Associated with the economist, A. A. Alchian who likens economic competition to a Darwinian survival-of-the-species game of natural selection, in which the amorally defined 'fittest' agents survive. See A. A. Alchian and W. R. Allen (1964). Of course, Marx and Engels had, more than a century ago, savagely ridiculed the crude naturalism of such statements.
3 For a disclaimer see Joseph *et al.* (1990). Also, for the first *non-Eurocentric* account of the incredible, but forgotten, contributions of non-European mathematics, by the same author, see Joseph (1992).
4 For a ringing critique of perhaps the most egregious piece of such rewriting – in this case, of African history – see Davidson (1987), and Bernal (1987).
5 See Marx (1969), for an extended discourse on this subject.
6 Marx and Engels (1968).
7 For this claim see Bhaskar (1989a: Chapter 1).
8 Bachelard (1968).
9 For a fiery denunciation of this phenomenon, see Feyerabend (1978).
10 See Philip Mirowski (1988) for an exaggerated statement of this idea.
11 Usually David Hume is seen as the originator of this orientation with his passionate injunction to 'commit unto the flames' that which could not be quantified.
12 Malthus, for instance, employed his spurious mathematical progressions (purporting to represent ratios of population growth and food supply increments) with great effect, the maths being viewed generally as the clincher in an otherwise wholly specious argument. Even today, economics employs quite unnecessarily complex mathematical tools to keep the laity (and fellow social scientists) in humble wonderment.
13 For a humanist critique of scientism, Feyerabend (1978); for a more tendentious perspective see Hayek (1942: 43).
14 For a fuller statement of this argument see Kanth (1986; also Chapters 7–11 in Kanth 1992).
15 See Arrow (1987) for a full specification of the (capitalist) 'rationality' postulate.

16 It is the critical importance of these premises to the coherence of the neoclassical paradigm that leads Friedman to propose a spurious 'methodology' of ignoring the realism of premises in economic argument.

17 Senior, Mill, Cairnes, Robbins, and the Austrians, all shared this fundamental conviction, if in varying degrees. For the very best single source on the history of methodology in economics, see the work of Blaug (1992, 2nd edn) despite the fact that, true to his personal conservatism, the (potential) contributions of radical critiques (especially Bhaskarian realism) remain quite unspecified.

18 Friedman (1953).

19 The *a priori*, axiomatic, nature of these pronouncements is obvious and continuous from Ricardo, through Cairnes (1965), and Robbins (1935, 2nd edn). For latter-day apologetics, in this vein, defending the metaphysics of the 'rationality' postulate, see Boland (1981).

20 Lange (1945).

21 Popper (1972).

22 The Lakatosian methodology of 'scientific research programmes' would have little difficulty in disposing of neoclassicism as a degenerate science; of course, that is missing the point: Neoclassicism always was a *political* research programme.

23 A famous *Methodenstreit* between Carl Menger and Gustav Schmoller debated the deductivist versus inductivist problem as early as in the 1880s (see Hutchison 1973); closer to our times, similar issues were 'debated' between Terence Hutchison (see Hutchison 1956; also 1973) and Fritz Machlup (1978: 143–144), and yet again between Lester and Machlup in 1946.

24 For a clarification, see Blaug (1992, 2nd edn: Chapter 6).

25 As is well understood by the profession, any form of empirical research in the macro-economy has to abandon all pretence of neoclassicism; there economists have to function as classical (or even Marxian!) economists paying all due attention to *non-rationalist* and *non-individualist* social agents.

26 Many have long recognised this all-too obvious truth; in times of yore, Letwin (1964). More recently, the amazingly candid reflections of Blaug (1992). For a detailed study on the Ricardian roots of this orientation see Kanth (1986). Of course, macro-economics, in *practice*, is almost, by definition, *contra* the conceits of neoclassicism.

27 I am being only partly satirical here; truth is that entire social economies, tribal and precapitalist forms generally, have been based precisely on such considerations (fitting easily within a postulated 'Gandhian' economics, for example) until they were ruthlessly swept away first by capitalist colonialist depredations, and later, by equally virulent socialist crusades. Today, of course, the anti-human monstrosity of capitalist ideology is visited upon the entire planet.

28 It is not often recognised the extent to which economists' discussions of 'social welfare' are based on prior adherence to the postulate of *methodological individualism*, consciously or unconsciously, explicitly or implicitly. As such the whole bag of Paretian postulates are vitiated by an arguably false ontological assumption (this applies as much to the work of Kenneth Arrow as John Rawls). See Hennipman (1976) who continues to view Paretian ideological jugglery, akin to much of the economics mainstream, as a positive, 'analytical' tool.

29 The reasons for the gaping emptiness of the black hole of neoclassicism are all political and historical; briefly, capitalist economics entered the world *defensively*, suffering the scorn of conservative criticism first and radical socialist critiques later. Now that the the socialist bloc has collapsed, and with it, the apparent extinction of all its enemies, perhaps economics will slowly shed its ideological wraps and begin the quite novel task of emulating a true science, which is to begin with real facts, not arbitrary premises.

30 The best single source for an understanding of the Marxian system remains the old classic of Paul Sweezy (1970).

31 Thus, for the simple Marxist, religion can be explained in economic terms, but economics cannot – legitimately – be explained in religious terms.

32 If we include so-called 'radicals' alongside the Marxists, their record, at least in the US academy, of providing a serious alternative to mainstream science (apart from mainstream *politics*) is quite pathetic. See Bronfenbrenner (1970) and Lindbeck (1971) for an early, and largely accurate, survey of issues. Quite aptly, therefore, Mark Blaug characterises the whole group as simple-minded 'voluntarists' (see Blaug 1990: Chapter 3).

33 It is in this area that Bhaskarian Realism comes into its own, irrefutably showing the individualist epistemic – the so-called *methodological individualism* – of capitalist economics as being fatally flawed in an *ontological* sense. See Bhaskar (1989, 2nd edn).

34 The presumptions of this school are neatly summarised in Martin Hollis and Edward Nell (1975).

35 See Schumpeter (1976).

36 I have shown this in the case of Ricardo (Kanth 1986, op. cit.), but it can, I think, be demonstrated for any and all paradigms.

37 The great error of both capitalist and Marxist theorising is to extract the 'economy' from its cultural base and then treat it as the determining foundation of the latter. The truth is ineluctable: the economy is always embedded in a cradle of values (no more or less so, be it capitalism, or for that matter even socialism).

38 The so-called Carnegie–Mellon school, in economics, aside from most business schools, takes this approach although the scientific scope of their research agenda remains as 'bounded' as their vaunted doctrine of 'bounded' rationality. See Simon (1957).

39 Indeed, this much is apparent even in standard oligopoly theory where the existence of self-conscious strategies invites not new modes of economic theorising but the application of political and military codes of gamesmanship in a Machiavellian world of power struggles.

40 One important caveat is due: the fact that this chapter, basically, offers an external critique of science does not, by any means, preclude it also from holding existing pretenders to Eurocentred science to the latter's own *internal* canons of acceptable scientific practice. There is no 'contradiction' between the two types of critique; rather, they are complementary.

41 For rejection of the notion of equilibrium Joan Robinson (1962) at her acerbic best is unsurpassable. For the empirical irrelevance of neoclassicism, except as a guide to a *praxiology*, see Lange, op. cit. and Hollis and Nell, op. cit.

42 Frank Hahn (1985: 19–20) blithely assures us that General Equilibrium theory is of 'great practical significance'; and yet he could still yield that

the theory 'makes no formal or causal claims at all' (1984: 47–48)!! In point of fact, the notion of 'General Equilibrium' is purely and simply an ideological construct: it has no practical or theoretical significance at all.

43 As a nineteenth-century observer of the Ricardians remarked, the strength of the economists lay directly proportional to their distance from the facts!

44 On the generally negative findings in this area, see Fisher (1991), in Oswald (1991). For similar discoveries vis à vis the 'rationality' postulate see the summation of evidence in Frey and Eichenberger (1989); significantly, empirical counter-evidence is, in mainstream economics *newspeak*, invidiously titled 'anomalies'!

45 See Latsis (1972; and 1976, ed.) for a flat rejection of the 'immunising stratagems' of neoclassicism, the clever ruses indicating the latter's status only as a 'degenerating' research programme.

46 Marx was fond of saying that if appearance and reality coincided there would be no need for science; however less subtle Marxists have taken this to mean that appearances are not a part of 'reality'. Perhaps Bhaskar (1989b) offers the best clarification here with his stratification of reality into the real, the actual, and the empirical dimensions.

47 As Brown and Deaton (1972: 1168) argue, 'theory', in this sphere, was little more than a 'fable'. Importantly, the positivism of economics does not allow for the entirely plausible ontological possibility, in economics behaviour, that 'anything goes'; hence the clinging to a determinist theory in face of the merry dance of chaos that is reality.

48 Samuelson (1966: 61).

49 On the vagueness of this schemata, see Thurow (1975).

50 The strategy of neoclassicism in dealing with its counterfactualities is instructive. First, it models the untruths (say, e.g., perfect competition) as canonical edifices, then it drags in the truth (the *contra* empirical evidence) as infelicitous 'anomalies', or 'externalities', to be worked into the models by way of exception! In effect, the so-called 'anomalies' are simply egregiously lapidary *refutations* of the 'models'!

51 I speak of Bhaskar's 'scientific', 'transcendental' or, as I will refer to it henceforth, '*critical*' realism quite exclusively in this chapter; of course, there are many other forms of realism as well; and the economics establishment has its own resident realist in the form of Uskali Mäki. For recent developments in the Critical Realist project in Economics, led by Tony Lawson, see Lawson, T. (1994 a, b); Lawson, C. (1994) and Fleetwood (1995, 1997, 1998), and Pratten (1993).

52 For the relevance of Bhaskar to economics see Kanth (1992).

53 This has profound, and ultimately negative, implications for the Marxian theory of revolutionary change. For a full explication see Kanth 1997b.

54 Many of these propositions will, of course, be denied as being *really* 'Marxian' by defenders of the faith. I shall refrain from quoting chapter and verse.

55 Bhaskar is incomparable in this area as well; in fact, arguably his chapter titled 'Societies' in Bhaskar (1989, 2nd edn) is possibly the best single treatment of the subject in modern times, beginning, so to speak, where Marx leaves off.

56 Of course, intellectual critiques, even at their best, can hardly dent the neoclassicist monolith (as the Sraffians discovered to their naive dismay

decades ago); the neoclassical has always lived quite securely, and opulently, in contempt of ordinary canons of common sense. The realists must understand that stating the truth does not, by itself, bring down the citadel of untruth.

57 More, perhaps, than other writers I treat the framework of transcendental Realism as almost exclusively instituted by Bhaskar, thereby neglecting many of his precursors (including Marx). While this posture may or may not be correct, it is certainly undeniable that Realism reaches its greatest philosophical sophistication in his writings. With Marx the speculation comes as a heady *aperitif*; with Bhaskar it's the last, gratifying sip of cognac.

58 Scientists have many (carefully cultivated, and largely self-serving) virtues; self-criticism is not, unfortunately, one of them.

59 On the whole problem of intellectuals *vis à vis* the state, see the excellent critique in Chomsky (1986).

60 On these issues see Watts (1983); and Illich (1970).

61 For some specifics, see Bodley (1982).

62 See Lyotard (1984).

63 See Kanth (ed. 1994) Postscript, for more on this theme.

64 This is directly *contra* Bhaskar's assertion (1989b: Chapter 1), echoed also in Lawson's work (Lawson, T., op. cit.), of the indispensability of science to emancipation. At any rate, matters here are quite simple; by Bhaskar's own admission, *Realism is simply an under-labourer for science – therein, the inherent, almost terminal, limits of both philosophy and philosophising.*

65 For some passionate notes on this subject see Shiva (1989).

66 See Feyerabend (1987) for a lyrically impassioned appeal to flee the realm of corporate reason before it's too late.

67 For it is only in his XIth Thesis on Feuerbach that Marx is arguably, and supernally, superior to any, and all, varieties of scientific realism.

Bibliography

Alchian, A. A. and Allen, W. R. (1964) *University Economics*, Belmont, CA: Wadsworth Publishing Company.

Arrow, K. J. (1987) 'Economic Theory and the Hypothesis of Rationality', in J. Eatwell *et al.* (eds) *The New Palgrave: A Dictionary of Economics*, vol. 2, pp. 69–74.

Bachelard, G. (1968) *The Philosophy of the New Scientific Mind*, New York: Orion Press.

Backhouse, R. E. (1994) *New Directions in Economic Methodology*, London: Routledge.

Bernal, M. (1987) *Black Athena: The Afroasiatic Roots of Classical Civilisation*, vol. 1, London: Free Association Books.

Bhaskar, R. (1986) *Scientific Realism and Human Emancipation*, London: Verso.

—— (1989a) *The Possibility of Naturalism*, 2nd edn, London: Verso.

—— (1989b) *Reclaiming Reality*, London: Verso.

Blaug, M. (1990) *Economic Theories: True or False?*, Aldershot: Edward Elgar.

—— (1992) *The Methodology of Economics*, 2nd edn, Cambridge: Cambridge University Press.

Bodley, J. H. (1982) *Victims of Progress*, Menlo Park, California.

Boland, L. (1981) 'On the Futility of Criticising the Neoclassical Maximisation Hypothesis', *American Economic Review* 71.

Bronfenbrenner, M. (1970) 'Radical Economics in America: A 1970 Survey', *Journal of Economic Literature* 8: 747–766.

Brown, A. and Deaton, A. (1972) 'Models of Consumer Behaviour: A Survey', *Economic Journal* 82: 1145–1236.

Cairnes, J. E. (1965) *The Character and Logical Method of Political Economy*, London: Frank Cass.

Chomsky, N. (1986) *Towards a New Cold War*, New York: Pantheon .

Davidson, B. (1987) 'The Ancient World and Africa: Whose Roots?', *Race and Class* XXIX(2): 1–15.

Eatwell, J., Milgate, M. and Newman, P. (eds) (1987) *The New Palgrave: A Dictionary of Economics*, London: Macmillan, 4 vols.

Feyerabend, P. (1978) *Science in a Free Society*, London: Verso.

—— (1987) *Farewell to Reason*, London: Verso.

Fisher, S. (1991) 'Recent Developments in Macroeconomics', in A. J. Oswald (ed.) *Surveys in Economics*, vol. I: 1–47.

Fleetwood, S. (1995) *The Political Economy of Hayek: The Socio-Economics of Order*, London: Routledge.

—— (1996) 'Order Without Equilibrium: A Critical Realist Interpretation of Hayek's Notion of Spontaneous Order', *Cambridge Journal of Economics* 20(4): 729–747.

—— (1998) 'Critical Realism: Marx and Hayek', in W. Keizer, B. Tieben and R. Van Zijp (eds) *Austrians in Debate*, London: Routledge.

Frey, B. S. and Eichenberger, R. (1989) 'Should Social Scientists Care About Choice Anomalies?', *Rationality and Society* 1(1): 101–122.

Friedman, M. (1953) *Essays in Positive Economics*, Chicago: University of Chicago Press.

Fukuyama, F. (1989) 'The End of History', *National Interest* Summer: 4.

Hahn, F. (1984) *Equilibrium and Macroeconomics*, Oxford: Basil Blackwell.

—— (1985) *Money, Growth and Stability*, Oxford: Basil Blackwell.

Hayek, F. A. (1942–43) 'Scientism and the Study of Society', *Economica*.

Hennipman, P. (1976) 'Pareto Optimality: Value Judgment or Analytical Tool?', in J. S. Cramer, A. Heertje and P. Venekamp (eds) *Relevance and Precision: From Quantitative Analysis to Economic Policy*, Amsterdam: North Holland, pp. 39–69.

Hicks, J. R. and Weber, W. (eds) (1973) *Carl Menger and the Austrian School of Economics*, Oxford: Clarendon Press.

Hollis, M. and Nell, E. J. (1975) *Rational Economic Man*, Cambridge: Cambridge University Press.

Hutchison, T. W. (1956) 'Professor Machlup on Verification in Economics', *Southern Economic Journal* 22.

—— (1973) 'Some Themes from Investigations into Method', in J. R. Hicks and W. Weber (eds) *Carl Menger and the Austrian School of Economics*, Oxford: Clarendon Press.

Illich, I. (1970) *Deschooling Society*, New York: Harper and Row.

Joseph, G. G. (1992) *The Crest of the Peacock*, London: Penguin.

Joseph, G. G., Reddy, V. and Searle-Chatterjee, M. (1990) 'Eurocentrism in the Social Sciences', *Race and Class* 31(4): 1–26.

Kanth, R. (1985) 'The Decline of Ricardian Politics: Some Notes on Paradigm-Shift in Economics from the Classical to the NeoClassical Persuasion', *European Journal of Political Economy* 1/2: 157–187.

—— (1986) *Political Economy and Laissez-Faire*, Totowa, NJ: Rowman and Little-field.

—— (1991) 'Economic Theory and Realism: Outlines of a Reconstruction', *Methodus* 3(2), Dec.: 37–45.

—— (1992) *Capitalism and Social Theory*, New York: M. E. Sharpe, Inc.

—— (ed.) (1994) *Paradigms in Economic Development*, New York: M. E. Sharpe, Inc.

—— (1997a) *Breaking with the Enlightenment: The Twilight of History and the Rediscovery of Utopia*, New Jersey: The Humanities Press.

—— (1997b) *Against Economics: Rethinking Political Economy*, London: Avebury Publishers.

Lange, O. (1945) 'The Scope and Method of Economics', *Review of Economic Studies*.

Latsis, S. J. (1972) 'Situational Determinism in Economics', *British Journal for the Philosophy of Science* 23: 207–245.

—— (ed.) (1976) *Method and Appraisal in Economics*, Cambridge: Cambridge University Press.

Lawson, C. (1994) 'The Transformational Model of Social Activity and Economic Analysis: A Reinterpretation of the Work of J. R. Commons', *Review of Political Economy* 6(3):1–25.

Lawson, T. (1994a) 'A Realist Theory for Economics', in R. E. Backhouse (ed.) *New Directions in Economic Methodology*, pp. 257–285.

—— (1994b) 'The Nature of Post-Keynesianism and its Links to Other Traditions', *Journal of Post Keynesian Economics* 16(4), Summer: 503–538.

—— (1995) 'The "Lucas critique": A Generalisation', *Cambridge Journal of Economics* 19(2): 257–276.

Letwin, W. (1964) *The Origins of Scientific Economics*, New York: Doubleday & Co., Inc.

Lindbeck, A. (1971) *The Political Economy of the New Left: An Outsider's View*, New York: Harper and Row.

Lyotard, J. F. (1984) *The Postmodern Condition: A Report on Knowledge*, Minneapolis: University of Minnesota Press.

Machlup, F. (1978) *Methodology of Economics and Other Social Sciences*, New York: Academic Press.

Marx, K. (1969) *Theories of Surplus Value*, London: Lawrence and Wishart.

Marx, K. and Engels, F. (1968) *The Communist Manifesto*, New York: Monthly Review Press.

Mirowski, P. (1988) *Against Mechanism*, Totowa, NJ: Rowman and Littlefield.

Oswald, A. J. (ed.) (1991) *Surveys in Economics*, Oxford: Basil Blackwell, 2 vols.

Popper, K. (1972) *Conjectures and Refutations: The Growth of Scientific Knowledge*, London: Routledge and Kegan Paul

Pratten, S. (1993) 'Structure, Agency, and Marx's Analysis of the Labour Process', *Review of Political Economy* 5(4): 403–426.

Robbins, L. (1935) *An Essay on the Nature and Significance of Economic Science*, London: Macmillan, 2nd edn.

Robinson, J. (1962) *Economic Philosophy*, London: C. A. Watts.

Samuelson, P. A. (1966) *The Collected Scientific Papers of Paul A. Samuelson*, Cambridge, MA: MIT Press, vol. 1.

Schumpeter, J. (1976) *Capitalism, Socialism and Democracy*, London: George Allen and Unwin.

Shiva, V. (1989) *Staying Alive*, London: Zed Books.

Simon, H. (1957) *Models of Man*, New York: Wiley and Sons.

Sweezy, P. (1970) *Theory of Capitalist Development*, New York: Monthly Review Press.

Thurow, L. C. (1975) *Generating Inequality*, London: Macmillan Press.

Watts, M. (1983) *Silent Violence*, Berkeley and LA: University of California Press.

12

CRITICAL ISSUES IN *ECONOMICS AS REALIST SOCIAL THEORY*[1]

Tony Lawson

Introduction

There are numerous facets to the project of *critical realism* as it has been developed in economics. Most obviously it offers a conception and analysis of the nature of reality, both natural and social. And through drawing on this analysis, specific claims are made regarding, amongst other things, the possibility of (and possibilities for) economics as social science, the relation of the study of social phenomena to certain (successful) natural sciences, the nature and relevance of contemporary mainstream economics, and the character of social, including emancipatory, change. Various aspects of this realist project are challenged in the previous four chapters. However, it is possible to discern five areas which receive the greater part of the criticism. These are (1) the role of transcendental argument in establishing the relative advantages of the broad perspective sustained; (2) the (philosophical) manner in which the perspective on social science is supported; (3) the analysis and critique offered of the nature and relevance of modern mainstream economics; (4) the account provided of social scientific explanation; and (5) the assessment made of the role of science in society, specifically in relation to any project of human emancipation. I use these five areas of critical focus to structure the discussion below.

Before setting out my response, however, I want briefly to acknowledge the constructive manner in which the contributors to this part of the volume (Chapters 8, 9, 10 and 11, respectively) present their criticisms. Some, Parsons and Hands in particular, adopt a somewhat aggressive rhetorical style. But in each case the criticisms offered are pertinent; they reveal a commitment to furthering the various debates and understandings. Of course this is how it should be. I record my appreciation explicitly only because all too often in recent years, methodological disagreement, whether in articles, book reviews or whatever, has (with some obvious exceptions) to a significant degree failed to engage. Rather arguments, evaluations and/or theses have tended to be summarily dismissed (or supported), usually on the basis of little more than assertion 'backed up' by authoritative posturing by the reviewer. Such stances are rarely insightful or facilitating of progress and the contributions to the discussion in the preceding pages show that they are unnecessary. I hope I succeed in repaying the compliment of engagement. In fact, and like the authors of the four chapters in question, I shall mainly concentrate on our differences and I offer criticism back. This, though, should not mask the fact that we do share a good deal in common, as I briefly indicate at relevant points in the discussion.

The use of transcendental argument in evaluating philosophical perspectives

In the realist project under scrutiny here, transcendental argument is employed in providing support for a particular perspective on reality and science. My assessment is that this aspect of the project has achieved some success. However, Tom Boylan and Paschal O'Gorman (Chapter 8) and also Steve Parsons (Chapter 9) are not convinced. Here there is disagreement both over the interpretation of transcendental argument and, connectedly, over what can be achieved through employing it. Let me consider these two aspects in turn.

The nature of transcendental argument

By transcendental argument I understand a process of reasoning concerned to elucidate the conditions of some generalised feature of experience. This form of argument is employed in the realist project in providing what I take to be a fallible, non-foundationalist account of reality and science. This assessment is immediately seen as problematic by both Boylan and O'Gorman and also Parsons for whom transcendental analysis is inherently bound up with the quest for 'incorrigible foundations'. In making sense of my position, the inclinations of Boylan and O'Gorman are to assign me to the foundationalist camp which they associate with transcendental argument. It is true that immediately after so doing they allow that I 'qualify' my stance in recognising explicitly that the conclusions I reach are '. . . like all cognitive claims, also fallible and corrigible'. However, they conclude that 'the spirit, if not the letter' of my position 'is that of neo-Kantian transcendental realism' (p. 139).

Parsons, in appearing to formulate the same dichotomy between the status of the results of transcendental analysis and fallibilism, instead places me firmly in the fallibilist camp. Parsons' complaint is precisely that, given that the realist orientation I adopt admits to being a fallible perspective, one that supports contingent, practically conditioned results, there are few grounds for my assuming the transcendental label in describing my position.

But transcendental argument is being interpreted too narrowly here by both sets of authors. And this can be seen even if we concentrate on Kant. In initiating his programme of immanent metaphysics Kant sought an alternative to the misguided (as he saw it) goal of revealing the nature of being. In its place he substituted the project of investigating the presuppositions of our knowledge of being. This way of proceeding was identified by Kant (in his account of transcendental idealism) with the determination of the conceptual conditions in terms of which anything knowable must be thought. However, it is clear that the two features identified here are in principle distinct. That is, the transcendental method of enquiry is conceptually distinct from the individualist and idealist mode or form in which Kant framed his own specific transcendental enquiries. It is this distinction that is recognised in transcendental realism, and the former, general transcendental procedure that is borrowed.[2] The two aspects ought not to be conflated.

Now once transcendental argument *is* conceptually disengaged from the specific idealist and individualist mode in which Kant framed his own investigations, and is accepted as involving reasoning that elucidates the conditions of possibility of some especially significant or pervasive aspect of experience, a rather wider set of implications inevitably follow than are allowed by (or are easily recognised by concentrating on) Kant's specific applications. In fact, we can identify transcendental enquiry as one instance of the class of enquiries into the necessary conditions of human activities as conceptualised in experience, where, despite Parsons' objections, this is indeed but a sub-species of retroductive argument, i.e. the move from a description of some phenomenon to an account of something by which it is produced or otherwise conditioned. Furthermore, the process of analysing human activities in this way can elucidate not merely conceptual powers or categories but also powers people possess as physical, biological and social agents. In this, clearly, the activity, its conceptualisation and analysis may each be fallible, spatially localised and transient.

Thus, transcendental analysis may produce (transcendental) realist, not idealist, and epistemically relativist, rather than absolutist, results. It is the case then that both premises and conclusions are contingent facts, the former (but not the latter) necessarily being social. It is thus only in this relative or conditional sense that synthetic *a priori* truths can be established. Philosophy gets going only on the basis of prior specific conceptualisations of actual determinate social practice.[3]

The utility of transcendental enquiry

If transcendental enquiry *can*, then, furnish us with practically conditioned, contingent, fallible knowledge there remains the question of its practical worth in discriminating between philosophical positions. Now how is the superiority of one particular philosophical position ever to be rationally demonstrated to a proponent of an alternative? One strategy, and perhaps the only one, turns on finding a set of premises accepted by both (or all) parties to the debate and demonstrating that these premises support (i.e., presuppose conditions or entail consequences that can be accommodated by) only one of the contending philosophical positions. It is in this context that transcendental argument displays significant utility.

Boylan and O'Gorman recognise the limitations of the empiricism against which (amongst other positions) transcendental realism has situated itself. But these authors appear to be of the opinion that transcendental argument is not needed to establish the superiority of alternative projects, their own *causal holism* included. They do not, however, suggest how philosophical opponents might be persuaded of the errors of their ways.

Parsons, on the other hand, not only questions the need for transcendental argument but also denies that it *can* provide support for the transcendental realist position over the Humean[4] or empirical realist one against which it is sometimes situated. The gist of Parsons' argument, as I understand it,[5] is that the transcendental realist is necessarily impaled on the horns of a dilemma. This turns on the difficulty of determining appropriate premises for a transcendental argument to (relative support for) transcendental realism. If the set of premises chosen is *rejected* by the empirical realist, then nothing can be made of it by the transcendental realist. However, reasons Parson: 'A transcendental argument that starts from a premise concerning observations acceptable to both parties cannot establish natural necessity' (p. 162).

Parsons does touch on the crux of what philosophical analysis can achieve here. To initiate a transcendental (or indeed any) argument from premises that opponents do not both (or all) accept is unlikely to persuade, or even to constitute an engagement. For this reason claims which invoke merely the authority of a source (of a text or its writer or even a distinguished interpreter [for example of Hume or of Kant]; of a contributor with training in philosophy or in science, or of someone with an expertise in the 'cutting-edge' of science, or in the history of science, etc.) advance the debate very little. But it would be wrong to suppose that where a set of premises is shared by disputants in a debate, it must lend equal support to the various positions sustained by the disputing parties. All knowledge and reasoning is fallible: each can involve inconsistencies or presuppose metaphysical and other absurdities, amongst other errors. And it is precisely because of this that Kant was able to allocate to philosophy the task of analysing concepts and claims that are given but confused.

Philosophy, then, takes the form of resolving confusions, inconsistencies and tensions, in short of *immanent critique*. Transcendental arguments are fundamental in this, being most potent when they take the form of, or involve, the transcendental refutations of actually or potentially competing positions. For such arguments to work, shared premises are essential. This is the truth in Parsons' assessment. And it is quite consistent with the arguments made for transcendental realism. Because there appears to remain some doubt about this latter claim, however, let me briefly run though the premises adopted, and describe the use which is made of them, in the transcendental argument for the conception of a structured, open and differentiated reality as systematised within transcendental (as against empirical) realism. After so demonstrating the utility of the type of analysis in question, I return to Parsons' specific objections to the particular strategy adopted.

Arguments for transcendental realism

Now it is certainly an essential feature of the strategy adopted that, by its focusing on activities which opponents themselves have historically picked out as the most significant in science, it avoids siding arbitrarily with some external criterion of, or claim to, knowledge. The philosophical orientations that I have identified as *most capable* of grounding the mainstream (deductivist) project in economics are empiricists and transcendental idealists, which, for current purposes, can be grouped together as empirical realists. And these sponsor the activities and results of controlled experimentation as fundamental to science. The assessment that experimental activities and results have had a significant role in successful science is a premise the transcendental realist can also accept. And given the fact of this shared premise, the intention has been to demonstrate how these sponsoring philosophies cannot, whilst a transcendental realist analysis can, sustain the intelligibility of the sponsored activity without generating metaphysical absurdity.

213

The argument made turns fundamentally on the interpretation of event regularities. According to the empirical realist tradition, empirical regularities are at least necessary and perhaps sufficient conditions for causal laws; and causal laws, etc. are analysed as dependent upon, or just as, constant conjunctions of events or states of affairs. According to transcendental realism, in contrast, there is an ontological distinction between causal laws and patterns of events. And support for transcendental realism is achieved by way of a transcendental demonstration that such an ontological distinction is a condition of the intelligibility of experimental practices and its results. In this way an immanent refutation of empirical realism in its various guises is achieved along with a vindication of the transcendental realist ontology.

The argument itself is fairly simple. It relies on the two-part observation that (1) (strict) constant conjunctions of interest in science[6] are both rather rare and spatio-temporally restricted, being mainly confined to situations of experimental control, while (2) law-like knowledge appears to be generally available and widely applicable and some of it experimentally corroborated.

For the empirical realist, the observed confinement of most scientifically interesting event regularities to the experimental situation, including supposed *laws of nature*, commits her or him to the absurdity that human beings, through experimental activity, cause and even change the laws of nature. This absurdity can be avoided only if a conception along the lines of the transcendental realist account of the world as open and structured is allowed. For, from such a perspective, the experiment can be recognised (and rendered intelligible) as a situation in which non-empirical factors (structures, powers, mechanisms, tendencies) of interest are insulated from other, perhaps countervailing, factors and thereby *empirically identified*.

The second component of the above noted observation is equally problematic for the empirical realist. Indeed, for such a person the observation that our law-like knowledge, even where experimentally established, is regularly practically applied in systems that can be characterised as open, where constant conjunctions of events do not obtain, is simply inexplicable. Once more, he or she is committed to metaphysical absurdity: that either outside experimental-like situations nature and society are radically indeterministic, or science has yet to find any laws. And as before, such absurdity is avoided by accepting the perspective of transcendental realism. For, a condition of the successful application of science in open systems is that, against empirical realism, causal laws be analysed as expressing not event regularities, but tendencies of things that may be active unrealised because of the action of countervailing tendencies. In other words, in citing a law one is referring to the transfactual activity of mechanisms, that is to their activity as such, and not making a claim about the actual outcome which in general will be co-determined by numerous mechanisms. Such mechanisms, when triggered, may continue to be operative outside of, as well as inside, the experiment. In short, the non-invariance of conjunctions is a condition of a successful experimental science, and the non-empirical nature of laws is a condition of a successful practical one.

Where does Parsons demur from all this? Central to Parsons' objection is a conjecture that the empirical realist will refuse to go along with the observation, emphasised by transcendental realists, that most scientifically interesting (strict) event regularities are produced in experimental situations (although Parsons sometimes misconstrues this observation as a claim that event regularities occur *only* under these conditions). It is noticeable that Parsons does not challenge the basic premise for the transcendental argument sustained, one that is seemingly acceptable to all relevant parties, namely that experimental activities and results are significant aspects of much successful science. Rather he questions the observational claim utilised alongside this premise, that scientifically significant event regularities are spatially–temporally restricted and, at least outside astronomy, mainly occurring in situations of experimental control. Or to be more precise, Parsons questions the assumption that this observational claim is acceptable to the empirical realist.

Parsons in this way strives to saddle the transcendent realist with the following dilemma: that the transcendental realist must either (1) accept that event regularities are not systematically confined but ubiquitous – in which case support for the transcendental realist account of a structured reality, etc. cannot be justified (even if correct), i.e., that the transcendental realist and empirical realist accounts are necessarily equally evidentially grounded; or (2) accept premises about the spatial–temporal confinement of event regularities in the knowledge that these premises are rejected by the empirical realist. In the latter case, there is no warrant for the empirical realist to engage in discussion; in neither case is the empirical realist compelled to accept the transcendental realist conception of reality.

Now if the transcendental realist were to conclude that event regularities are ubiquitous, then it would indeed be difficult to provide justification for the transcendental position. Of course, I do not so conclude. Interestingly, however, Parsons seems to include a supplementary line of argument to the effect that the transcendental realist must. Because this claim, if correct, would serve to undermine my argument, I must now briefly consider the reasoning involved.

If I understand it correctly, Parsons' challenge here comprises two parts: (a) because scientific activity produces constant event conjunctions in the laboratory, it is held that, in such laboratory conditions, causal relations relate events, and laws refer to constant conjunctions; and (b) because all causal relations outside the laboratory can, it is supposed, be expressed in the constant conjunction form, there are no grounds for concluding that reference to mechanisms is required here either, nor for supposing that event regularities are other than ubiquitous.

In support of (a) Parsons writes:

> if scientific activity produces constant event conjunctions then, in the experimental situation, causal relations would seem to relate events, and laws refer to constant event conjunctions. Indeed, why would science produce such conjunctions, unless the causal relation relates events? Consequently, in the experimental situation, laws refer to constant event conjunctions, and the causal relation relates events.
>
> (p. 159)

Such reasoning is hardly sustainable. It is precisely because causal laws operate irrespective of actual events and their patterns that scientists are often able, knowledgeably and capably, to intervene, through the experiment, in order to produce certain event conjunctions. In other words, the recognition that 'scientific activity *produces* constant event conjunctions (emphasis added)' is intelligible only if we first accept that the world is open and structured – allowing the possibility of its being amenable to experimental closure. Why (Parsons asks) should science produce such conjunctions? This is an excellent question. It *can* do so because the world is open, structured and differentiated; it *seeks* to do so in order both that the workings of non-empirical mechanisms be identified, and/or that additional evidence be made available for assessing hypotheses of how mechanisms work, etc. This is the only intelligible answer to Parsons' question that I am aware of, and it severely undermines any inference that 'in the experimental situation, laws refer to constant event conjunctions, and the causal relation relates events'.

What of Parsons' additional argument (b), that event regularities are ubiquitous outside the experimental situation, and that this is (or should be) accepted by the transcendental realist? Now it can be readily accepted that outside the laboratory regularities of sorts sometimes emerge, and that a central aim will often be to explain them. But this is a far cry from supposing, as Parsons seems to (and for his argument needs to), that the experimental and non-experimental results are essentially identical in form. Of course, *ex posteriori* we find that, even in an open system, certain mechanisms of interest occasionally shine through; but rarely if ever do they do so continuously or always. Taking up Parsons' examples, the effects of certain viruses may sometimes be manifest as skin spots, but not always; the effects of certain genetic codes may sometimes be manifest in puppies turning into dogs, but not always (fatal accidents occur); the British system of industrial relations may often have resulted in productivity growth that is relatively slow compared to that of certain other countries, but not always. In addition, Hume's billiard ball at rest need not (and does not) always move when struck by a second one (whether it is next to the cushion and struck in a particular manner, or I simply hold onto it).[7] Even with examples such as these, then, the transfactual tendencies in question are unlikely to be continually actualised, to support event regularities.

In consequence, it simply does not follow that 'There is thus no observable difference between the world as it appears to the transcendental realist and the world as it appears for the Humean analysis', at least if Parsons is (as he seems to be) interpreting the latter as an undifferentiated world in which event regularities are ubiquitous. For the world – as the transcendental realist finds it certainly – is indeed one in which strict (and near strict) event regularities are found to be restricted to certain conditions (and not others), while scientific knowledge is applied rather more widely. Of course, such event regularities as occur are not restricted only to the experimental situation. But they are not ubiquitous either; they are found only under certain identifiable conditions. These are fundamental insights which are continually reaffirmed in the transcendental realist project. They point to a set of contrasts that warrant explanation. And the achieving of the latter, as we have already seen (and as is easily further demonstrated),[8] requires accepting the transcendental, as opposed to the empirical, realist account of reality, science and its objects.

We must thus return to the central point of difference, to Parsons' conjecture that the empirical realist will refuse to acknowledge the empirical claim in question, that scientifically interesting regularities are hardly ubiquitous, but largely confined to the experimental situation. In fact, we have in contention here not one empirical question but two; whether event regularities are spatio-temporally restricted, and (even if they are) whether the empirical realist will accept that they are. But I think the two questions can be addressed together. For it is equally necessary to ask why the empirical realist so sanctifies the experiment. And the answer can only be because it is in this context that most scientifically significant regularities are produced *and* the empirical realist recognises that this is so. Certainly there is little doubt that the experiment is central to those of this orientation. And it is regularly observed that claims held as knowledge by this tradition are to a large degree restricted to the experimental situation. As the entry on *empiricism* in Flew's *A Dictionary of Philosophy* records, for example:

> Empiricism . . . has taken several forms; but one common feature has been the tendency to start from the experimental sciences, as a kind of prototype or paradigm case of human knowledge. . . . As a result, *empiricism has characteristically seen the acquisition of knowledge as . . . limited by the possibilities of experiment and observations.*
>
> (p. 105, emphasis added)

At one point Parsons asks 'If opponents of transcendental realism believe that constant conjunctions of events are "ubiquitous" in non-experimental situations, then why should they accept the thesis that they are not?' (p.158). But the more relevant question, surely, is why, if opponents really were to believe this, would they distinguish the experimental situation at all? I thus remain sceptical about Parsons' assertion that the empirical realist will contest the point in question.

That said, it is still open to any individual opponent of transcendental realism to question whether or not event regularities are yet ubiquitous, of course, whatever empiricists in general might have concluded. For in the end, if to repeat, the location of strict event regularities is always an empirical matter. If Parson himself is sceptical about the empirical assessment in question I invite him to check out whether it is not in the experimental situation that strict event regularities of interest in science are mainly located (short of this, he and I will have to find a different way to develop our particular debate). I repeat once more, though, that I have not at any stage denied that regularities of sorts can and do occur to a degree in non-experimental contexts. But I find the experimental/non-experimental contrast is fairly systematic and striking on this score. Moreover, the transcendental realist analysis of the experiment helps us understand and explain such event regularities as occur elsewhere. The goal of the realist, contra Parsons' assertions, is not to deny *a priori* that event regularities can occur in non-experimental situations but to explain them *ex posteriori*, i.e., if and where they do. And this means making sense of any temporal and spatial specificity involved.

Arguments in support of a perspective on social reality and (social) science

A second feature of critical realism that comes in for criticism in some of the preceding chapters is the manner in which a perspective on social reality and its science is achieved. Specifically, there is a scepticism that insights gained through philosophical reflection on the natural realm can carry over to the social one. This appears to lie behind Boylan's and O'Gorman's worries. They, and perhaps Parsons as well, doubt that anything follows from philosophical reflection on the natural realm. Boylan and O'Gorman, indeed, appear sceptical that anything is to be gained from philosophical analysis at all: 'our objection to critical realism is not to its social ontology, it is rather to its commitment to particular modes of philosophical argument *vis-à-vis* this ontology' (Boylan and O'Gorman, this volume: p. 141).

I have some sympathy with this last objection. If I may inject an autobiographical note here, like numerous others I originally embarked upon social scientific research informed implicitly by a directly determined perspective on the nature of social being (see e.g., Kilpatrick and Lawson 1980; Lawson 1981b). However, I was surprised to find that the main criticisms offered of this research were not of the form 'this is wrong' but rather 'this is not economics'. It seemed that for research to be sanctioned as 'proper economics' it was necessary to produce formalistic models, and preferably models in which someone somewhere was optimising something. It was because this formalistic-modelling orientation seemed to me so obviously questionable as a general tool for investigating social phenomena, yet promoted so uncritically by the majority of our discipline, that I soon turned to study methodological issues. My aim, in part, was to understand this puzzling situation.

Now if it was difficult when I 'started out' to do social scientific research which did not conform to the conventional mould, my impression is that it is certainly no easier to do so today. The point, in other words, is that economic research, like everything else, always take place in a context, and an enduring aspect of the situation in economics is a widespread belief that it is the formalistic (deductivist) modelling approach (along with its implicit ontology) which constitutes the appropriate procedure. Thus, it is unfortunately not enough to set to work with an alternative account of social reality and science, however much more relevant it may be than that bound up with mainstream economics. So dominant is the latter project that *any* deviations require justification. Thus, whilst I can agree with Boylan and O'Gorman that critical realist analysis, or, more generally, sustained philosophical/methodological reflection, may not be essential for a more relevant research project in economics to be formulated or even to proceed, analysis of this sort does seem to be a strategic require-ment for a more relevant approach to be at all understood and accepted in the modern environment.

Alternatively put, all methods, etc., rest upon a philosophy of science grounding of some sort, whether or not the latter is explicitly acknowledged. If I am correct in concluding that the characteristic feature of the mainstream project in economics is its (deductivist) *method*, then a philosophical critique is required if that project is to be actively undermined. And given the current dominance of that project, it does seem necessary that its untenability be revealed if alter-native paths are even to be seriously contemplated.

The question of naturalism

If the foregoing sketch indicates why I take the view that philosoph-ical argumentation is more or less strategically inevitable in fashioning and defending a more relevant economics, I have yet to justify the specific strategy of drawing on insights gleaned through analysing the natural realm and natural science. I pursue this issue now.

First, I ought to indicate why I do not employ a transcendental argument from shared premises concerning successful *social* scientific practices directly (even if as only part of the exercise). This way, it would surely be possible to derive a conception of social reality without any need to consider the situation in natural science? The reason this strategy is not adopted is simply that it is not available: there are no social scientific practices, certainly not in economics, that are accepted by the opposing parties as unambiguously successful. This is precisely the matter in contention.

Second, I want to be clear about the manner in which any insights gleaned from reflecting on the natural sciences are employed. It is categorically *not* the case that these are imposed upon, or unquestion-ingly accepted for, the social domain. Rather, the strategy is to *question* whether the conceptions developed through reflecting on the natural realm have relevance in the social domain. It is the *modal* status of the results achieved that is important. The results serve not as injunctions but as facilitators of lines of enquiry. The actual possibilities of, and for, social science can be determined only by reflecting upon social life itself.

But, of course, this manner of proceeding serves more purposes than the constructive role of generating lines of investigation. It is simultaneously corrective of prevalent conceptions of natural science.

And this is important. For it is frequently supposed that support for the mainstream (deductivist) approach arrives by way of an appraisal of the methods of natural science. As Hahn, for example, asserts of the deductivist method, 'In any case all theory in all subjects proceeds in this manner' (1985: 9). Or as Allais supposes, 'the existence of regularities' is the phenomenal situation in economics, and 'This is why economics is a science, and why this science rests on the same general principles as physics' (1992: 25). In similar fashion others have (erroneously) accepted the characterisation of natural science as deductivist, but, on recognising the openness of the social domain, more or less rejected the possibility of a science of social phenomena (e.g. Hayek 1942–44; Hicks 1986). Given the prominence of such lines of reasoning it is strategically vital to set the record straight, to provide a more adequate conception of natural scientific method (indeed this is the primary reason I choose to contemplate the natural sciences at all).

In short, a questioning (and typically the asserting) of the possibility of naturalism, i.e. that economics can be a science in the sense of natural science, is already on the agenda. As such, the conception systematised as transcendental realism provides a more relevant basis for such questioning. It is because deductivist injunctions so dominate the normative scene in economics that the transcendental realist sublation of this perspective is rather important. But, to repeat, the aim is no longer to impose; it is *merely* to question whether science in the relevant sense is possible with regard to the social realm. In this way, the transcendental realist assessment of natural science can be effective in the social realm, but only in shifting the terms of the debate, by allowing the question of the possibility of naturalism to be more accurately and fairly put.

The social domain

As I have noted, in the end the possibilities of, and for, social science must be determined by reflecting on the social realm directly. Notice that by the social realm I mean (as usual) the domain of matter whose existence depends, at least in part, on intentional human agency. Once we turn to the social realm the evidence suggests that it is an open system. For example, if fifty years of econometric failure have demonstrated anything, it is that those aspects of social reality of interest to economists are open and hardly susceptible to local closure; event regularities of the sort that economists pursue seem not to exist to be uncovered.

Now it should be clear, though I emphasise it anyway, that this failure to turn up enduring social event regularities of interest is an *ex posteriori* state of affairs. At one point, Parsons interprets me as

supposing that the statement 'event regularities ... do not ... generally occur in the social realm' is an 'argument' and one which follows
from the further argument that 'knowledge presupposes sufficient
endurability in the objects of knowledge to facilitate their coming to be
known'. But of course I make no such supposition. The former is a
(fallible) observation, not an argument as such. It plays a role as one of
the elements of a set of premises for a transcendental inference.
Simply put, I merely suggest that if enduring generalities at the level
of events and their patterns are not widely in evidence, and if the
capable activities of agents that we observe depend upon a degree of
knowledgeability, where this knowledgeability in turn presupposes
relatively enduring (intransitive) objects of knowledge, then such
enduring objects of knowledge must both exist and lie at a different
level to events and their patterns.

Even this conclusion is insufficient for purposes of establishing the
possibility of social science, of course. For it does not follow from it
that the structures which govern human life include social ones. How,
then, is it possible to establish the reality of specifically *social* structure? It is vital to recognise at this point that if we can come to know
non-empirical features of reality at all it can only be through their
effects. For example, it is only because of their effects on objects of
direct experience that we can establish the reality of gravitational and
magnetic fields. But by the same criterion we can establish the reality
of social structure such as social rules, relations and the like. Rules of
language are known through the speech acts which they facilitate.
And it is precisely this ability to make such acts possible that indicates
their reality (just as the fact that they pre-exist any given speech act
testifies to their relative autonomy). Through the generalised employment of reasoning along these lines it is easy enough to see that social
rules and relations can be established in every domain of human life.
Of course, delimiting their mode of being is complicated by the fact of
their reciprocal dependency on human agency and also, as indicated
elsewhere (Lawson 1997a), their dynamic and totalising nature.[9] But
for our purposes it is sufficient to note that the possibility of social
research being scientific in the sense of natural science is, in the
manner described here, established.

Notice, incidentally, that because social structure is existentially
dependent upon human agency (as well as vice versa) the procedures
of social science are likely to differ in various ways from those of
natural science. However, it does *not* follow from this that social structures are other than intransitive. To describe certain objects or features
as intransitive is merely to indicate that they exist at least in part independently of any knowledge claims of which they are the referents.

222

Thus intransitive objects of knowledge need be no more fixed or enduring than transitive ones. If I am studying the thought of a second person, for example, her or his thought constitutes an intransitive object of my enquiry. Thus the following statement by Boylan and O'Gorman is not quite right:

> [Lawson] uses linguistic structures (language) and their relationship to specific speech acts to illustrate how social structures function, especially how they are reproduced or transformed. In view of this, social structures are clearly not intransitive objects postulated by transcendental realism. The *modus operandi* of social structures are different from the structures of intransitive objects and consequently the ontology of critical realism does not coincide with the ontology of intransitive objects 'guaranteed' by transcendental realism.
>
> (p. 141)

At the moment a social investigation is initiated the putative objects of that enquiry either do, or do not, exist, and, if the former, possess whatever properties that they do, quite independently of the process of investigation which eventually ensues. This is true, even if that investigation, in due course, informs a transformation in the object concerned. In short, the social sciences are concerned to study intransitive objects in exactly the way of natural ones. Being, or existence, means the same in both contexts even if the forms of being are different, if the categorical features of the objects of two domains are to an extent distinct.

The nature and relevance of the contemporary mainstream project in economics

I mentioned above that I originally turned to methodology because I was puzzled by the widespread yet unquestioning adoption of a (formalistic modelling) perspective in economics that seemed almost irrelevant to the analysis of social phenomena. I early on (e.g., Lawson 1981a) characterised a prominent strand of it in a manner that I now refer to as *deductivist*. And after reaffirming my initial perceptions of the limitations of the modelling project I set about pursuing an alternative.[10] Thus my characterisation of mainstream economics according to its method has been important to all that has followed since. It is precisely my conception of mainstream economics that Hands takes to be the feature of my analysis that is most wanting. It is Hands' critical appraisal that I turn to consider next.

Actually Hands' criticisms largely derive from one basic misunderstanding. The crux of it is that Hands interprets me as claiming that mainstream or 'neoclassical' economists are all empirical realists, or are imbued with an empirical realist vision.[11] This interpretation is simply wrong. However, I do bring empirical realism into my argument. But it is important to understand my purpose in so doing. I thus propose to go over relevant features of my argument in the hope of rendering my objectives clearer.

Let me first indicate what has been my intended object of criticism. Although I think little, if anything, turns on it in this particular exchange, unlike Hands I tend to avoid making reference to *neoclassical* economics. Instead I refer only to the contemporary *mainstream* project. Certainly, I find that contributions, journals and individuals are regularly identified by economists according to their attachment or not to something referred to as 'the mainstream', even if the criterion being employed frequently remains tacit or is poorly articulated. The category *neoclassical*, however, is more problematic, unnecessarily bringing into play, amongst other things, matters of historical lineage and questions of fit with that lineage. I am more concerned to criticise the modern orthodoxy for what it actually does, however it interprets itself and its origins.

Now my central claim with respect to contemporary mainstream economics is that it is most accurately characterised as deductivist. By deductivism I understand a mode of explanation which involves deducing the explanandum from a set of initial conditions plus regularities that take the *form* 'whenever this event or state of affairs then that event or state of affairs'. Let me elaborate something of what I do or do not suppose in advancing this thesis.

I do not deny that mainstream economists may employ the rhetoric of structures. Nor do I doubt that, at some level, they are likely committed to a structured ontology. Of course, this is inevitably the case when they are away from the academy. But it can figure in their 'economics' musings as well. For example, it is conceivable that a mainstream economist will, if pushed anyway, allow that rationality is a *capacity* or *potential* possessed by structured individuals. However, the need to formulate results of 'the whenever this then that' form in terms of actualities, so that deductions/predictions of events or states of affairs can always be made, constrains what can be made of this in analysis. If a capacity of sorts is posited, then, if deductivist (typically formalistic) modelling is to proceed, it must be supposed that this capacity in the given situation is always exercised and its activity invariably realised or *actualised*. Thus within the mainstream project we usually find that rational *behaviour* is an *a priori* premise on which explanation is built, not a hypothesis to be examined *ex posteriori*; it is not a conjecture based on the *possibility* that rational capacities have been exercised *and* fulfilled.

In short, even if features of reality are described as capacities, for purposes of analysis, i.e., if the usual modelling activities are to proceed, they can be treated only in a capacity-which-is-exercised-and-realised form. The priority given to the event regularity *structure* of explanation, which the acceptance of deductivism necessitates, entails that any depth to the ontology explicitly acknowledged always remains superfluous to substantive explanation.

Notice that the fictitious nature of much economic modelling does not undermine the relevance of this distinction between capacities, on the one hand, and their exercise and fulfilment. Thus, even where capacities attributed to (say) human individuals are acknowledged as quite fictitious, it remains the case that, in modelling exercises, such capacities are necessarily assumed exercised and fulfilled in individual behaviour (or at least in demands, etc., expressed). It is this reduction of any potential to the *level of the actual* that is relevant here, not the question of whether claims about actual behaviour are, or even could be, born out empirically. What I am taking as essential to deductivist explanation is the *structure* of explanatory claims, not their empirical adequacy. 'Theorists', for example, frequently divide their premises between axioms and assumptions, where the former are often considered (however dubiously) to be empirically grounded and the latter acknowledged to be less secure in terms of empirical adequacy (see e.g. Hahn 1984, 1985). But the logical structure is the same in each case. The empirical adequacy of a claim is not essential when modelling in conformity to the deductivist mode.

Notice too that I do not deny that there are numerous nominal differences in mainstream economics, i.e., differences which lie at a *substantive* level. Sometimes groups adopting distinct substantive features may even be nominated schools (often associated with specific academic institutions). My concern is with what is common, and indeed essential, to *all* such contributions as are simultaneously recognised as part of the mainstream (whatever the nominal differences). And this, I argue, is their adherence to a particular (the deductivist) method in the context of addressing economic phenomena.

Finally, I do not claim that mainstream economists (typically) support their (usually implicit) deductivism with philosophical reasoning. Given in particular the hostility displayed by most mainstream economists to 'methodology', I doubt that many are even knowledgeable of any such reasoning. Thus, neither do I impute to them positivist reasoning nor do I suppose that they necessarily build upon any explicit acceptance or 'vision' of the empirical realist ontology. I suspect in fact that the deductivist method is accepted by mainstream economists because it is a precondition of mathematical modelling (for which [unthinking] enthusiasm continues unabated) and/or it is perceived (erroneously of course) to be the essential method of the successful natural sciences while no other way of proceeding has occurred to them.[12]

In short, I do not deny that mainstream economists, whatever their particular nominal or substantive orientation, may allow a structured ontology, even if their deductivism renders any such ontological commitment largely superfluous to substantive analyses, and I do not impute to them a knowledge of philosophical analysis. Why then do I bother formulating and criticising the empirical realist position at all? Why even *consider* the empirical realist conception of reality as constituted by events given in experience and their putative constant conjunctions? More generally, why consider any philosophical position, if economists are not philosophically minded?

The answer to the last question is once more because all methods and practices are underpinned by some or other philosophical analysis or reasoning, whatever the level of awareness of that philosophical reasoning might be. And where, as in the modern mainstream project in economics, the method adopted is actually fundamental to the constitution of that project, then any critique of relevance will necessarily be methodological or philosophical. Moreover, where an approach is as dominant as deductivism is in economics, it will be natural for its advocates to suppose that its philosophical justification is beyond question, whatever it is. In this light, rendering explicit the nature of the philosophical underpinnings of mainstream economics is itself a task worth undertaking.

As it happens, positivist analysis, as I understand the latter, represents the most compelling attempted grounding of the deductivist position. If, as in Humean positivism as I interpret it, knowable reality is restricted to atomistic events given in experience, then the only conceivable generalities are correlations, or regularities in the connection and succession, of these events. This is the Humean or positivist conception of 'causal laws'. This is the perspective of empirical realism. If it were a correct theory, my own understanding of science and knowable reality would be in error and deductivism as an approach to economics would appear to stand vindicated (irrespective of the empirical adequacy or otherwise of existing models). Thus I have drawn attention, and have attempted to contribute, to arguments which show, at one and the same time, that this empirical realist conception is flawed and the transcendental realist alternative is vindicated. From this demonstration it follows that the primary aim of science is the identifying of underlying causal mechanisms, and that *prima facie* at least, the *explanatory usefulness* of the deductivist approach is restricted to certain identifiable conditions, conditions which, in the social realm, may hardly hold at all.

In short, the critique of empirical realism removes one fundamental philosophical crutch upon which any deductivist approach might be expected to rely. But, I repeat, to argue this, and to draw out the ultimately unfortunate consequences of this reasoning for the deductivist approach of modern mainstream economics, does not necessitate that I believe orthodox economists are imbued with an empirical realist, or indeed with any explicit philosophical, theory or 'vision'. Hands is simply wrong in his interpretation of my position on these matters.[13]

With these clarifications laid out I can quickly deal with Hands' more specific criticisms. Briefly stated they run as follows. According to Hands: (i) I do not substantiate my characterisation of mainstream economics; (ii) when mainstream or 'neoclassical' economics is closely examined it is found not to conform to my characterisation of it; (iii) the view that mainstream economics does not conform to my characterisation of it is shared by other 'methodologists'; and (iv) mainstream economics is actually akin to the position I myself defend.

It seems clear from Hands' text that charges (i), (ii) and (iii) stem in large part from the mistaken assessment that I am attributing an empirical realist vision to mainstream economists, when in fact the only essential feature that I associate with them is an adherence to the deductivist *mode* of explanation, i.e. one which relies on 'whenever this then that regularities' couched in terms of actualities (rather than capacities) as an essential component. However, this presumably cannot be the whole story. For Hands actually supposes in charge (iv) that at least some of mainstream economics conforms to the (explicitly non-deductivist, transcendental realist) perspective which I myself defend. Let me then briefly consider Hands' four charges further.

In regard to the first claim that I do not substantiate my characterisation of mainstream economics, it surely is sufficient to point both to the bulk of econometric modelling and to all the contributions within the project that is characterised as 'economic theory', to establish my thesis. Remember, my characterisation of the mainstream is that it is deductivist, necessitating elaborating regularities of the 'whenever this then that form' *at the level* of actualities. Such closures can be in terms of events and states of affairs that are recorded or purely hypothetical, and/or the claimed correlations themselves can be known to be quite imaginary.[14] I refer to a *structure* of 'laws' or premises, one to which most econometric hypotheses, and all 'economic theory' axioms and assumptions, in my assessment, clearly conform. Deductivism so understood seems to me to be essential to *all* current attempts at formalistic economic modelling.[15]

Now such an apparently bold claim, if false, should be easy to undermine via a counter-example of course. And the latter is something that Hands endeavours to provide. In the process he both draws on the arguments of other methodologists/philosophers (in particular on Hausman and Mill who figure most prominently in charge (iii)) and also makes the claim that the mainstream project in question is actually an example of the transcendental realist analysis I defend. This is useful because all four charges listed above are thereby brought together in one illustrative argument. I am thus able to reply to these four charges in one go, by demonstrating that the illustrative example provided by Hands is not a counter-example of my thesis at all, but an illustration which serves only to reinforce my own analysis and conception.

Hands' focus is Arrow and Hahn (1971), apparently because this is the canonical text of a genre (general equilibrium theory) that Hands acknowledges I have previously explicitly addressed. The bulk of Hands' remarks are confined to a discussion of Chapter 2 concerned with the 'existence' of equilibrium.[16] Hands writes:

> In this chapter the authors [Arrow and Hahn] provide a simple existence proof for the general equilibrium price vector (p*) in a Walrasian economy characterised in terms of continuous aggregate excess demand functions. Their main concern is 'the description of situations in which the desired actions of economic agents are all mutually compatible and can all be carried out simultaneously, and for which we can prove that for the various economies discussed, there exists a set of prices that will cause agents to make mutually compatible decisions' (Arrow and Hahn 1971: 16). Where is the event regularity that this exercise is supposed to explain?
>
> (Hands p. 175–6)

The posing of this last question by Hands is significant. For of course the purpose of the exercise is not to explain an event regularity. Rather, while the exercise in question *presupposes* a set of already elaborated claims taking the *form* of such regularities,[17] its purpose is not to explain anything at all. All that is demonstrated by the equilibrium analysis to which Hands refers is that a set of variable values can be determined which renders the equations of the system mutually consistent in some sense; the system as a whole is shown to possess a particular formal property.[18]

Why is this significant? Most mainstream modellers who reflect seriously on this issue themselves have difficulties answering this question. My own assessment is that it is merely something to do for a project that does not really know where it is going. For, given a system of such regularities, which hardly relates to the open social system in which we live, just about the only question to provide a challenge is whether such a system 'solution' can be determined. But whatever the point of the exercise, there is nothing in this that challenges my characterisation of mainstream economics as a deductivist project – and one moreover that is floundering due to the open nature of the social world.

How or why does Hands view these matters differently? Mostly it turns on a recognition that the specific premises or hypotheses of the theory are not borne out empirically. And it should by now be clear that this does not undermine my characterisation of the project as deductivist. But in some part Hands' assessment seems also to rest on his evaluation, interpreted above as charge (iv), that existence proofs have 'a transcendental realist role' in mainstream analysis. I have already indicated that the nature of Arrow and Hahn type modelling is perfectly consistent with my characterisation of the overall mainstream project. Whatever Hands is getting at here, my basic thesis is already seen not to be undermined. However, it may be illuminating of the issues involved to consider this particular claim of Hands in detail, to examine the reasoning behind it.

How, then, does Hands infer a 'transcendental realist role' for the activity of determining existence proofs? Drawing upon some arguments by Hausman (1992), who in turn is drawing upon Mill, Hands writes:

> Such existence proofs show that certain things are *possible* in certain hypothetical worlds (worlds that are admittedly far simpler than ours). Such proofs provide, as Daniel Hausman has argued, a type of 'theoretical reassurance'; such demonstrations of existence 'give one reason to believe, in Mill's words (1843, 6.3.1), that economists know the laws of the "greater causes" of economic phenomena' (Hausman 1992: 101). This is a transcendental realist role, not an empirical realist role, for such existence proofs. We want our economic theories to isolate the underlying 'greater causes' of the phenomena that we observe, and one way that we can obtain the 'reassurance' that we have in fact isolated these greater causes is to see if it is *possible* that such causes would be consistent with the type of coordinated activity that seems to

prevail in a market economy. Existence proofs provide us with some reassurance that we are 'on the right track' (Hausman, 1992: 101) in this essentially realist endeavour.

(p. 176)

But this misrepresents the exercise. First of all, solution concepts of models, including equilibrium formulations in Arrow and Hahn type models, do not express real phenomena that require explanation. They do not initiate the exercise. Rather, as I have already noted, they express nothing more than (possible) consistency properties of models. Their form is necessarily model dependent, and determined during the modelling exercise. Of course, the goal of explaining, of identifying the real conditions of, coordinated market activity as it occurs in reality, is of the sort encouraged in transcendental realism, and particularly in the enlarged project of critical realism. This much of Hands' analysis is correct. Indeed, it constitutes a task that is being carried through.[19] But this is not a concern of the formalistic modelling project; its solution concepts do not express any actual situation. Indeed, for this reason it is hard to disagree with Hahn's (1970) own criticism (published at about the time that Arrow and Hahn (1971) would have been in press) of the widespread focus on equilibrium states:

it cannot be denied that there is something scandalous in the spectacle of so many people refining the analyses of economic [equilibrium] states which they give no reason to suppose will ever, or have ever, come about. It probably is also dangerous. Equilibrium economics ... is easily convertible into an apologia for existing economic arrangements and it is frequently so converted.

(1970: 88–89)

Second, the formalistic equations that constitute the model structure are usually so obviously fictitious, and widely recognised as such by their formulators, that there can be no reasonable pretence that they might express real world conditions of such (real world) actualities as are experienced (whatever the nature of the latter). The exercise is merely about exploring the purely logical possibilities of constructions recognised by almost everyone as having little or no relevance to reality. This view of mainstream 'modelling' is not an exaggeration. The 'hypothetical worlds' in question are not merely 'simpler than ours', they bear almost no relation to it. Even Hahn appears to acknowledge as much when recently reflecting upon the sorts of models that 'theorists' like himself have always concentrated upon (even if he still mistakes his opponent's criticism of the *misapplication* of formal methods for an 'anti-mathematics' stance):

> there is . . . a lesson which has only gradually been borne in on me which perhaps inclines me a little more favourably to the 'anti-mathematics' group.
>
> The great virtue of mathematical reasoning in economics is that by its precise account of assumptions it becomes crystal clear that applications to the 'real' world could at best be provisional. When a mathematical economist assumes that there is a three good economy lasting two periods, or that agents are infinitely lived (perhaps because they value the utility of their descendants which they know!), everyone can see that we are not dealing with any actual economy. The assumptions are there to enable certain results to emerge and not because they are to be taken descriptively.
>
> (Hahn 1994: 246)

Clearly, if a construction is *known* to be descriptively quite false, with core aspects bearing very little relation to any feature of reality, and does not constitute a really possible counterfactual scenario – and this is inevitably the case with regard to all examples of the closed-systems modelling in question – then Hands, like Hausman, is deluding himself in drawing theoretical, or any other kind of, 'reassurance' from the analysis. Indeed, it is a mistake to suppose that we can learn anything more than the properties of certain obscure formalistic constructions.

Formally, if x is mainly false as an expression of reality, and it can be demonstrated that x implies y, we can learn nothing from this demonstration about y as a claim about reality. This is so even if y happens in reality to be true (which of course is not the case with the usual model solution concepts). No more should the farmer, concerned with whether he or she can afford to take all the pigs to market, be influenced by the (known-to-be-false) hypothesis that pigs can fly, than should an economist conclude that a market-clearing set of prices or whatever is (or is not) feasible by exploring its possibility in the sort of absurd hypotheses in question. In each case, because the conditioning hypothesis is known to be absurdly false as a claim about reality, it can provide no insight on the real possibility of the hypothesis' consequent. This type of exercise really has nothing in common with transcendental realist explanation, and there is no basis in any such endeavour for reassurance, concern, or anything of the kind.

In short, it is the case neither that an equilibrium state of affairs or model solution as typically formulated is analogous to an *ex posteriori* observation requiring explanation, nor that formalistic models of the sort in question are designed to explain any actual phenomenon. And this is widely recognised. In consequence, existence proofs in Arrow and Hahn type models can no more be interpreted as having a 'transcendental realist role' than they can be looked to for theoretical reassurance. Of course, the lack of relevance of the whole project is undesirable. But this failure to illuminate is not surprising once the project's deductivist nature is appreciated, given the openness of the social system. Certainly I find little here that undermines my basic assessment of the contemporary mainstream position.[20]

Hands finishes with two further 'concluding points'. The first is that my interpretation of much mainstream economics as fictitious in nature does not, and cannot, follow from ontological arguments such as those systematised as critical realism. Any substantive claims, such as my evaluation that 'universal perfect competition, linear expected profit functions, Cobb-Douglas production functions, etc. are not intended to capture the mode of operation of real economics mechanisms', must follow rather from my practices as a social scientist. This is true enough; critical realism does not license any particular substantive theory, as I have often taken pains to emphasise (e.g. Lawson 1996: 417 [this volume, Chapter 1: 14]; 1997a). This is a point on which we agree.

Hands' second 'concluding point' is basically that any self-respecting transcendental realist would wish to explain 'the theoretical behaviour of the economics profession'. But that is exactly what is going on here. I and others do find constructions of mainstream economists (Cobb-Douglas production functions, omniscience, three commodity worlds, people living forever, etc.) to be fictitious. So too, it seems, do many who produce 'theories' of this nature. From my perspective at least, a relevant question is why it is that such theories are entertained and even prevail? This is one of the many puzzling phenomena that I have been concerned to explain. My answer, for what it is worth, is that constructions of this sort are forced upon mainstream 'theorists' because of their unthinking acceptance (at least in their formal rhetoric and modelling practices) of deductivist methods in a misguided attempt to address phenomena generated by a quintessentially open social system (see Lawson 1997a, especially Chapters 7–9).

If this assessment is correct, then, certainly for anyone of a transcendental realist inclination, the question subsequently arises as to why deductivism should be so widely accepted in economics. I have speculated upon reasons for this elsewhere (e.g. Lawson 1997a – see also the discussion on the need for, and role of, science in the following section). Of course, if methodologists of the calibre of Hands are yet to be convinced by my characterisation of the mainstream project as deductivist, or if I have yet to formulate my thesis with sufficient clarity, I should not be too hasty in moving from defending this assessment to explaining it. But whatever the level at which an explanation of some phenomenon is put forward, this explanation itself will likely warrant investigation, sooner or later. All analysis is partial, and couched in terms of features which themselves are eventually likely to attract/require further study. There may not be any absolute stopping point this side of any 'big bang'; it is likely there will always be reason to agree with Hands' final 'criticism' that 'One would expect a transcendental realist to look deeper', at least in due course.

The nature of social scientific explanation

If critical realism as developed in economics assumes a negating role in revealing the limitations of the contemporary mainstream project in economics, it simultaneously generates constructive insights for the conduct of social analysis. It is this aspect of the critical realist contribution that Boylan and O'Gorman question in the third part of their chapter, where they also indicate something of their own perspective on the conduct of social analysis. My reaction is that, whilst there may well be differences between our respective projects, they do not after all turn on the points these authors identify here. Rather they seem to turn on quite different points put forward in their excellent recent book (Boylan and O'Gorman 1995). Let me first, then, consider the reservations of Boylan and O'Gorman as formulated above and indicate why, on the issues they raise, I think we are actually in broad agreement.

I accept, first of all, that events play a causal role. I do argue that the primary aim of science and explanation is to identify and understand underlying structures, capacities and mechanisms, etc., which causally bear upon (facilitate, influence, produce) surface phenomena, including events, of interest. But this in no way compromises a recognition that events too are causal. In the social world, indeed, the moving forces upon which everything turns are human practices. Even the reproduction and transformation of social structures are events of sorts. If I have previously failed to emphasise this sufficiently, let me acknowledge explicitly that Boylan and O'Gorman are of course correct in emphasising the (efficient) causality of events.

Let me also acknowledge that if and where event regularities are detected, they may well be useful in science. Indeed, I have argued that event regularities of sorts are essential to the initiation of scientific endeavours and to the process of assessing theories. This is as true in the social realm as any other.[21] However, I have observed that those available to social science (which I now think are most aptly termed *demi-regularities*) are usually of a relatively enduring, partial, rough and ready, and (especially) contrastive (see below) nature. And I have argued that these are all we need once we adopt explanatory rather than predictive criteria of theory assessment and recognise that our primary aim is to uncover but one relatively distinct causal process involved (see e.g. Lawson 1997a, especially Chapter 15).

Boylan and O'Gorman further suggest that they and I part company when they adopt a (Wittgensteinian) approach whereby all explanation is held to be dependent upon the scientific context. From their text on pages 142–144 it seems clear that these authors are suggesting several things here. First, they point out that most if not all explanation is inherently contrastive: the question addressed implicitly takes the form of 'why this outcome *rather than that one*'. Second, they note that the particular contrast adopted in any study will depend on context, and (implicitly) the presuppositions and interests of whoever is asking the question. Third, they observe that the causes of phenomena will typically be numerous, with different ones identified by different investigators, according to their individual areas of expertise. In fact, the only part of all this that I have problems with is the assumption that such insights are somehow at odds with my own position. Let me briefly elaborate.

The possibility that events may be multiply determined is more or less the situation that is captured by an open system. It is *contrasted* to a closed system situation, i.e., one in which a single set of factors is insulated from the actions of other mechanisms and thereby empirically identified. Only in the latter case (at best) can it be supposed that events may not be determined by a multiplicity of factors. Of course, if Boylan and O'Gorman are suggesting that any explanations put forward are *merely* dependent on the investigators, i.e., that all explanation inevitably fails to reference any thought-independent mechanisms, then we do part company. But if, in contrast, as seems to be the case, they are recognising that various real causes can jointly bring about an eventuality, theirs is a scenario towards which critical realism is very much oriented.

Nor is the contrastive and interest-dependent nature of explanation a problem for my conception of the explanatory process. To the contrary, *these features are essential to it*. For just about the only enduring rough and ready regularities of scientific interest that occur in the social realm take the form of contrasts. These are the stylised facts or demi-regularities that are held as being essential both in initiating analyses and in assessing competing causal explanations. In the absence of possibilities for the experimental manipulation and insulation of individual causes, any hope of being able to identify individual causes rests on situations where two or more outcomes or aspects, i.e., the 'fact' and the 'contrast' (or 'foil'), are such that our background knowledge leads us to expect them to be similar (or more generally that they stand in some definite predictable relation), but where *ex posteriori* our expectations are not confirmed. Under such conditions, there is at least *prima facie* evidence of a hitherto unknown or anyway unexpected mechanism at work, and resources can meaningfully be devoted to pursuing it. The question of *which* contrasts are focused upon in any context, of course, *will* rest upon the interests and understandings of the individual scientists. Most especially, the chosen (set of) contrast(s) will frequently be that which engenders the greater experience of surprise, doubt, and general curiosity on the part of the individuals involved.

Boylan and O'Gorman do not indicate why they suppose that any of this is inconsistent with critical realism, or at least with my own contribution to that project. Probably it is because at the point in time at which these authors were formulating their critique, this aspect of critical realist explanation was left largely implicit. In case this is so, I hope I will not appear too indulgent if I reproduce certain recently published passages of my own, which these authors did not have access to in preparing their essay:

> I am suggesting that scientific explanation is inherently contrastive. We have seen that in accounting for some social phenomenon the aim could not be to provide its complete causal history. Rather, we can only aim to identify one (set of) causal mechanism(s). And to this end the obvious strategy is to seek out two (or more) situations where the outcomes might have been expected to be related in some manner other than turns out to be the case, and to attempt to determine the reason(s). Typically, this will involve identifying at least one mechanism that operates, or does so in a particular fashion, in the one (set of) situation(s) only.
>
> In consequence, we can now see even more clearly than hitherto that explanatory projects are inherently dependent on the interests of those involved. For it is now evident that the interests of the investigator influence not only the choice of phenomenon to be explained, but also, by selecting the contrast, the *particular* explanatory mechanism to be researched. For example . . .
>
> (Lawson 1997a: 209)

I turn at this point to a rather significant feature of the approach I am developing, one that has been implicit throughout this chapter and is bound up with the interest-dependent nature of all scientific practice, but which, mainly for ease of exposition, I have yet to elaborate upon explicitly. I refer to the fact that inquiry will usually be initiated not just by any partial regularities and/or contrasts, but those that, along with other beliefs, occasion certain contradictions, inconsistencies, experiences of surprise and ultimately doubt.

(ibid.: 210)

Turning to the question of explanatory logic, I should emphasise that I do not deny the place either of inductive logic (if grounded in causal necessity) or deductive logic in science, the latter being particularly significant in the process of theory assessment. The point of contention seems to be whether Boylan and O'Gorman accept a role for retroduction. In my framework this is fundamental in explanation where the aim is to redescribe phenomena occurring at one level in terms of causal features existing at a different, deeper level. I do not see why Boylan and O'Gorman would wish to deny the utility of this mode of reasoning even allowing for the causal holist reluctance (which of course I do not share) to make epistemic commitments to unobservables (see below). Boylan and O'Gorman do seem to be wanting to interpret the category of induction rather more broadly than I do, as something like ampliative inference, and thereby to assimilate retroduction to it. Certainly something like this seems necessary for their acknowledgement that phenomena of interest may be redescribed in terms of observable causes, where the latter can constitute quite different kinds of things to the phenomena to which they give rise.

I should emphasise, though, the usage of metaphor, which Boylan and O'Gorman seem cautious about assimilating to their under-standing of inductive reasoning, is a fundamental feature of the retroductive approach I defend. For, to the extent that science does seek to explain surface phenomena in terms of underlying causes, and that it turns out that sets of causes of interest are both unobservable and as yet unknown, little may be gained by referring to these causes using labels or terms that carry no prior sense. It is frequently the case in science that objects of one domain of study display features, or manifest effects, that have parallels in some other domain. *Prima facie* this indicates a possibility of fruitful advance through borrowing (or abducting) from one domain to another. Scientists have found it useful to view the brain as a computer, the cause of computer malfunctioning as a virus, and so on. In other words, science draws necessarily upon metaphor in the course of many of its investigations.

But it is essential to recognise that if a metaphorical expression is developed because parallels between source and target domains have been perceived, in the target domain the metaphor is useful to the extent it can *generate* new lines of analogical or other thinking, i.e., be suggestive of new paths of investigation. Notice too that in the target domain the senses of the borrowed terms themselves become transformed. Thus, when terms like 'evolution' or 'equilibrium' bring predetermined senses to a new or 'target' domain of usage, these senses can soon become transformed as understandings of the target subject matter develops.[22]

In short, as Martin-Soskice (1985) has formulated the matter, and as Lewis (1996 [also this volume, Chapter 5]) has elaborated it with significant insight, metaphor is a figure of speech that allows us to speak of one thing in terms which are suggestive, if only suggestive, of another. And a significant point here is that in working through the interaction of two different domains or contexts, metaphorical reasoning produces emergent cognitive content. This process seems essential to retroductive reasoning as emphasised in critical realism, whether or not it can be assimilated to inductive inference broadly interpreted.[23]

Finally, I agree yet further with Boylan and O'Gorman when they insist that there is much more to explanatory endeavour than abstraction. Abstraction understood as focusing on certain aspects of a concrete entity or situation to the (momentary) neglect of others is always fundamental. But it is not sufficient. The manner in which abstraction can be most usefully deployed inevitably depends on context and explanatory objectives, amongst other things. Thus, when accepting the critical realist perspective, I have emphasised the importance of abstracting what is essential to (i.e., the underlying cause of) some phenomena rather than that which is merely most general. To a positivist, however, this evaluation presumably makes little sense. And even where, for non-positivists, this assessment is accepted, abstraction is nothing like sufficient for getting us there, for furnishing a hypothetical cause. This, of course, is where retroduction comes in, operating under a logic of analogy and metaphor amongst other creative processes. But, in the scientific process abstraction will always be involved. I repeat, though, that any assessment of whether or not abstraction is most usefully employed in 'this manner or that' depends on the context and framework as a whole.

So where *do* critical realists and causal holists like Boylan and O'Gorman part company in their accounts of the social scientific explanatory endeavour? Here I draw directly from Boylan and

O'Gorman's recent book. If there is a significant difference between us it seems to me to turn on contrasting epistemic attitudes towards claims involving 'unobservables' or 'non-empirical entities'. Specifically, Boylan and O'Gorman refuse to allow theories couched in terms of non-empirical entities to count as scientific knowledge. They write:

> In particular, there is no question of theoretical economics furnishing approximately true descriptions of non-empirical generative structures, powers or mechanisms. The causal holist objection . . . is to the Lawsonian realist thesis that structured entities which possess these powers are claimed to be non-empirical. If one postulates non-empirical entities, how can economists go on to furnish theoretical descriptions of these and know that their descriptions are correct or approximately true? Quine has taught us that it is not beyond the ingenuity of economists to construct a range of incompatible economic theories such that each one is compatible with the empirical evidence. Given this pluralism, causal holists do not see any rational way of deciding which non-empirical referents they should choose nor which theoretical descriptions are true of these non-empirical entities . . .
>
> . . . our sophisticated linguistic capacities in general and our analogical capacities in particular, clearly allow the Lawsonian realist the possibility of economic theories postulating non-empirical entities. In causal holism, however, Quinean considerations prevent us from extending our scientific knowledge to these entities.
>
> (Boylan and O'Gorman 1995: 211–213)

As Boylan and O'Gorman acknowledge here, it is certainly possible to use analogical, metaphorical and other creative forms of reasoning to come up with (in my terminology to retroduce) accounts or theories of causal hypotheses with non-empirical referents. Such theories, then, clearly provide hypothetical descriptions of the causal hypotheses in question.[24] Boylan and O'Gorman, however, doubt that there is any 'rational way of deciding [between] non-empirical referents'.[25] It is this scepticism that underpins their unwillingness to allow theories with non-empirical referents to count as scientific knowledge. But competing theories with non-empirical referents can be assessed according to their relative explanatory powers (using critical realist terminology) with respect to 'observables', i.e according to their relative successes in illuminating a range of empirical phenomena. In other words, a theory invoking unobservables may be accepted if it proves capable of accommodating many observable aspects of reality it bears upon; if it is empirically adequate at the level of its detectable consequences (see Lawson 1997a: Chapters 14 and 15).

Of course, in principle it could have turned out that in science we are always in the possession of a multitude of competing causal hypotheses couched in terms of unobservables, all of which achieve similar explanatory power in this sense. But *ex posteriori* this has not been the situation. That is, even if we accept (the weakest version of) Quine's underdetermination thesis as a real possibility, the fact of the matter is that we start from a situation in science in which few of the maintained causal theories involving unobservables fit all the available empirical 'facts' they bear upon.[26]

If and where competing theories do achieve the same degree of empirical adequacy in terms of their consequences and conditions, *ceteris paribus* the correct epistemic attitude is to suspend judgement. On this we can agree. But this, in my experience, is not the typical scenario. Even when competing theories invoking unobservables have seemed, at some point, to be equally supported by empirical evidence, it has usually proven possible to discriminate between them sooner or later.[27]

Critical realism, science and human freedom

The relevance of critical realism and its conception of science to human freedom, is a topic taken up by Rajani Kanth. Although there is much I agree with in Kanth's piece (Chapter 11 in this volume), there are notable points of divergence between us. We are at one, it seems, in concluding that mainstream economics provides a somewhat poor account of reality and that the perspective sustained in critical realism is (easily) superior. Disagreement creeps in when we turn to examine (1) the *need* for, and (2) the *role* of, science in human society. Human freedom is in fact Kanth's primary concern. And he is explicitly of the opinion that *'scientific knowledge is neither a necessary nor a sufficient condition for human emancipation'* (p. 200). At the same time he concludes that the role assumed by science in practice renders it actually undesirable.

I too take the *'position that freedom is a far higher order value than science'* (p. 200). But I am not yet convinced of an inevitable conflict between the two. Scientific knowledge, we can all agree, could never be a sufficient condition for human emancipation. But it does seem to me to be quite necessary. Before considering Kanth's argument to the contrary let me briefly consider his stronger claim that science, including any economic science informed by critical realism, is necessarily an obstacle to human freedom in practice.

Science as an impediment to human emancipation

In fact Kanth urges us to recognise (1) that the real purpose of scientific models in the social sciences is merely to serve as *'ideological constructs to help recruit and consolidate scientific communities '*(p. 198); (2) that the scientific establishment, whatever the dominant paradigm, is everywhere corrupt; and (3) that in practice science *'is simply another name for the systematic record-keeping and surveying requirement of a predatory system built upon unlimited greed wedded to virtually limitless power'* (p. 199, emphasis in the original). Thus, in the modern 'corporatist' era, *'science is become now simply the master tool of corporate enslavement'* (p. 199). In consequence, reasons Kanth, we must recognise that getting better at science is 'no guarantee that the resulting process/products will either extend, or even preserve, the domain of freedom for humbler people' (p. 199). It 'is this disconsolate fact, in this period of world mastery of capital, that dictates an attitude of extreme caution with regard to scientific paradigms, *en général'* (p. 199).

Even if the above italicised phrases capture real tendencies, the repeated use of the qualifier 'simply' renders them problematic. What evidence or argument is provided that science is always so disreputably motivated (or completely hijacked)? Mainly, Kanth's reasoning is inductive, based on a view of how science in general and mainstream economics in particular, have operated to date. Now evidence of something happening in the past is, by itself, insufficient grounds for expecting the same to continue. At the very least an explanation grounded in causal necessity is required for such an inference. This is absent from Kanth's analysis, and this observation alone gives reason to doubt that Kanth's speculations are sound. But in truth I do not suppose that science in general or even mainstream economics has in fact operated wholly in the manner that Kanth describes. As we are primarily concerned with economics here, let me briefly consider the hypothesis that the constructions of the mainstream project in economics, as Kanth believes, are deliberately fixed so as to generate results which support the *status quo*. Kanth writes:

> To state the moral: *the entire enterprise of neoclassical economics is rigged to show that laissez-faire produces optimal outcomes, but for the disruptive operation of the odd externality (a belated correction) here and there.*
>
> (pp. 191–192)

Now sometimes mainstream economics may be rigged with this intent; but certainly not always. Even allowing equilibrium theory its absurd assumptions, an equilibrating solution in this framework is not guaranteed or presumed; its possibility is merely examined. The scandal of the mainstream deductivist project is not its conclusions but its lack of relevance: its inability to provide an understanding of the real world. In order to facilitate the deduction of statements in terms of actual phenomena, social life, in this mainstream framework, is necessarily transformed beyond recognition. In ensuring that closure is achieved, so that deductivist modelling is able to proceed, realistic assessments are unavoidably abandoned in favour of, in effect, formulations in terms of isolated crypto-atoms. And with the criterion or goal of realisticness so abandoned it is easy enough to produce models that generate anything you want.

Of course, some *may* treat this state of affairs as an opportunity to 'show' the optimality of the existing social order. But, whilst economists tend not to take each other's results seriously anyway, in practice a range of contrasting results are generated – by mainstream 'Marxian' and other opponents of (aspects of) the current social system as well as by the latter's defenders. Equally apparent is the ability of different econometricians to employ a given set of data to reach quite divergent conclusions. And even amongst econometricians, as Leamer observes: 'hardly anyone takes anyone else's data analysis seriously' (1983: 37). Moreover, in places Kanth himself acknowledges the variety in positions so supported. For he writes:

> Indeed, for the longest time, Marxists (in the US) had to live in the academic dog-house for not being familiar with matrix algebra, until keen (if not always scrupulous) Marxist minds, with academic tenures at stake, realised the enormous (and inexpensive) potential of this tool for restating Marxian ideas in formalised language and instantly acquiring the gloss of high science, the latter-day pundits of repute here being Roemer in the US and Morishima in England, who were of course soon emulated by a host of lesser lights to whom this switch in language alone promised hours of (well-funded) computerised fun and games.
>
> Of course, all the formalisms did not advance a critical understanding of the *organon* of Marxian system, and its many difficulties, one iota; but it did succeed in generating grudging respect for the Marxist by the even more facile and shallow savants of neoclassicism.
>
> (p. 189)

In truth, where a project can support everything it ends up supporting nothing. An *inability* to contribute to the policy discussion is I think a fairer characterisation of the modern economic orthodoxy. If it is the case that mainstream economics plays an inescapable ideological role, I suspect this is achieved in a manner that is rather more implicit: the deductivist emphasis upon surface phenomenon, to the inevitable relative neglect of deeper structures, including social (class, gender, race, etc.) relations, sustains an impression that society is rather more harmonious than it really is. In acknowledging this, however, I am still not willing to adopt too functionalist or conspiratorial an orientation, at least prior to sustained investigation.

Of course, if conspiracy to sustain the *status quo* does not explain the nature and persistence of the modern mainstream in economics, there remains the puzzle of what does. This is the question raised above by Hands. Undoubtedly, there are numerous forces at work, including, at times, ideological ones. My own assessment (see Lawson 1997a) is that a causal factor of far greater significance is the inspirational role of mathematics in western culture, certainly since the Enlightenment, and especially amongst economists (there were of course numerous attempts to mathematise the discipline long before the apparent successes of Walras and others – especially in France). Currently, new students to economics are not so much taught the supposed virtues of deductivism directly as immersed in mathematical techniques to an extent which presupposes the widespread relevance of deductivist method.[28] Any justification for this training appears to rest on little more than an uncritical enthusiasm for formalism on the part of those who direct the discipline – individual academics who, by and large, appear quite blind to the fact that specific formalistic systems are necessarily limited in their scope of application.[29]

Once more significant aspects of my assessment actually receive support in Kanth's own discussion. Our differences in this turn mainly on matters of emphasis and direction of (primary) causality. Kanth supposes that 'The apparent rigour of mathematics was recruited avidly by neoclassicism to justify and defend its truistic, axiomatic, and almost infantile, theorems that deeply investigated but the surface gloss of economic life' (p. 189), whereas I am more of the view that the pursuit of mathematical formalism for its own sake is primary, with the concentration on surface (measurable) phenomena an inevitable corollary. Resolving these differences, though, is a topic in the history of thought, best left to a further occasion. It is at least clear, though, that the defence of the existing social order is not a characteristic of the (highly variable) modelling results that mainstream economists explicitly generate.

The supposed non-necessity of science for human emancipation

If Kanth's assumption that science must prove harmful to any project of human emancipation seems insufficiently grounded, at least in the worst case scenario of economics, what of his belief that science is in any case not a requirement for it? To address this issue we need first to consider what any emancipatory project involves.

Most obviously the possibility of human freedom presupposes the existence of shared human objectives, i.e. real interests, needs and motives. If everyone's needs are, for example, merely subjective, with the possibility of being irreconcilably opposed, then projecting the goal of social emancipation is likely to be question begging from the outset. The condition of shared real interests is a presupposition of all emancipatory proposals (whether supporting [relative] change or [relative] continuity) whatever perspective is accepted. Thus, we can observe that every national government, popular liberation front, local collective, trade union, individual policy spokesperson, and so on, professes to act on behalf of a specific group of people, supposing that certain interests of the members of the relevant constituency are the same. To be sure, such claims and conceptions warrant unpacking. But all programmatic stances with respect to (changing or sustaining) any aspect of the economic and social order rest upon some implicit moral realism, they carry presuppositions of shared real interests of all individuals which exist by virtue of a common human genetic make-up, or as a result of shared occupancy of specific societal (national, regional, cultural, gender, etc.) positions.

These are issues addressed in critical realism, where a moral realist orientation is indeed explicitly accepted (Lawson 1997a, Chapters 13 and 19). In particular, the possibility of moral theorising, grounded in a recognised common human nature, is acknowledged; a conception is sustained which recognises the existence of rights of all human beings as human beings, by virtue of a common nature grounded in our biological unity as a species. Of course, it is also recognised that this common nature is always historically and socially mediated, so that needs will be manifest empirically (as wants) in potentially many ways. It follows, accepting this perspective, that the pursuit of social goals always takes place in a context of conflicting position-related interests. Certainly, conflicts centring on the interests of class positions, age, gender, nation states, regions, culture, and so forth, are as real and determining as anything else. Even so, different groups may co-operate and persistently reproduce relations of trust, and so on. But opposed, position-related, interests exist. And it may be upon our unity as a species and the more generalised features of our social and historical experience and make-up, that the greater possibility of unambiguous and more enduring progress rests. The point, though, is that any emancipatory project presupposes the existence of shared interests at some level.

Second, the possibility of emancipatory social change requires not merely shared real needs and interests but, equally, an awareness of these needs and interests. Needs and rights can be formulated as goals or wants or demands, and treated as legitimate or illegitimate, only under definite historical conditions. As such, they may be poorly, and even misleadingly, formulated. Specifically, real needs can be manifest in a variety of historically contingent wants, which may then be met by any of perhaps a multitude of potential satisfiers. To assume that either actual satisfiers (e.g. specific commodities purchased or perhaps acts of violence) or expressed objectives (such as owning more than others) are defining of human needs is to commit an ethical version of the epistemic fallacy – to reduce needs to wants and wants to the conditions of their being satisfied or expressed.

I am not suggesting that wants as expressed in actions bear no relation to underlying needs, of course. Indeed, although certain activities sometimes appear quite undesirable from the point of view of facilitating human development and potential, it is often easy enough to see how they are nevertheless motivated by various real needs on the part of the perpetrators – for example, to obtain respect from others, inner security or simply a release of frustration. But it is important that real needs and expressed wants are not conflated.

A third condition for emancipatory, or indeed of any intended, change is that particular goals pursued (or least movement towards such goals) constitute real possibilities, and possibilities whose conditions are adequately understood.

A fourth condition is an inclination to act in accord with real interests, if indeed they can be correctly identified and their pursuit rendered practically feasible. In any actual situation, emancipatory action may involve a large cost, a degree of risk, or just an effort of will. Not every person grasps every opportunity that is recognised as coming her or his way.

There are other conditions, but the above are certainly central: human freedom requires that real needs exist, that they are known (at least under some [fallible] description), that their fulfilment (or engineering the conditions of the latter) is a real and recognised possibility, and that there is a will to act in accordance with them.

Of these four sets of conditions it is only the latter that receives explicit attention by Kanth. Indeed, immediately after asserting that 'scientific knowledge is neither a necessary nor a sufficient condition for human emancipation', Kanth adds, as if to explain: 'The latter [human emancipation] stems from a moral, spiritual, and personal resolve to struggle against iniquity, injustice and oppression.'

Now resolve is certainly necessary. But by itself it is hardly sufficient. It cannot just be assumed that the nature of both human needs and existing conditions of oppression are everywhere understood without the aid of systematic investigation. Of course, I recognise that any process of struggle, as with all human practice, will itself contribute to human understanding. And I do not wish to over-emphasise the revelatory power of formal science. Nor do I want to exaggerate the possibilities of an economics informed by critical realism. Indeed, I am in full agreement with Kanth when, earlier in his text, he writes:

> even if economic theory were true, and its 'science' valid, in some acceptable sense, *it would still represent only one manner of interpreting the myriad facts of social life*; and it would not, *ipso facto*, have the right to impose its special discernments, such as they are, on other traditions by force.
>
> (p. 190)

But to accept all this is merely to acknowledge that science could never be (anything like) sufficient. It remains the case that emancipation requires that real needs and interests be recognised and conditions of their achievement understood and feasible. And it is with regard to facilitating this recognition and understanding that science, meaning systematic study, has an essential role.

Let me endeavour to make my position as clear as possible. I am not suggesting that scientists, policy makers, or anyone else can know the choices that individuals should make. Even less am I suggesting that the latter group normally be empowered to take more decisions on behalf of others. Rather, I am merely arguing that systematic study is a condition of an adequate understanding of both real needs and the possibilities for their realisation – allowing individual choices to be made in (more) informed ways (possibly in some democratic forum). For, to repeat, a condition of emancipatory social change is a self-awareness of real human needs and interests, along with an understanding of the real possibilities for their pursuit.[30] Theory is a necessary complement to practice.

As I say, Kanth never raises the question of the degree to which human needs are understood. Nor does he explicitly consider the conditions of their fulfilment. He does, though, present a picture of modern developments wherein everything appears to be widely known. According to Kanth: *'the domain of the macro is always subject to apparent regularities – "laws" and "controls" and so forth'* allowing the course of capitalist development to be widely discerned (p. 196), albeit under the control of the corporations in this 'period of world mastery of capital'[31] (p. 199). It is this perception that encourages the view that any future science of economics can have nothing to add to our understanding.

But, in truth, there is little evidence that the requisite regularities are to be found either at a micro or at a macro level (see for example Hutchison 1994; Kay 1995; Leamer 1983; Rosenberg 1992). And contra Kanth, this situation is quite comprehensible from the perspective I have argued for within the umbrella of critical realism. In other words, although Kanth claims the support of critical realism for his global perspective, the conception of social reality supported in this realist project is actually quite different. Let me expand on this.

In one passage (pp. 196–197) Kanth seems to suggest (1) that the individual and society relationship as elaborated within critical realism reduces, in economics, to that between micro and macro economics; (2) that macro economics is governed by regularities or laws; (3) that individual behaviour is erratic; (4) that it is a realist discovery that macro and micro theory could not be brought into sync. As I have observed, in fact there is little evidence of these regularities at either the macro or the micro level. But in truth, I am uncomfortable with each of the four assessments listed above.

Most problematic is the presumption that the individual/society relation reduces to a micro/macro opposition. Far from being a critical realist discovery, this opposition, like so many others, derives from contending and quite inadequate philosophies of science and society. Over the last century philosophical thinking about society has veered towards one or other crude conception of either individualism or undifferentiated collectivism. In economics, this has taken precisely the guise of (an opposition between) micro and macro economics. At one extreme we find a micro-foundationalist individualism assuming a deductivist format. At the other is a macro-foundationalist collectivism assuming an equally deductivist format. From the perspective of a version of the former, macro or aggregate phenomena can be as erratic as you like, and from a version of the macro-foundationalist pole, micro or individualist phenomena can be ignored as erratic. There are numerous intermediate positions. Some economists appear to assume that deductivist relations can be discerned, or at least legitimately formulated, for any and every level of analysis, and the object is to uncover aggregational or integrability conditions to place on the system's initial conditions which allow this. Others assume that the same assumptions which guarantee 'whenever this then that' type regularities at the level of the individual can achieve a parallel result at the level of the collective merely by framing the analysis in terms of something called the average or 'representative' individual. All such approaches are fundamentally deductivist, couched in terms of surface phenomena, whether real or imaginary. And Kanth's suggestion (in the relevant passage at least) appears to come surprisingly close to a macro-foundationalist variant of this familiar schema.

The perspective systematised in critical realism is somewhat different. Thus in opposition to the atomistic individualism of micro economics and the undifferentiated collectivism (or idealised individualism) of macro economics the focus in critical realism is on human agency and social structure and their inter-dependency: society is viewed as consisting of a network of relations, rules, positions, and so forth, which not only depend upon, and are reproduced and/or transformed through human activity, but also condition it. In short, society, on the transformational and relational conception elaborated in critical realism, is recognised as being far more complex and dynamic than Kanth's macro assessments allow.

A result is an acceptance that, although society is a skilled accomplishment of active agents, many aspects of it may yet be opaque to the social agents upon whose activities it depends. Consequences of action may be quite unintended and unrecognised and its structural conditions unacknowledged. Indeed, human beings slot into a number of inherently conflictual as well as cooperative social/cultural/political positions, where it is always likely that many operative modes of determination (including oppression) are poorly or inadequately misunderstood. And while human beings skilfully negotiate their everyday tasks within these conditions, the future, like society, remains truly open and (especially at the level of events) inherently unpredictable.

It is with the intention of advancing our understanding of this complex situation and the possibilities for its investigation that critical realism is being developed. And it is with addressing concrete aspects of this situation that any emergent science of economics will presumably concern itself. None of this is to guarantee that Kanth's speculations will not be fulfilled; I mainly indicate that the bases on which they are formed are wanting. It is quite conceivable that Kanth is identifying real tendencies at work. But even if so, it remains the case that an effective and realisable aspect of any strategy for pursuing emancipatory goals, is to work to harness science rather than abandon it.

Notes

1 For helpful comments on an earlier draft I am very grateful to Steve Fleetwood, Steve Pratten and Jochen Runde.

2 I am not sure that the suggestion that transcendental argument can be conceptually disengaged from Kant's specific mode of application is particularly contentious. I note that it is quite consonant for example with the entry on *transcendental argument* in the *Cambridge Dictionary of Philosophy*. Of course, although modern familiarity with transcendental argumentation derives from the manner it was taken up by Kant, its employment is found in philosophy stretching back through the Middle Ages to the ancient Greeks. Over time its interpretation has evolved with new understandings just like any other concept. And the interpretation accepted here is certainly continuous with that running up to the present day through Kant.

3 Notice, incidentally, that in fact all claims to knowledge, including Kant's own, are fallible. This applies to mathematical argument, forms of logical derivation, and any other cognitive claim; all rely on fallible human elucidation, application or execution. Thus Parsons is quite wrong if he is suggesting that my emphasis on the fallibility of knowledge is *evidence* that I employ transcendental argument differently to Kant (whether or not I do). In any case, no sooner does Parsons seem to suggest this than he himself admits that

> the arguments presented by Strawson, or Kant himself, may be mistaken. However, in these cases, the mistake is a philosophical failure to correctly illuminate, say, the logically necessary conditions of experience. With transcendental realism, the term 'mistaken' pertains to the empirical failure to elucidate the 'causally necessary' conditions of scientific phenomena.
>
> (p. 155)

Clearly if the arguments made by Kant and others may be mistaken, then it is admitted his method is fallible, and thus incoherent to hold that fallibility is a peculiarity of the causal orientation that I am adopting. All cognitive claims, to repeat, are fallible, including claims to knowledge of necessities of *any* mode.

Notice too that *all* argument involves logic, including reasoning involved with the identification of causal conditions, the demonstration that certain premises lead to metaphysical absurdity, or whatever. There are times when Parsons appears to suggest otherwise. But if it is important to distinguish, or to avoid conflating, causal and logical necessity, it is just as vital to avoid supposing that an analysis of the former can proceed without invoking the latter.

4 It is true that, in my writings, a critical contrast is drawn sometimes with Hume's own arguments and sometimes with those of others adopting an empiricist perspective of the sort which Hume encouraged. Frequently, as in the 1994 publication from which Parsons mainly quotes, I both sketch a position I am criticising *and* indicate how Hume (if I mention him at all) encourages such a position (see Lawson 1994: 111). But I cannot understand why Parsons supposes any of this to be a problem. On a related point, I do agree with Parsons that if arguments are to be directed against

an analysis by Hume (or indeed any author), they should strive to show a 'sensitivity to the subtleties and complexities of [that] . . . analysis' (p. 156). But I am yet to be convinced by Parsons that I fail in this regard with respect to Hume (or even that Parsons himself displays any greater sensitivity). Parsons' evidence against me on this is presented as follows:

> For example, it is argued that Hume denied: 'The possibility of establishing the independent existence of things' (Lawson 1994: 111). Compare this to Hume himself: 'As to what may be said, that the operations of nature are independent of our thought and reasoning, I allow it' (Hume 1969: 219).
>
> (pp. 155–156)

But there is surely a difference between 'establishing' something and 'allowing' it. By the former I of course mean (and meant) establishing via philosophical argument, i.e., by way of sustaining a philosophical account of being. And in the context of the 1994 paper I was referring specifically to the possibility of establishing necessary connections, the operation of natural necessity. In fact, a fuller version of the passage by me from which Parsons quotes runs as follows:

> Hume encouraged this perspective with his attempted critique of any philosophical account of being, of ontology, with his denying the possibility of establishing the independent existence of things, and specifically of the operation of natural necessity.
>
> (Lawson 1994: 111)

Nor can Hume's use of the term 'allow' be interpreted along the lines of 'establishing' in any philosophical manner. Indeed, Hume was quite prepared to 'allow' all manner of unknown 'qualities' in reality, even those designated *'powers'* and *'efficacy'*, as long as we did not claim to be able to establish a clear or intelligible idea of them: 'I am, indeed, ready to allow, that there may be many several qualities both in material and immaterial objects, with which we are utterly unacquainted; and if we please to call these power or efficacy, 'twill be of little consequence to the world' (Hume 1969: 218). But when, according to Hume, we make such terms signify something of which we have a clear idea, ultimately 'we are led astray by false philosophy' (ibid.: 219). Hume immediately adds that: 'This is the case, when we transfer the determination of the thought to external objects, and suppose any real intelligible connexion betwixt them; that being a quality, which can only belong to the mind that considers them' (ibid.: 219).

5 For reasons of space I restrict myself to responding in explicit fashion mainly to Parsons' central arguments as I understand them. There are numerous additional critical (often largely assertive) asides in Parsons' piece, which I do mostly address – sometimes explicitly, but more often without making direct reference to Parsons' text.

6 Of course, determining which are the scientifically interesting event regularities, etc., is a matter that is always dependent on context (see the section headed 'The nature of social scientific explanation' below). However, I doubt (re Parsons' concluding question 5) that there are many contexts in which the repeated production of the symbol 5 whenever a

given keyboard key is pressed, will be regarded as particularly curious (although fanciful scenarios are not out of the question).

7 This is not a trite remark. My ability, wherever I go, to undermine event patterns that would otherwise have occurred, but not their underlying causes, bears precisely on the point in question. It is because the world is open that event regularities can be produced and also obstructed.

8 The example of billiards which Parsons mentions in discussing Hume, is a case in point. Although no pattern must hold, there clearly are numerous patterns frequently found to hold connecting events occurring on billiard tables. Ultimately, with this example, there is a need to make sense of the implicit contrast that the observed regularities are largely confined to billiard balls on billiard tables in billiard halls; they do not in general hold away from the billiard table. Thus, for example, such regularities as are in question are rarely associated with plastic balls (or even billiard balls) on the beach. The contrast is what makes the case of the billiard balls on the billiard table, etc., striking. The case of billiard balls is significant precisely because event regularities are not ubiquitous. Now an achievement of the transcendental analysis of the experiment is an understanding that event regularities are mainly confined to conditions where certain stable (typically) non-empirical mechanisms are effectively insulated from the countervailing actions of other mechanisms. And, of course, we can see that such an insulation, this closing-off of the situation from countervailing factors, is precisely what is achieved (or anyway aimed for) in constructing the billiard table. Put differently, the explanation of the *confinement* of the event regularities in question to the billiard table, is that this is a location in which certain causal factors can be effectively insulated from potentially interfering mechanisms. Far from undermining transcendental realism, such considerations strengthen it; a transcendental realist perspective, but not an empirical realist one, can explain the systematic confinement of any event regularities concerning the movements of billiard balls to a certain set of conditions. The transcendental realist account can be shown via numerous such illustrations to be the more explanatory powerful.

9 Natural science's experimental successes are suggestive that the natural realm is differentiated, and populated by, if amongst other things, relatively stable structures and mechanisms. This seems to be a necessary condition for the experimental isolation of some mechanisms, and the *ex posteriori* successes of scientists in generating event regularities. The failure to achieve this in the social realm itself suggests that *if* social structure exists it is either not differentiated in this way, i.e., it is holistic, or insufficiently stable, or both.

10 Eventually, albeit quite a while later, I came across the works of Bhaskar of course. Because our perspectives are so similar, and Bhaskar's work was already having a big impact in various spheres of philosophy and science, I found it convenient to borrow much of his terminology as well as draw upon his ideas. It goes without saying that I am greatly indebted to Bhaskar's work.

11 At one point Parsons seems to make the same mistake. However, this is not crucial to Parsons' criticism which turns on the philosophical argument for preferring transcendental realism to empirical realism (rather than the question of how the latter relates to mainstream economics).

12 To repeat Frank Hahn's assessment: 'If one is kind to . . . critics [of deductivism] one interprets them as signalling that they do not care for these axioms and these assumptions. In any case all theory in all subjects proceeds in this manner', that is they 'consist of logical deductions from axioms and assumptions' (1985: 9).

13 In my papers I repeatedly stress that deductivism does not presuppose knowledge of any philosophical reasoning in support of that position. In the paper from which Hands mainly quotes I even speculate that if positivist reasoning were known to economists it would likely be rejected by many (1994: 112). It does seem to me, though, that the modern subject is imbued with unnecessary restrictions and confusion, and that the resolving of this is something in which philosophy can, and perhaps must, play an essential role.

In truth Hands' uneasy mixing of deductivism and empirical realism is immediately noticeable merely in his manner of portraying my position. Specifically, when he interprets my assessment of mainstream economics Hands regularly employs the category of empirical realism; when he quotes my text the language is that of deductivism or of results rooted in positivistic reasoning, or some such. Thus, for example, when Hands accuses me (erroneously – see below) of not substantiating my characterisation of the mainstream, he writes:

> Regrettably the intensity of Lawson's commitment to this *empirical realist* reading of contemporary economics is not matched by either the quantity or the quality of the evidence that he garners in defence of his reading. In fact, Lawson offers very little evidence to support his claim that positivism has an overarching impact on modern economics. He frequently makes statements such as 'I do not think it contentious to observe that *deductivism* so understood characterises contemporary economics' (1994: 260) or that it is 'the misguided adherence to this conception of science, . . . including accepting the universal applicability of the *deductivist* form of explanation, that constitutes the fundamental problem in the economic scientific project' (1995: 18) but there is seldom any real defence of these statements . . . ; let us consider neoclassical economics more carefully and see if *empirical realism* is as influential as Lawson claims in these repeated assertions.
> (pp. 174–175, emphasis added)

14 It is because they can be, and often are, fictions that Solow, in assessing the axiomatic deductive method can conclude: 'It would be a useful principle that economists should actually believe the empirical assertions they make. That would require more discipline than most of us now exhibit, when many empirical papers seem more like virtuoso finger exercises than anything else' (1986: 23).

15 If case study evidence is required regardless, a good example of such is provided by Fleetwood's (1997a) recent critical survey and assessment of some mainstream analyses of trade union activities.

16 Because the points Hands makes in the context of Chapter 2 of Arrow and Hahn are identical in nature to, if more extensive than, those relating to ensuing chapters, I focus on Hands' discussion of this chapter.

17 Or rather it presupposes a set of functional relationships. But to the extent that such functional relations as are formulated can make claim to referents at all, the latter must be of the form of correlated actualities.

18 This corresponds precisely with the notion of equilibrium employed by Arrow and Hahn (1971: 22). Of course, the whole gamut of equilibrium conceptions and other solution concepts that have occupied the mainstream project from Arrow and Hahn onwards (and before) involves finding 'solutions' of this consistency sort.

19 Thus, and with Hands, I do not deny that a 'type of coordinated activity ... seems to prevail in a market economy'. What is false is the implied presumption that the coordination involved is of the 'solution concept' sort associated with deductivist modelling. Indeed, perceived from the perspective of these fictitious worlds of mainstream models the market activity we actually observe in the real world can hardly be interpreted as coordinated at all. This, I presume, is why the more reflective of 'theorists' do not generally suppose that an equilibrium, as they understand it, obtains (see main text below).

Perhaps, however, there is an onus on me here to indicate something of my own conception of such coordination as occurs in market economies, along with its conditions. In my assessment, consistent with the perspective systematised within economics as critical realism, all coordination of human action, when it occurs, is an *ex posteriori* achievement, and takes the form of knowledgeable and capable human beings simultaneously each more or less successfully negotiating her or his daily affairs (in a quintessentially open social system) drawing upon shared networks of social structures, including, of course, social rules. These rules, as with all social structures, are both constraining and enabling. Communication is facilitated by shared rules of language, conventions of turn-taking in conversation, and so forth; trade is facilitated by rules governing the exchange of property rights, quality guarantees, etc. Now according to this conception, social structure (rules, relations, etc.) is both a condition of (transformative) human agency and also a consequence. Social structure which facilitates coordinated human action, then, can in principle be reproduced, transformed or even radically undermined by human action. Thus an essential aspect of the conception of social order in question is precisely social reproduction, i.e, the *reproduction* of coordinated-action-facilitating social structure. Social life is a process, and social order cannot be reduced to a set of outcomes, whether hypothetical or otherwise.

Of most significance to economics, perhaps, is the reproduction of those social structures most immediately implicated in the coordinated production, exchange and distribution of the material conditions of wealth or well-being (see Lawson 1997b). And because it is always an *ex posteriori* achievement, where it occurs, and not an *a priori* given, social reproduction itself requires explanation. I have discussed the conditions of social reproduction with respect to certain identified social structures elsewhere (Lawson 1997a). Let me just note, though, that the social ontology elaborated under the head of critical realism is of a complex internally related network of dynamic totalities. Clearly, if the assessment in question is correct, elucidating the nature of social order at a systems level is a complicated issue, as Marx and Hayek amongst others have earlier demonstrated. However, that is no excuse for collapsing this complex ontology onto a set of supposedly correlated surface manifestations, assumed describable via a set of equations, whereupon the notion of order is reduced to a system-of-equations-specific solution concept (for a detailed discussion of social order conceptualised along these lines, one which focuses upon Hayek's insights [and limitations] in particular, see Fleetwood, 1995, 1996, 1997b).

20 To put all this somewhat differently, I acknowledge, of course, that *if* (for the sake of argument) we were (1) to grant the presumption that some-thing like an equilibrium situation prevailed in the real world, and (2) to allow a social reality (per impossible) of a nature such that the 'laws of the "greater causes" of economic phenomena' could be expressed as event regularity formulations, then, by demonstrating the logical possibility of an equilibrium in a particular model not known to be other than empiri-cally adequate, we might thereby gain reassurance of having 'isolated' the 'underlying "greater causes" of the phenomena that we observe' (whether or not economic modellers would conceive their project in this way). Or at least, we might gain some reassurance from this result *if* we were not simultaneously in the possession of a host of contending (equally empiri-cally adequate) Arrow and Hahn type models each allowing such a logical possibility. In other words, Hands is not wrong in his intuition that the transcendental realist orientation could well retain insight in conditions of closure, i.e., under conditions which the deductivist must everywhere presuppose (whatever may be the *actual* goals and practices or ways of proceeding of contemporary mainstream modellers). In granting this scenario we would merely have rendered many of the transcendental realist insights (temporarily) inapplicable – those addressing the open, dynamic, and holistic nature of reality – by fashioning a world in confor-mance to the presuppositions of the deductivist. The error here would lie merely in assuming that such conditions could have relevance for any real social system.

21 As Parsons correctly recognises in formulating his concluding question 4.

22 Two related errors are easily made in all this. The first is to draw metaphorically from a source domain without regard to prior insights of the target one; in the belief that the nature of the material to be investi-gated is irrelevant to the manner of its investigation. This error, the scientistic fallacy, regularly occurs in economics. A modern form is abduc-tion that occurs *merely* on the criterion that terms involved are drawn from, say, the cutting edge of other sciences (e.g. the borrowing of concepts of automata and/or simulacra from the 'cyborg sciences'). The second is to suppose that the senses of terms borrowed must be rigidly fixed according to usage in the source domain (e.g. by insisting that the term 'evolution' must retain the sense it has in [the latest or any other specific] developments in biology).

23 According to critical realism, then, because metaphor allows us to say something that cannot be expressed in any other way, metaphor is recog-nised as performing an indispensable cognitive role. Thus, while the observation that use of metaphor is pervasive in successful science (and social life in general), is clearly intelligible from the realist perspective, this observation is presumably something of an embarrassment for those oppo-nents of critical realism who are unable to find any essential role for metaphor in (their conception of) science.

24 So that, for Boylan and O'Gorman, being *describable* and being *empirical* presumably do not amount to the same thing. However, if, for Boylan and O'Gorman, these categories *are* considered identical (so that anything that can be known under some description is empirical), there may not be any significant differences of substance between us after all.

25 Presumably, when Boylan and O'Gorman assert, 'there is no question of theoretical economics furnishing approximately true descriptions of non-empirical generative structures, powers or mechanisms', their understanding entails (the impossibility of) such theories being epistemically on par with theories of observables that are descriptively adequate. If they mean only that being formulated in terms of observables is a *necessary* requirement for (aspects of) any theory to be held as true then, by definition, theories invoking unobservables cannot be held as true. (Of course, even our most descriptively adequate theories may be false in some way or other. Certainly, many theories and observations (flat earth, setting sun, motionlessness as the natural state) that previously were held to be descriptively adequate, are so no longer, at least from the vantage point of modern science.)

26 We should not be deflected by the findings of econometrics here. As is well known, with a given set of data, econometricians with different theoretical commitments often run thousands of regressions in order to come up with formulations coherent with their prior convictions. But, even ignoring the fact that such procedures are inconsistent with the classical theory of inference which most econometricians profess to be acting upon, the fact of the matter is that econometricians as a rule simply ignore the vast array of evidence, much of it contrastive, which the hypotheses behind their models bear upon. The one set of 'alternative evidence' that is regularly observed comprises additions (available with the passing of time) to time series data of the type used in the original model estimation process. This alone, however, is usually sufficient to undermine the previously held specification.

27 We might also note that many scientific claims referencing observed entities were in fact originally formulated at a time when the entities in question were unknown and/or unobserved. Thus, to the theorist, they were epistemically on par with the inherently unobservable. As such, the *ex posteriori* realisation that many such hypothesised entities have been subsequently observed, i.e., have come to be accepted as scientific knowledge according to Boylan and O'Gorman's descriptive adequacy criterion, is surely something of an embarrassment for the view that 'there is no question of theoretical economics furnishing approximately true descriptions of non-empirical generative structures, powers or mechanisms'.

28 Compare for example with the experiences of Strassmann (1994).

29 I do not (of course) criticise the use of maths *per se*. The trait I refer to here is that of wielding mathematical formalism in contexts where it is transparently inappropriate to do so. In truth, an expert crafts-person knows the limits of her or his tools. Mainstream economists appear not to recognise even that there are any limits to applying their formalisms.

30 We might further note that if, as Kanth emphasises, numerous groups are significantly oppressed, and if, as I am suggesting, not only real interests but mechanisms and relations of oppression may hardly be understood, the relative advantage of laying such matters bare presumably accrue to

the dispossessed. For those in a position to benefit from such processes are doing so already whether or not there is a clear understanding of what is going on.

31 The picture presented by Kanth is certainly questionable. In the modern world, of which two thirds is yet to be industrialised; with numerous localised wars based on ethnic, religious, tribal and other differences; with technology throwing up ever new possibilities; with worker organisation and militancy springing up in areas where previously they were hardly recognised; with industrial decline well under way in various traditional industrial strongholds generating often concomitant erosion of civil order, spread of racist, fascist and other destabilising tendencies; with revolutions followed by counter revolutions (Iran, old Soviet Union, Albania); with continuous destruction to the environment, the emergence of new diseases (some as a direct result of capitalist agricultural practices) and growth and spread of military capacities including those for world-wide destruction, and so forth, I am not convinced that we are in or approaching a 'period of world mastery of capital', even if Kanth is correctly identifying operative tendencies.

Bibliography

Allais, M. (1992) 'The Economic Science of Today and Global Disequilibrium', in M. Baldassarri *et al.*, *Global Disequilibrium in the World Economy*, Basingstoke: Macmillan.

Arrow, K. J. and Hahn, F. H. (1971) *General Competitive Analysis*, San Francisco: Holden-Day.

Bhaskar, R. (1986) *Scientific Realism and Human Emancipation*, London: Verso.

—— (1989) *Reclaiming Reality*, London: Verso.

Boylan, T. A. and O'Gorman, P. F. (1995) *Beyond Rhetoric and Realism in Economics: Towards a Reformulation of Economic Methodology*, London: Routledge.

—— (1997) 'Critical Realism and Economics: A Causal Holist Critique', *Ekonomia* (Chapter 8 in this volume).

Fleetwood, S. (1995) *Hayek's Political Economy: The Socio-Economics of Order*, London: Routledge.

—— (1996) 'Order Without Equilibrium: A Critical Realist Interpretation of Hayek's Notion of Spontaneous Order', *Cambridge Journal of Economics* 20(4): 729–747.

—— (1997a) 'Why Trade Union Models are Inadequate: A Critical Realist Perspective', *Labour* (forthcoming).

—— (1997b) 'Critical Realism: Marx and Hayek', in W. Keizer, B. Tieben and R. Van Zijp (eds) *Austrians in Debate*, London: Routledge.

Flew, A. (1979) *A Dictionary of Philosophy*, London: Pan Books in association with The Macmillan Press.

Hahn, F. (1970) 'Some Adjustment Problems', *Econometrica* 38: 1–17, January, reprinted in Hahn (1984), (page references to the latter).

—— (1984) *Equilibrium and Macroeconomics*, Oxford: Basil Blackwell.

—— (1985) 'In Praise of Economic Theory', the *1984 Jevons Memorial Fund Lecture*, London: University College.

—— (1994) 'An Intellectual Retrospect', *Banca Nazionale del Lavoro Quarterly Review*: 245–258.

Hands, W. D. (1997), 'Empirical Realism as Meta-Method: Tony Lawson on Neoclassical Economics', *Ekonomia* (Chapter 10 in this volume).

Hausman, D. (1992) *The Inexact and Separate Science of Economics*, Cambridge: Cambridge University Press.

Hayek, F. A. (1942–44) 'Scientism and the Study of Society', *Economica*. Reprinted in *The Counter-Revolution of Science*, Indianapolis: Liberty Press.

Hendry, D. F., Leamer, E. E. and Poirier, D. J. (1990) 'The ET Dialogue: A Conversation on Econometric Methodology', *Econometric Theory* 6: 171–261.

Hicks, J. (1986) 'Is Economics a Science?', in M. Baranzini and R. Scazzieri (eds) *Foundations of Economics*, Oxford: Basil Blackwell: 91–101.

Hume, D. (1969) *A Treatise on Human Nature*, London: Penguin Books.

Hutchison, T. W. (1994) 'Ends and Means in the Methodology of Economics', in R. E. Backhouse (ed.) *New Directions in Economic Methodology*, London and New York: Routledge.

Kanth, R. (1997), 'Against Eurocentred Epistemologies: A Critique of Science, Realism and Economics', *Ekonomia* (Chapter 11 in this volume).

Kay, J. (1995) 'Cracks in the Crystal Ball', *Financial Times*, 29 September.

Kilpatrick, A. and Lawson, T. (1980) 'On the Nature of Industrial Decline in the UK', *Cambridge Journal of Economics* 4: 85–102. Reprinted in D. Coates and J. Hillard (eds) *The Economic Decline of Modern Britain*, Brighton: Harvester Press, 1986. Also reprinted in C. Feinstein (ed.) *The Economic Development of Modern Europe Since 1980*, Cheltenham: Edward Elgar, 1998.

Lawson, T. (1981a) 'Keynesian Model Building and the Rational Expectations Critique', *Cambridge Journal of Economics* 5: 311–326.

—— (1981b) 'Paternalism and Labour Market Segmentation Theory', in F. S. Wilkinson (ed.) *Dynamics of Labour Market Segmentation*, London: Academic Press.

—— (1994) 'Why Are So Many Economists So Opposed to Methodology?', *Journal of Economic Methodology* 1(1): 105–133.

—— (1996) 'Developments in *Economics as Realist Social Theory*', *Review of Social Economy*, LIV(4): 405–422 (Chapter 1 in this volume).

—— (1997a) *Economics and Reality*, London: Routledge.

—— (1997b) 'Economics as a distinct social science?, On the nature, scope and method of economics, *Economie Appliquée*, tome L, no. 2: 5–35

Leamer, E. E. (1983) 'Let's take the Con out of Econometrics', *American Economic Review* 73(1): 34–43.

Lewis, P. A. (1996) 'Metaphor and Critical Realism', *Review of Social Economy*, vol. LIV, no 4: 487–506 (Chapter 5 in this volume).

Martin-Soskice, J. (1995) *Metaphor and Religious Language*, Oxford: Clarendon Press.

Parsons, S. (1997) 'Why the "Transcendental" in Transcendental Realism?', *Ekonomia* (Chapter 9 in this volume).

Rosenberg, A. (1992) *Economics – Mathematical Politics or Science of Diminishing Returns?*, Chicago: University of Chicago Press.

Solow, R. E. (1986) 'Economics: Is Something Missing?', in W. N. Parker (ed.) *Economic History and the Modern Economist*, Oxford: Basil Blackwell.

Strassmann, D. L. (1994) 'Feminist Thought and Economics; Or, What do the Visigoths Know?', *American Economic Review, Papers and Proceedings* 84(2): 153–158.

NAME INDEX

259

SUBJECT INDEX

271

Printed in the United States
by Baker & Taylor Publisher Services